Rogue Elephant

*How Republicans Went
from the Party of Business
to the Party of Chaos*

Paul Heideman

V

VERSO
London • New York

First published by Verso 2025
© Paul Heideman 2025

The manufacturer's authorized representative in the EU for product safety
(GPSR) is LOGOS EUROPE, 9 rue Nicolas Poussin, 17000, La Rochelle, France
contact@logoseurope.eu

The moral rights of the author have been asserted

1 3 5 7 9 10 8 6 4 2

Verso
UK: 6 Meard Street, London W1F 0EG
US: 207 East 32nd Street, New York, NY 10016
versobooks.com

Verso is the imprint of New Left Books

ISBN-13: 978-1-80429-408-6
ISBN-13: 978-1-80429-410-9 (US EBK)
ISBN-13: 978-1-80429-409-3 (UK EBK)

British Library Cataloguing in Publication Data
A catalogue record for this book is available from the British Library

Library of Congress Cataloging-in-Publication Data
A catalog record for this book is available from the Library of Congress

Typeset in Sabon by MJ & N Gavan, Truro, Cornwall
Printed and bound by CPI Group (UK) Ltd, Croydon, CR0 4YY

Contents

Acknowledgments

I have acquired many debts in writing this book. Though I can't hope to clear them all in this short section, I can at least begin making payments.

This book has its origins in an article Vivek Chibber asked me to write for the journal *Catalyst* around the time of the 2020 election. I owe him my thanks for pushing me to take on the topic of GOP's evolution. He also gave this manuscript a detailed read, which has improved it greatly. More broadly, I'm in debt to Vivek for modeling a refusal to be satisfied with easy or politically convenient answers, and for insisting on the same from his students.

Corey Robin's work on conservatism has shaped my thinking for well over a decade. During the first Trump administration, his call to analyze what Trump did rather than what he said exemplified the kind of research I hoped to do. Corey was also generous enough to read a draft of the manuscript, and I am grateful for our conversations about it.

As a researcher working outside of academic institutions, I have relied on a number of people and institutions for access to academic research. Gerard di Trolio's help was invaluable in this regard. The staff of the New York Public Library provided access to all manner of material, and I also benefited from Alexandra Elbakyan's efforts to make academic journal articles more widely available. David Vance and Liz Iacobucci at Common Cause were also gracious in helping me track down old reports on the political donations of the tobacco industry. Peter Lucas provided a heroic last-minute research save.

I owe Ben Mabie for first suggesting expanding my article into a book. My agent, Jonathan Agin, was tremendously supportive throughout the writing process. My editor at Verso, Asher Dupuy-Spencer, personified grace and forgiveness when it came to deadlines.

I want to thank Jonah Birch, Matthew Nichter, Jeff Goodwin, Nathan Tankus, Eric Blanc, and the participants in NYU's Economic and Political Sociology seminar for answering questions and providing feedback on various ideas in this book. I probably should have taken even more of their advice.

On a personal level, I owe a tremendous amount to my parents, Robert Heideman and Kathy Muntner for too much to list. This book is dedicated to my wife Marie and our daughter Nina.

Introduction

Going Rogue

Donald Trump and Joseph McCarthy have their differences. New York City born and bred, Trump exemplifies parvenu extravagance. McCarthy, on the other hand, was born on a farm in rural Wisconsin. Trump is a teetotaler, famously abstaining from alcohol and other intoxicants. McCarthy struggled with alcoholism for much of his life and would die of cirrhosis of the liver. McCarthy was laid low by television, collapsing in popularity after the Army-McCarthy hearings of 1954. Trump has thrived on television, prolonging his celebrity through reality TV and benefiting massively from his ability to dominate news coverage through controversy.

Yet the similarities are noteworthy as well. Both were Republican politicians whose conduct deeply divided their party. Trump gave rise to the Never Trumpers, Republicans who would rather support a Democrat than Trump. McCarthy polarized much of the party against himself as well, and was despised by party leaders like Dwight Eisenhower and Robert Taft. Both Trump and McCarthy practiced a demagogic mode of politics, caring little whether what they said was true or false, so long as it inflamed their supporters against their enemies. In so doing, both of them also drew considerable opposition from the American elite, from corporate boardrooms to the military bureaucracy.

This last similarity reveals, in turn, another difference. Where elite opposition effectively ended Joe McCarthy's political career in 1954, leaving him politically friendless and without influence, the opposition to Donald Trump among the power elite has been far less successful. It failed to prevent him from winning the presidency in 2016, and even after his attempt to overturn the results of the 2020 election drew universal condemnation from business leaders, he has retained more or less total control of the Republican Party, purging it of opponents and identifying the party with his personal political fortunes. The different results elite opposition to a right-wing demagogue produced in these two cases reveal a great deal about how American politics in general, and Republican Party politics more specifically, have changed over the last few decades.

Joe McCarthy came to prominence in 1950, when he gave a speech in Wheeling, West Virginia, claiming to have a list of 205 Communists working in the State Department. McCarthy possessed no such list, but as it turned out, this hardly mattered. The Cold War had begun a few years earlier under the administration of Harry Truman, and by 1950 anticommunist hysteria was running wild. The House of Representatives had voted in 1945 to establish the House Committee on Un-American Activities on a permanent footing, and in 1946 Truman had given the FBI, headed by anticommunist fanatic J. Edgar Hoover, carte blanche to begin investigating the backgrounds of federal employees. In this environment, the existence of McCarthy's list mattered less than his claim to have one.

What distinguished McCarthy, and what made his name synonymous with anticommunism, even as others had been far more important in its development, was the ferocity of his accusations. For McCarthy, anyone who doubted his crusade was, at best, a naive dupe of the Reds. At worst, they were an active accomplice to the communist conspiracy. McCarthy always had a new accusation to make the jobs of the headline writers, both those who supported him and those who opposed him, easier. Claiming that he alone had the dedication to root out communists from positions of influence in American life, he embarked on a campaign that sustained itself on a never-ending crop of new sources of subversion that needed to be investigated.

The recklessness of McCarthy's methods was what brought him into conflict with the American elite; it posed two threats.

First, many of them feared McCarthy's irresponsible attacks would discredit anticommunism, making the crusade against the Reds more difficult. Whittaker Chambers, the former communist turned *National Review* editor, gave voice to this worry, writing to a friend: "We live in terror that Senator McCarthy will one day make some irreparable blunder which will ... discredit the whole anti-Communist effort." Second, in his zeal, McCarthy had at times attacked institutions and persons with which the American establishment was actually quite happy. For example, in 1951, he attacked George Marshall, World War II general and architect of the Marshall Plan (ironically, a device by which the American government hoped to maintain political and economic hegemony in Europe). He accused Marshall of membership in "a great conspiracy ... to diminish the United States in world affairs ... To what end? To the end that we shall be contained, frustrated and, finally, fall victim to Soviet intrigue from within and Russian military might from without." Similarly, in 1953, he attacked the Army for being soft on subversives, beginning the conflict that would ultimately undo him.[1]

These actions drew increasing opposition from the American business elite, whose role in McCarthy's downfall, though little appreciated, was central. To be sure, there were plenty of business leaders who supported McCarthy. The anticommunist crusade had deep roots in American business, who were only too happy to use it as a general weapon against labor and against activist government. However, the leaders of many of the country's largest corporations saw McCarthy as damaging the cause of responsible anticommunism. As the historian Ellen Schrecker has observed, they thought "the Wisconsin senator was *bad*, but he wasn't *wrong*." These figures were, in the postwar United States, organized as they had never been before, with organizations like the Committee for Economic Development (CED) and the Business Council connecting corporate titans to one another and to the government. These bodies proved key to McCarthy's downfall, as men in these networks worked, generally behind the scenes, to undermine the senator from Wisconsin.[2]

Opposition to McCarthy from these quarters began early. In the fall of 1951, Connecticut Senator William Benton, an advertising executive and key figure in the founding of the CED, launched an attack on McCarthy. Benton submitted a motion to have McCarthy expelled from the Senate, a rebuke never before exercised by the Senate. McCarthy, pugnacious as always, responded (in decidedly Trumpian fashion) by calling out "Little Willie Benton, Connecticut's mental midget" and filed a $2 million libel suit. The episode did little to build broader opposition to McCarthy in the Senate; one member quipped that it had the makings of "an ideal double murder."[3]

Benton's failure, however, galvanized other opponents of McCarthy. One of them was Maurice Rosenblatt. Rosenblatt was a founder of a group called the National Committee for an Effective Congress (NCEC), a liberal organization formed in 1948 in reaction to the Republican surge in the 1946 midterms. Initially focused on defeating a resurgence of isolationism in Congress, the group turned its attention to McCarthy in the wake of the failure of Benton's initiative. Rosenblatt would later describe how he saw "men with good intentions, like Bill Benton ... attacking McCarthy—and not making a dent ... it was inevitable that the committee and I would become involved with Joe McCarthy." In the spring of 1953, Rosenblatt founded the McCarthy Clearinghouse as a project of the NCEC. Its goal was to gather opposition research on McCarthy, disseminate it among his enemies, and coordinate the campaign against him. The Clearinghouse was funded by Benton, along with fellow CED founder Paul Hoffman, the former president of the auto manufacturer Studebaker.[4]

At the same time that business elites were backing the McCarthy Clearinghouse, they were also putting pressure on President Eisenhower to take a firm stand against McCarthy. Eisenhower came out of the business-elite wing of the Republican Party. Before becoming president, he had served on both the CED and the Business Council. The campaign to draft Eisenhower to run for president on the GOP ticket had been organized by precisely the kinds of titans of industry who were growing increasingly concerned about McCarthy in the early 1950s. Though Eisenhower himself had, in his brother's words, "loathed McCarthy as much as any human being could possible loathe another," he nonetheless enabled McCarthy by, for example, dropping praise for George Marshall, Eisenhower's mentor, from a speech after McCarthy attacked him and more generally by refusing to publicly denounce the Wisconsin senator. However, the corporate leaders who backed Eisenhower began putting pressure on him in late 1953 to take action against McCarthy. Hoffman told Eisenhower that "McCarthyism has passed far beyond being merely a nuisance and has now become a deadly menace." He was joined by General Electric Chairman Philip Reed, another founder of the CED, who warned Eisenhower that "people in high and low places see in [McCarthy] a potential Hitler."[5]

In 1954, the White House's posture began to shift. Before this moment, the army had acceded to McCarthy's inquisition in much the same way the administration as a whole had. Indeed, Army Secretary Robert Stevens, soon to be known as McCarthy's greatest enemy, had been invited to McCarthy's wedding the previous year. After McCarthy publicly abused a general he was questioning, however, the military's response to his campaign changed noticeably. Under the direction of the White House, Stevens issued a statement proclaiming that he would never allow his personnel to be abused. Furthermore, when McCarthy demanded more army men come before his committee, Stevens struck back, accusing McCarthy of using his influence to pressure the military to give a favorable posting to a recently drafted aide of the senator's. These accusations and counteraccusations were what led to the televised Army-McCarthy hearings in the spring of 1954.[6]

Though these hearings produced plenty of drama, the real action was behind the scenes. In April of 1954, McCarthy had his famous confrontations with Secretary of the Army Stevens. Stevens, however, was not a soldier. Before his appointment in the Eisenhower administration, he had been president of one of the largest textile firms in the country and had been the chair of the Business Council (his brother was also a trustee of the CED). After his confrontation with McCarthy, Stevens was flown to a meeting of the Business Council; a delegation of American corporate leaders met him at the airport to expressing their support. Shortly afterwards, these same men subjected White

House officials "to a torrent of abuse for caving in to McCarthy's grandstanding media tactics." These meetings "gave the administration the courage it needed to finally take a strong stand against McCarthy."[7]

The killing blow would come not from the White House, however, but from a fellow senator. In March of 1954, Republican Ralph Flanders of Vermont, a friend of William Benton's and fellow CED member and former vice president of the Business Council, launched an attack on McCarthy on the Senate floor. The usually soft-spoken legislator excoriated McCarthy, comparing his demagoguery to the rise of Hitler. In June, after McCarthy's dramatic exposure in the Army-McCarthy hearings, Flanders introduced a motion to censure McCarthy. He was backed up by the NCEC, who wrote speeches for him and helped coordinate the opposition on Capitol Hill. Flanders himself would describe how he was "well prepared by the NCEC" to take down McCarthy. The network of business leaders who opposed McCarthy sprang into action to support Flanders's motion. Paul Hoffman of the CED put together a twenty-three-member committee, which sent a telegram to every senator, urging them to support the motion. Six of the members of this committee were trustees of the CED, and eight others were executives of various sorts. In response, the Senate voted to establish a select committee to hear Flanders's charges against McCarthy. In December, it finally voted on the charges, convicting McCarthy of treating fellow senators with contempt by a margin of sixty-seven to twenty-two.[8]

The vote broke McCarthy, who would drift through the Senate for two and half more years, friendless and ignored, before dying of alcoholism in 1957. Though McCarthy had, of course, destroyed any number of lives with his crusade and had reshaped American politics as part of the broader anticommunist backlash, when he became viewed as a threat by the nation's business elite, he was effectively put out to pasture. Some six decades later, however, another right-wing demagogue would show himself to be rather more unyielding.

∾

Donald Trump also drew significant opposition from the nation's business elite. Like McCarthy, he certainly had backers among businesses, including various far-right billionaires and some firms who hoped to benefit from his promises of more tariffs. But from the time he declared his candidacy in 2015, Trump faced massive opposition from employers. Even staunchly conservative pro-business groups, like the Club for Growth and the Koch brothers, who had been pushing the Republican Party to the right, declared their opposition to Trump. In the general election, there was something resembling a stampede of business donations towards Hillary Clinton, allowing her to outspend Trump two to one. Once elected, this opposition continued. To be sure, business found many areas of agreement with the Trump administration, from his massive corporate tax cuts to his see no evil approach to enforcing regulations. But in spite of this, tensions with business continued throughout the administration. After Trump defended the Charlottesville rally—a march protesting the removal of statues of the Confederacy, which included open white supremacists—business leaders quit en masse from various advisory councils the administration had set up, leading Trump to dissolve the councils. Unsurprisingly, when the 2020 election rolled around, donations from business were as lopsided as in 2016.[9]

The biggest break, however, came after Trump's attempt to overturn the results of the 2020 election. Over 123 firms on the Fortune 500 list announced their boycott of Republicans who backed Trump's effort. These firms collectively accounted for over a quarter of American GDP. Leading business organizations like the Chamber of Commerce and the Business Roundtable denounced the riots at the capitol and called on Trump to ensure a peaceful transfer of power. The National Association of Manufacturers even called for Trump's cabinet to remove him via the twenty fifth amendment. For a moment, it looked as if Trump would join McCarthy in the halls of Republican infamy, remembered as a historical embarrassment and defended only by posterity's controversy mongers.[10]

Trump, however, was not felled so easily. His grip on the Republican Party, it turned out, would only tighten over the next four years. In 2024, he won nearly every GOP primary while refusing to debate the other candidates. Republicans who once declared their contempt for Trump now behaved like trembling supplicants. Big business, it seemed, could no longer sway the Republican Party as it had six decades earlier.

Business's failure to discipline the Republican Party in the aftermath of January 6 raises profound questions about the relationship between the party and American capitalists. Traditionally, the Republican Party has been the preferred party of American business. Throughout the twentieth century, the Republican Party had generally been able to command the support of most of American business: J. P. Morgan had the White House at his beck and call; Eisenhower was cozy with the mid-century corporate elite; and George W. Bush cultivated a massive corporate coalition. By the time of Trump, however, something had clearly changed.

This shift is but one aspect of the broader transformation of the Republican Party over the last few decades. For some time now, political scientists have been pointing out that the polarization of American politics—the increasing distance between the positions of the two parties—has been driven primarily by the Republican Party moving further to the right. There has, by contrast, been relatively little movement by the Democratic Party. It would be a mistake, therefore, to see Trump as a sui generis development in Republican politics. He is rather the culmination of a decades-long Republican trajectory traveling ever further rightward.[11]

At the same time that the Republican Party has become more conservative, it has become more internally divided. This is a somewhat counterintuitive development. After all, the increasing polarization of the parties means that, by definition, they are more internally politically coherent than they were before the 1970s. Nonetheless, the growth of internal conflict in the GOP is striking. There were already signs of growing tension in 1997 when Newt Gingrich, generalissimo of the 1994 Republican Revolution, faced a coup attempt from his own members hoping to remove him as Speaker. This was a highly unusual maneuver, and though Gingrich was able to quash it before it came to a vote, it spoke to a new fractiousness in the Republican Party. Conflict would explode in the second George W. Bush administration, when Bush found himself at loggerheads with his own party more often than with the Democrats, on issues from immigration reform to the response to the financial crisis of 2008. From that time forward, the Republican Party was dominated by conflict between different wings. As of this writing, the last three Republican Speakers of the House have been brought down by internal opposition. Even when the Democrats were divided between Southern Dixiecrats and Northern liberals during the 1950s and 1960s, this level of intraparty conflict did not exist.[12]

The party's shift to the right and its escalating intraparty clashes join with another recent development suggested by business's opposition to Trump. Since the 1990s, the party has increasingly come into conflict with its historic benefactors in the business community. During the 2008 financial crisis, a majority of House Republicans refused to support the financial bailout bills, despite the demand for them by virtually every major business organization in the country. During the Obama administration, the GOP forced a government shutdown and threatened to begin defaulting on US debt if their budget priorities were not met—moves that were intensely opposed by leading business organizations like the Chamber of Commerce and the Business Roundtable. Trump's conflict with business is thus also rooted in the party's recent history.

The last few decades of Republican Party history thus present three developments in need of explanation.

1. The Republican Party has become much more conservative.
2. The Republican Party has developed much higher levels of intraparty conflict.
3. The Republican Party has found itself increasingly in conflict with American business leaders.

This book attempts to explain these developments. In contrast to much recent work on the Republican Party and American conservatism more generally, it does not look to trends in voter opinion or to currents in intellectual history for an explanation. Instead, it looks to the evolution of key institutions in American society and argues that two have created the context for the Republican Party's transformation: the American party system and the leading organizations of American business, like the CED and the Business Council of McCarthy's time.

American political parties have always been weaker than parties in comparable countries. The constitutional structure of a presidential, divided-powers system, combined with American federalism, militates strongly against nationally unified parties. Little more than coalitions of regional elites until the early twentieth century, American parties have traditionally lacked either the programmatic or institutional foundations of leading parties in other bourgeois states.

This began to change in the period from the New Deal to the civil rights movement. The New Deal consolidated the Democratic Party as a coalition of labor and its supporters, the most progressive bloc in the country, with Southern Dixiecrats the most reactionary bloc. Over the next three decades, liberals in the Democratic Party fought to expel the Dixiecrats and create a unified liberal party. At the same time, conservatives in the GOP were fighting to wrest control of their party from the so-called kingmakers of the Eastern Establishment, supporters of moderate Republicans like Dwight Eisenhower who had made their peace with the New Deal. In the mid-sixties, the civil rights movement facilitated the exodus of conservative Southern whites out of the Democratic Party and into the Republican Party, giving the polarizers in both parties what they wanted. For the first time in American history, an ideologically cohesive party system was created, with conservatives in one party, and liberals in the other.[13]

However, just as the parties were reorienting, they were also becoming weaker. Reforms of various sorts, like the introduction of the primary system in the early twentieth century, had weakened the parties considerably from the height of their organizational vitality in the nineteenth century. Reforms in the 1960s, pushed strongly by liberals in the Democratic Party, extended the primary system to presidential nominations. The Republican Party, meanwhile, exhausted from the factional fights of the mid-1960s, embraced the model of the service party, wherein the party apparatus existed not to make decisions about the course of the party but to provide services to candidates running on the party's ballot line.

Looming above all of this was the vertiginous rise in campaign costs from the 1970s onwards. Combined with a new legal framework for campaign finance that privileged the candidate's campaign committee above the party, this created a system in which parties responded more readily to the whims of their donors than they acted as decision-makers in their own right. Supreme Court decisions like *Citizens United v. FEC* legalized so-called super-PACS, fundraising committees that, unlike candidate committees or parties, could accept unlimited funds from donors so long as they did not directly coordinate with campaigns. This spawned an entirely new ecosystem of campaign finance, in which the parties themselves played a shrinking role.

In this new environment, party leaders could exert less control than ever over party members and nominations. If a candidate or a rogue representative could raise the necessary funds, there was little the party leadership could do to control them. In the Republican Party today, this means that a grotesque like Marjorie Taylor Greene, who embarrasses the party and actively hinders it by stoking intraparty conflict, cannot really be reined in, as she is also a highly successful fundraiser.[14]

While party weakness may explain why radicals like Greene can thumb their nose at the party leadership, it clearly cannot explain why the party as a whole has found itself in conflict with large sectors of American business. After all, if the party were simply following the money, one would expect it to be more subservient to business, not less. The other piece of the puzzle is the disorganization of American business.

Unusual among rich capitalist democracies, the US has never had a single peak-level employers' association. The reasons for this are rooted in the age-old question of American exceptional-ism. As scholars of business organization have recognized for some time now, employers organize in response to labor organi-zation. In the US, labor organization has always been weaker. As a result, business has felt less pressure to organize itself. In fact, the two main organizations of American capital for most of the twentieth century—the Chamber of Commerce and the National

Association of Manufacturers—were both organized externally, by Republican Party operatives, in order to help create closer links between business and the party.

In the 1970s, the disorganized world of American business changed. Rocked by global economic turbulence and a rank and file labor upsurge at home, American corporations organized like never before. They formed a new group, the Business Roundtable, to act explicitly as a representative not of specific firms or sectors but of business as a class. Organizations like the Chamber of Commerce ceased functioning as networking hubs for businessmen and became class combat organizations dedicated to overturning the legacy of the New Deal.

They got their way soon enough: Ronald Reagan's election signaled the end of accommodation with the forces of liberalism. But with their immediate foes defeated, business soon found it could not maintain the unity it had found in the heat of battle. Business organizations atrophied, their members asking what the point was with Reagan already giving them everything they wanted. Organizations began fighting amongst themselves over which sectors and firms would benefit most from the largesse of their friend in the White House. In the words of one Reagan advisor, business began acting less as a disciplined political force, and more like pigs feeding at the trough.[15] The model of organizing they had adopted in the 1970s fell apart in this new environment; a new one was plainly needed.

Business found it over the course of the 1990s, as leading organizations like the Roundtable and the Chamber stopped even pretending to be forces for the class-wide interests of business and instead devoted themselves to the most parochial and particularistic interests of their members. Nothing so exercised the Roundtable in the 1990s as a threat to CEO compensation proposed by the Clinton administration. The Chamber, meanwhile, found new life in reputation laundering for individual corporations. As a trade association, the Chamber was not required to report itemized donations for tax purposes, allowing it to keep its donors anonymous and lobby for unpopular causes on their behalf. Any pretense of representing the general interests of employers was left behind.

This new orientation by business cleared the way for conservative political entrepreneurs looking to pull the party to the right. Figures like Newt Gingrich, Paul Ryan, and Michele Bachmann sought to do so, and the increasingly disorganized and parochial character of business political action aided them in two ways. First, a fractured business community proved less able to discipline a Republican Party that was beginning to threaten its interests. With lines of power within the party scrambled and business organizations focused on sectional, short-term interests, reorienting the party away from needlessly confrontational politics proved difficult. Second, the disorganization of business led more firms to strike out on their own politically, pursuing their own idiosyncratic objectives regardless of the preferences of other employers. Firms like Koch Industries poured massive amounts of money into supporting politicians and causes that other large firms opposed. While political entrepreneurs seeking to pull the party rightward had existed since the New Deal, the changes in American parties and business organization since the 1970s empowered figures like the Koch brothers to achieve their ends.

The relationship between a conservatizing Republican Party and a fractured business elite has thus been complicated and dynamic. Some sectors of business actively fuel that conservatization. Others benefit from and support its stridently anti-labor and anti-redistributive politics, while balking at the instability caused by its pursuit of those ends.

The combination of an institutionally weak party and a fractured business class has created a cycle that has played out in the GOP since the 1990s. Insurgents in the party, able to draw on funds from sectors of business looking to push politics to the right, challenge the party leadership. Eventually, these insurgents manage to take leadership and succeed in their push. Then, a new crop of insurgents springs up, and the cycle begins again.

This cycle first took form with Newt Gingrich's rise in the 1980s and 1990s. Frustrated with the compromises of the Reagan administration, Gingrich launched a campaign to make the Republican Party even more intransigently conservative. What is less commonly appreciated is that this campaign was undergirded by a massive fundraising operation that took advantage of loopholes in campaign finance law to become, in the words of two political scientists, "a shadow [National Republican Congressional Committee]." When, in 1994, Gingrich led the GOP to its first House majority in nearly half a century, he became the establishment and quickly found himself confronted by Republican insurgents who wanted to push the party even further right.[16]

George W. Bush's presidency accomplished an impressive synthesis between the old party establishment, which his father had personified, and the insurgents. Bush's agenda combined the business Republicanism of corporate boardrooms with the cultural politics of the Christian right. His first term demonstrated the power of this alliance, leading Republicans to begin fantasizing about a permanent Republican majority. Yet during Bush's second term, the center could not hold. The party split over immigration politics, with a new, ferociously anti-immigrant contingent coming to dominate Republican congressional politics. This was particularly notable given that Bush had originally supported immigration reform at the behest of big business, who wanted more workers. Even more incredibly, the majority of congressional Republicans refused to follow business's lead during the financial crisis of 2008, steadfastly opposing bailouts to the financial sector, even as the whole of American business proclaimed their necessity.

Après Bush, le déluge. The years following the Bush presidency saw the most intense Republican factional conflict since the fights between Barry Goldwater and Nelson Rockefeller in the 1960s. A large section of the party repudiated the Bush administration, arguing that it had exemplified a fake conservatism. Rebranding themselves as Tea Party Republicans, the Republican right argued that even more strident conservatism was necessary. These Republicans plunged the GOP into ill-advised fights with the Obama administration, resulting in government shutdowns and confrontations over the debt ceiling that helped convince corporate America that the Republicans were becoming less and less reliable as stewards of their interests. At the same time, a new conservative donor network was growing up around the Koch brothers: petrochemical billionaires from Texas who pushed Republicans to declare all-out war on the welfare state. The infighting between Republicans who sought to stay the course mapped by the Bush administration and their insurgent rivals consumed the party for the entirety of the Obama administration.

This factional warfare paved the way for Donald Trump. With the establishment and the insurgents at each other's throats, neither saw the threat that Donald Trump's demagoguery posed to their control of the party. During the 2016 primaries, each side thought Donald Trump's presence in the race helped them, and so they concentrated their fire on each other. Trump understood, as neither the establishment nor the insurgents did, that a significant part of the Republican voting base had soured on free market economics, and Trump was able to win over his divided opponents, despite having virtually no support from the institutional Republican Party. This same rejection of budget-cutting Republicanism allowed Trump to eke out the narrowest of victories over Hillary Clinton, putting him in the White House and forcing the Republican Party to accommodate to his rule. What followed was an extraordinary process in which Trump was able to bend the Republican Party to his rule, establishing a degree of personalist control that is simply unprecedented in American history. This same personalism, however, proved singularly ill-suited for exercising control over the American state, leaving Trump with a weak and chaotic presidency that was largely consumed with crises of his own making.

Trump's control over the Republican Party only deepened after his defeat in 2020. While, as discussed above, the January 6 putsch alienated a large section of American capital, Trump continued as the indispensable man of the Republican Party. In the 2024 election, this resulted in Kamala Harris continuing the massive fundraising advantage her predecessors had maintained over Trump. As in 2016, however, this advantage was not sufficient to produce victory.

Though Trump had won little support from big business during the 2024 campaign, as it became clearer that he would likely win, CEOs began softening their stance towards him. Republican mega-donors, even those that had anathematized Trump after

January 6, had largely returned to the fold by the time the general election got under way. By the late days of the campaign, many corporate elites began to hedge their bets and tried to open lines of communication with the Trump camp. After Trump's victory, this coquetry evolved into shameless propositioning, as CEOs fell over themselves to win favor from the incoming administration. The fractured nature of corporate political action could not have been demonstrated with greater force, as each company scrambled to win favors for itself, with little thought as to the larger direction of American capitalism.[17]

As Trump's second term has begun, the dynamics described in this book have reached a frightening intensity. Trump's rule is as personalist as ever, and this time, one particular American capitalist—Elon Musk—has been empowered to set policy with a directness that would make J. P. Morgan blush. At the same time, this administration has demonstrated an even more forthright contempt for the rule of law than it did the last time around. It seems likely that the transformation of the Republican Party will result in a constitutional crisis more extreme than any since the secession of the South in 1861.

1

The Fractured Elite

The Republican Party's trajectory since the 1980s has been shaped by two institutional transformations that developed over the same period: the disorganization of American employers and the weakening of American political parties. Together, these forces have enabled a succession of conservative political entrepreneurs to take the party further and further right. Without an understanding of these transformations, it is impossible to understand what has happened to the Republican Party.

This chapter focuses on the disorganization of American employers. Though this disorganization has been particularly salient in American politics since the 1980s, it is nonetheless a more tectonic force in American society. American capitalists have, for some time now, been free of the burdens that weighed down their Western European counterparts, such as powerful labor movements and strong socialist parties. Assured of their dominance, American capitalists have not had to build the kind of disciplined, all-encompassing employer organizations that are the norm in Western Europe. Instead, American employers have tended to engage in far more sectional and self-interested modes of political action. This pattern was briefly disrupted during the 1970s, when American capitalists organized to confront the crises of that decade. However, with their decisive victory in the 1980s, the conditions that produced class-wide unity disintegrated, and disorganization prevailed once more. This disorganization yielded a politically fractured capitalist class, sections of which have been all too happy to fund the Republican Party's insurgent right.

Capital Organizes When Labor Does

Business organizations have existed almost as long as capitalism has. Already in 1776, Adam Smith noted in *The Wealth of Nations* that "masters are always and everywhere in a sort of tacit, but constant and uniform combination, not to raise the wages of labour above their actual rate." Keeping wages low is not the only reason capitalists organize, though it is a frequent goal. Business associations perform all kinds of services for their members, from representing them in negotiations with government to promoting the products of specific sectors to providing information and expertise.[1]

In all of this, however, business confronts problems. Some of these are the classic problems of collective action, like how to deal with free riders. Others are more specific to capitalists. Capitalists, after all, are often in competition with one another. It is not necessarily easy for Coke and Pepsi to cooperate, even where their interests overlap.

The job of business organizations is accordingly not merely to represent firms' interests but to play an active role in shaping collective interests that supersede the narrow interests of individual firms. As Wolfgang Streeck and Philippe Schmitter put it, business organizations use "organizational control mechanisms to ensure the day-to-day presence, internally as well as externally, of their collective interests as a class as opposed to their individual, and potentially self-destructive, interests." Where individual firms in a tight market might be best served by paying a premium for skilled labor, the collective result of such behavior would be a wage spiral that hurts all employers. Business organizations allow capitalists to coordinate their behavior to avoid such outcomes, as well as to formulate policy to reshape the labor market to their advantage. They enable capitalists to confront the problems capitalism creates in a collective fashion.[2]

Yet precisely because capitalists are, as Marx put it, "enemy brothers," business organizations do not form automatically. Instead, as the Adam Smith quote above suggests, they tend to form in response to collective action by workers. Claus Offe and

Helmut Wiesenthal summed up the dynamic of organization in capitalist society as follows:

> In all capitalist countries, the historical sequence is this: the first step is the "liquidation" of the means of production of small commodity producers and the merging of these into capitalist industrial firms; the second step is the defensive association of workers; and the third step is associational efforts that are now made on the part of capitalist firms who, in addition to their continued merging of capital, enter into formal organizations in order to promote some of their collective interests.[3]

Historical research has tended to confirm this account. Already in the early 1900s, when the new academic field of economics began to study employer collective action, researchers found that it generally arose in response to worker organizing. One economist began his 1906 chapter on employers organizations by noting "employer's organizations, formed solely for the purpose of dealing collectively with labor, come into existence only after organizations of employees have become strong enough to gain advantages in the making of the labor contract."[4]

By and large, business organizes when labor does. When there isn't a strong labor movement to confront, the competitive, short-sighted interests of firms are more likely to win out over longer-term, class-wide perspectives on the problems confronting employers.

Capitalist countries accordingly vary in the degree to which business organizations are present and in the role they play. In countries with strong corporatist institutions like those in Northern Europe, business organizations play a state-appointed role in collective bargaining and various tripartite (or bipartite) committees, which also include representatives from organized labor and the government. In these countries, business organizations are centralized and powerful, formulating policy for the capitalist class as a whole.[5]

In the United States, by contrast, business organization has always been decentralized and limited in coverage. There has never been a single, peak-level business organization representing even a strong plurality of American firms. Instead, the US has had various kinds of small councils of large companies alongside competing mass-membership business organizations. While these groups have often been incredibly powerful in American politics, they have not tended to transmute the individual interests of firms into a class-wide perspective. As Cathie Jo Martin has argued, it is "much harder for U.S. employers to think about their collective long-term interests than their counterparts elsewhere." As multiple organizations compete to represent business interests, business organizations have to themselves be concerned with their market share. They find it easier to "voice short-term objections than to endorse positive policy change."[6]

Employer Disorganization in the Early Twentieth Century

Large-scale organization by American employers emerged in the late nineteenth century, around the same time that the American union movement established itself on solid footing. Though the Knights of Labor had flared up spectacularly in the 1880s, reaching nearly three quarters of a million members, it quickly collapsed. By the turn of the century, however, the American Federation of Labor was surpassing the high water mark set by the Knights, and doing so on a more durable basis. Around this same time, two of the country's key employer organizations— the National Association of Manufacturers (NAM) and the US Chamber of Commerce—emerged. Yet as resilient as these organizations have proven to be (both continue to be influential today), a closer look at their history reveals that neither tended to function as all-encompassing, class-wide organizations and that, instead, they express far narrower interests.[7]

The NAM was founded first, in 1896. The timing is significant —1896 was an election year, and far from representing a push for collective action among employers, the NAM functioned largely as an adjunct of the Republican Party. The party was attempting to consolidate its position as the party of American business in these years. All the men involved in its establishment were deeply involved in the McKinley campaign, and after the fanfare of its founding, which included a parade for McKinley and a keynote address by the candidate, the organization stalled. In 1901, the NAM could claim 1,082 members, but the 1900 Census listed 296,400 manufacturing firms in the country. There was, as yet, little demand for what the NAM was selling.[8]

In response, the NAM changed its product line. The years around the turn of the century had seen an impressive surge in union organizing in the United States, with the American Federation of Labor (AFL) increasing in membership from under 500,000 in 1897 to over two million by 1904. When the NAM shifted towards a more anti-union stance, firms responded quickly. Membership rose quickly to 2,700 a few months after the new position was announced. As one study of the NAM's early years concludes, "it was not until the NAM became the standard bearer for vigorous antiunionism that it assumed a commanding position among economic interest groups in terms of number of members, amount of income, and scope of activities."[9]

Even in the context of the vicious anti-unionism of American employers before the New Deal, however, the NAM made little headway as a class-wide business organization. Its membership topped out at only 5,000 firms in the 1920s. Unable to cohere a positive program beyond anti-unionism, the organization drifted. Association officials admitted "we are a fragmentary body. We have officers but we lack numbers."[10]

The US Chamber of Commerce followed a similar trajectory. It, too, was organized more by politicians than by employers. In this case, it was officials in the Department of Commerce who saw US businesses slipping behind their European counterparts in organization and feared the impact on American exports. In 1912, the Secretary of Commerce organized a conference to found the Chamber, which featured President Howard Taft as a speaker.[11]

With its close links to the American economic policy apparatus, the Chamber was soon more influential than the NAM. It also distributed voting rights based on the size of local business organizations that affiliated with it, creating an incentive for powerful local groups to join. Calvin Coolidge and Herbert

Hoover praised it publicly and looked to it for advice privately. By 1929 the Chamber had over 13,000 individual/firm members and a budget of over two million dollars.[12]

Yet the Chamber was ultimately no more successful than the NAM in cultivating a class-wide program of action for American business. It was, as Colin Gordon has written, "superficially effective" at "disguising elite corporate and banking opinion as that of 'business' [as a whole]," but "as a means of organizing or representing broader interests, it was neither effective nor particularly interested." As a result, the organization came under severe stress during the Great Depression, as its members vacillated between cooperation with and opposition to the New Deal. It began losing members. In 1936, Edward Filene, a department store owner, announced his resignation in a public letter to the group's board of directors. The Chamber, he complained

> is not an organization of *business*, but rather an organization of *business men*—meeting not to study business in a business way, nor even to find out what the needs of business in general may be, but ... to promote the special views of certain prominent people in the business world ... The Chamber as at present organized may function as a successful club of business men when times are good, or as a potent center of reaction when changing times make some great new forward step necessary; but in neither role can it furnish any real help to business.

Filene wasn't alone in this opinion, and many firms learned to accommodate themselves to government's new role in the economy during the 1930s. The same year of Filene's letter, the Automobile Manufacturers Association, a founding member of the Chamber, announced its withdrawal from the group. Membership in the Chamber was no longer a means of gaining influence in government.[13]

The Committee for Economic Development

The most influential American business organization in the mid-twentieth century was the Committee for Economic Development. Founded during World War II by corporate moderates unhappy with the Chamber and the NAM, it quickly became a key source of policy planning for both the corporate community and the state, and its members regularly took high positions in the federal bureaucracy. Yet for all its influence, the CED tended to represent a minority viewpoint among American employers and was structurally incapable of producing greater coherence. More a think tank than an employers' organization, its successes themselves are indicative of the disorganized character of American business in the middle third of the twentieth century.

The CED was founded in 1942 by a group of business leaders concerned that the purely rejectionist approach of the Chamber and the NAM would lead business to have no influence over postwar policy planning. Its incorporation papers were based on those of the Brookings Institution, underlining its role as a think tank rather than a lobbying organization. Its leadership was drawn from the American corporate elite. Of the twenty-seven founding trustees, twenty-one came from corporate backgrounds, and of these, fourteen came from corporations that would be in the Fortune 500 in its inaugural year or a subsequent year. Three of the others came from major retailers or investment banks.[14]

The Truman administration was the period of the CED's greatest influence (in fact, so many members were appointed to administration positions that it "was forced to call a meeting to replenish its ranks"), and here it had several major successes in shaping the American political economy. The first successes concerned the United States' global role after the war. When the Bretton Woods agreement structuring international trade was being debated in Congress, the CED played a crucial role in mobilizing business support for it. President Truman himself praised the CED as "unequivocally ... determinative in passing the Bretton Woods Bill." Shortly thereafter, the CED helped win public and congressional support for the Marshall Plan. Finally, the CED mobilized behind the Cold War designs set forward in National Security Memorandum No. 68, which became a foundational document for American anticommunist global strategy. While congressional conservatives worried about the fiscal deficits required to maintain a permanent American troop presence in Western Europe, behind the scenes, the CED pushed to support increased expenditures both in Europe and for the Korean War. The CED was, in short, an important force in the formative years of American postwar global strategy.[15]

The CED's success in securing funding for the Cold War led directly to its next major contribution, which lay in achieving a durable accord between the Department of the Treasury and the Federal Reserve. After World War II, conflict had developed between the Treasury and the Fed over interest rates, with Truman and the Treasury demanding low rates to finance defense expenditures while the Fed preferred higher rates to ward off inflation. Into this conflict stepped the CED. The CED had close links with the Fed; many of its researchers had been employed at various points at the Federal Reserve banks, and the Fed's new chair, Thomas McCabe, was a founding trustee of the CED and an original member of its research committee. The CED had also, over the previous years, worked out a preference for a Federal Reserve that would be independent of the administration in power, writing in its 1948 report *Monetary and Fiscal Policy for Greater Economic Stability*, "The Federal Reserve should feel free to reduce the support level [of government bonds] unless it finds a superior alternative way of bringing about a monetary restriction." With the CED behind the Fed, the administration soon yielded, and an accord was reached whereby the independence of the Federal Reserve would be respected by subsequent administrations. This accord was of enormous importance. As Gerald Epstein and Juliet Schor write, "more than any other single event, [it] established the structure for the monetary policy regime of the postwar period."[16]

Despite these foundational successes, the CED never came close to establishing itself as the voice of a unified American employer class. It was constantly attacked from the right by other business groups. The *Wall Street Journal* accused the group of being "communistic" at one point, prompting the CED to release a statement reaffirming their belief in the free enterprise system. As Howell John Harris concluded of the group, the CED's "practical conservative and reactionary colleagues were more numerous and more immediately influential within the business community itself."[17]

The CED's success in shaping policy, while representing a distinctly minoritarian current of business opinion, underscores the disorganization of American business for much of the twentieth century. This disorganization does not denote an absence of business organizations; as described above, there were several. Moreover, these organizations were powerful enough that they were basically able to exclude organized labor from policymaking for this period, with few exceptions. Their very dominance, however, is what fostered disorganization. Largely unchallenged by working class movements, American employers never felt the imperative to unite in the way their European counterparts started to around the turn of the twentieth century.[18]

Dominance Disrupted

The historic dominance of American business was challenged in the late sixties and early seventies, as political and economic developments combined to bring gloom to corporate boardrooms across the country. In response, American employers would embark on an unprecedented campaign of class mobilization in the 1970s. There were three developments that spurred employers to action: the rise of regulatory policy, climbing construction costs, and economic turbulence.

The late sixties and early seventies saw a wave of regulatory legislation unlike anything that came before it. In 1969, Richard Nixon signed the Occupational Safety and Health Act (OSHA). In 1970, he signed the National Environmental Protection Act (NEPA). Consumer protection legislation, meanwhile, was defeated during this period but was nonetheless a constant worry for business.

Both OSHA and NEPA managed to pass Congress without a great deal of opposition from business. Though the Chamber had mobilized against OSHA, the CED did not take a position on it. As Charles Noble, the leading scholar of OSHA's passage, put it, their failure was "a result of an organizational lacuna ... No peak association existed that could speak for employers as a whole and negotiate these issues with organized labor and government. This was particularly important because employers were divided among themselves. These differences might have been resolved by class-conscious leadership, but none emerged." Environmental legislation, meanwhile, had significant support from business. The *National Journal* noted at the time that "there are indications that some corporate interests would welcome a centralization of environmental programs in the Federal government." A survey by *Fortune* magazine at the same time found strong support among chief executives for environmental legislation, "even if it means inhibiting the introduction of new products."[19]

After their passage, however, both laws drew significant opposition from business. In 1971, CEOs of some of the largest corporations were admitting that the new wave of regulation was becoming a serious problem. When two journalists sat in on meetings of the Conference Board, a discussion forum for business leaders, in 1974 and 1975, they noted that "almost every executive has some bureaucratic horror story to relate of his experience with some allegedly unreasonable official from ... the Occupational Health and Safety Administration." There was plainly a need for a counteroffensive, though it was not immediately clear who would lead it.[20]

Unlike environmentalism and occupational safety, consumer protection legislation was met with a united front of opposition from business. The modern consumer protection movement emerged in the 1960s, led by a young lawyer named Ralph Nader. Nader first announced his proposed agency with Senator Abraham Ribicoff of Connecticut in the spring of 1969. The corporate response to this campaign was nothing short of apoplectic. In 1970, the Chamber issued a filmstrip entitled "The Consumer Revolution" that began by listing the challenges the country faced, including "restless youth demanding sweeping changes ... militant minorities battling for social and economic change ... rioting in our cities ... bombing office buildings ...

marches on Washington ... angry consumers protesting rising prices and other problems of the marketplace." The American corporate leadership felt, for the first time in decades, that their hold on power might be slipping.[21]

Construction costs were also a cause of worry. Construction was an unusually decentralized industry; in the 1940s, *Fortune* magazine dubbed it "the Business Capitalism Forgot." In the late 1960s, in the context of record low unemployment, wages—and hence construction costs—increased rapidly. Workers on strike at a given worksite could easily sustain themselves by working for another company in the interim. The firms hiring the contractor, meanwhile, often placed more of a premium on completing a project on time than holding down construction costs, which reduced resistance to higher wage settlements. Concern began mounting about this situation in the mid-sixties. In 1964, the chair of the president's Council of Economic Advisors (CEA) sounded the alarm on construction costs. In 1966, the National Association of Manufacturers was getting theatrical in its jeremiads, warning: "For want of a nail, a kingdom was lost ... For want of someone to hammer nails, America ... may have some serious difficulties in reaching the potential its advancing technology ... indicate[s] to be possible." The Chamber of Commerce began calling on companies to shut down projects where there were local strikes, depriving workers of income while they struck. As will be discussed in more detail below, these initiatives eventually coalesced into a new organization, the Construction Users Anti-Inflation Roundtable (CUAIR), which would itself play a central role in the surge of business organization of the 1970s.[22]

The last challenge to the corporate elite in this period was the economic turbulence of these years, which manifested as declining profitability and increased inflation. Inflation rates had climbed during the late sixties, reaching 4.4 percent by January 1969 and topping 6 percent a year later. At the same time, American business was losing ground in international markets. Between 1965 and 1973, the "the U.S. share of the manufacturing exports of the main industrial countries fell sharply by a third." Constrained by this competition, manufacturing firms in particular were unable to raise prices, forcing their profitability downwards.

Meanwhile, declining American manufacturing competitiveness exacerbated the balance of payments problems threatening the economy since the 1950s, as money flowing out to other countries grew more quickly than money coming in.[23]

The first sign of the new employer recalcitrance manifested on the shop floor. Unfair labor practice complaints to the National Labor Relations Board (NLRB) rose sharply in the late 1950s as employers tried to squeeze more from workers during the recession of Eisenhower's second term. They continued to rise steadily in the 1960s, again increasing rapidly after the boom of the sixties ended. From 1965 to 1973, the NLRB's caseload doubled, as corporations engaged in what the board's chair later described as "sophisticated testing and probing ... to find every possible loophole in the statute."[24]

Employers conducted their battle outside of the plant as well. In 1965, a group of management lawyers and corporate executives formed an organization that would eventually be called the Labor Law Reform Group (LLRG). The LLRG had three objectives. First, it would identify weak points in existing labor law and statutes that needed to be changed. Second, it would convince Americans that unions had too much power, through a public relations campaign that included radio plays and storylines in comics like *Peanuts*. Finally, it would conduct a political campaign to elect Republicans who would carry through the desired legislative changes.[25]

The LLRG was necessary because the existing organizations of business were insufficient to coordinate the battle against unions. As the legal historian James Gross put it, "there was also no unanimity in U.S. employers' reactions to unionism and collective bargaining, which ranged from acceptance of organization and 'effects' bargaining, to preference for operating without a union and adoption of wage and personnel policies that made unions appear unnecessary, to resistance (lawful and unlawful), to unionization." In order for the crises that began in the late 1960s to be addressed, business needed to organize to create of a consensus towards collective bargaining.[26]

By 1970, then, a sort of consensus was building among employers. The state had gone too far with regulations and needed to be restrained. Similarly, employers were increasingly in agreement that the restoration of macroeconomic stability required the destruction of the beachheads of working class power built since the New Deal. As G. William Domhoff put it, "reducing union power became the primary concern for both moderates and ultraconservatives in the corporate community by 1968, whether the immediate issue was inflation, wage rates, profit margins, or foreign trade." By 1970, corporations had begun reorganizing themselves to accomplish these goals. But the following decade would see a resurgence of corporate organization that would remake the American political economy, as well as, ironically, sowing the seeds for the return to disorganization.[27]

Building an Army

The 1970s witnessed a reorganization and assertion of business power unprecedented in the twentieth century. As the associational forms of previous decades proved unable to meet the challenges at hand, old organizations faded and new ones were created. Most importantly, the CED, rent by internal disagreement, found itself largely irrelevant by 1980. Meanwhile, a new organization, the Business Roundtable had been founded, which was composed of the CEOs of the largest American corporations. Dedicated to combating labor as well as unwelcome governmental regulation, the Roundtable quickly established itself as a powerful voice in federal policymaking. During these same years, the Chamber of Commerce underwent a striking revitalization, vastly increasing its membership and funding to embark on a new campaign to reshape the American political economy.

At the beginning of the first Nixon administration, the CED appeared to be playing its customary role, supplying a number of appointees to various positions and issuing reports that shaped policy. However, the politics of inflation exposed a growing rift between the CED and the rest of the business community, and by the end of the decade, its power was considerably reduced. As inflation ticked up in the 1970s, the CED had recommended price controls as one instrument to combat it. In 1971, Nixon followed their advice, using authority granted him by the 1970 Economic Stabilization Act. The controls, however, failed to tame prices, and by the mid-1970s, the business community had turned decisively against them. Meanwhile, at the CED, support for such measures remained strong, with one trustee giving a speech endorsing the kind of corporatist arrangements that were common in Western Europe. In response, another trustee, the management theorist Marvin Bower (founder of McKinsey & Company), circulated a letter among the other trustees asking "whether CED should continue to be a proponent of Keynesian doctrine," attaching a recent speech on inflation by the libertarian economist Friedrich Hayek. At this point, leading members of the CED were questioning the embrace of Keynesianism, which had been the group's raison d'etre when it was formed.[28]

This episode precipitated a crisis in the organization. Its president, who had run the group since the mid-1950s, resigned. A survey of members revealed that the CED had lost the allegiance of many of its corporate sponsors, and the group had to cut its budget. Mark Mizruchi has chronicled the CED's declining power by tracking its mentions in the *New York Times*. As he concludes, "the frequency of attention given to the CED dropped sharply during the 1970s." Already by 1977, the conservative American Enterprise Institute, which was essentially a non-player a decade earlier, was receiving more attention. In under a decade, the CED had gone from being the premiere business organization in the United States to a beleaguered and divided group that could barely speak for itself, let alone the sprawling corporate community as a whole.[29]

The Business Roundtable was organized to play the role the CED could not—a disciplined organization of capitalists advancing their interests as a class. Two men were crucial to its founding. Winton Blount was an Alabama construction executive who had was elected head of the Chamber of Commerce in 1968. Shortly after his election, he gave a speech to a construction employers' association calling for all-out war on the construction unions. While there was considerable enthusiasm for his proposal, Blount himself was unable to lead the charge, having been appointed by Richard Nixon to be postmaster general. Attention turned to

Roger Blough. The longtime CEO of US Steel, Blough represented the pinnacle of corporate power in the US. He had been chair of the Business Council, a trustee of the CED, and also sat on the board of J. P. Morgan. In early 1969, corporate executives were calling on Blough personally to head up Blount's initiative.[30]

In May of 1969, at a meeting of the Business Council, a group of executives announced the formation of the Construction Users Anti-Inflation Roundtable. Blough had agreed to chair the group, on the condition that "all CEOs present in the meeting would support the organization and would personally participate on a Policy Committee." CUAIR's strategy was to organize employers to act as a class, supporting each other in their battles with unions. Members would refuse to hire workers striking other job sites and hold the line on overtime pay, even if it meant projects took longer to finish. As the *Wall Street Journal* reported in its scoop revealing CUAIR's existence, its members would "monitor each other in a sort of internal police system."[31]

CUAIR then merged with two other groups: the Labor Law Reform Group, discussed above, and the March Group. The March Group had begun as an informal gathering of CEOs originally convened by the CEO of General Electric in the 1950s. Rather than hiring staff to do research, like the CED did, the March Group would formulate policy directly through conversations among CEOs. In 1972, the merger of CUAIR and the LLRG created The Business Roundtable—For Responsible Labor-Management Relations, and the entrance of the March Group the following year completed the group's formation.[32]

From the beginning, the Roundtable was notably more centralized and coordinated than previous American business groups. Its ambition was, in the words of one historian, to be a "disciplined phalanx defending the interests of business as a class." This emphasis on discipline flowed from the complaints corporate leaders had with the disorganization of their class. As one Roundtable member put it, "Business was getting kicked around compared to labor, consumers, and other groups, and the constant cry within the business community was 'How come we can't get together and make our voices heard?'" The Roundable's ambition was not merely to amplify the voices of business leaders but to forge them into one voice. As another member summarized,

> The purpose of the Roundtable was to be much more catholic, not representing the banking industry nor the oil industry nor the steel industry, but representing the very fundamental business climate in the United States and, in effect, the survival of the free enterprise system.[33]

By 1970, the US Chamber of Commerce had a reputation as a predictable and not terribly effective business lobby. It was, as Thomas Edsall has written, "dismissed as a collection of unrealistic fiscal conservatives who were still fighting causes that had been lost in the 1930s and 1940s, unequipped to participate in ... highly complex contemporary battles." In the 1970s, this changed drastically.[34]

Discontent with the Chamber's position was rife among its membership. In response, the group moved to professionalize its leadership, changing its president position from a volunteer role to a full-time paid position. In 1975, Richard Lesher, a former NASA manager who was serving as the president of a trade association for the solid waste disposal industry, was hired for the job.[35]

Lesher was a true believer in the free market, and set about turning the Chamber into a formidable organ in defense of business. As one local chamber leader put it, "It's almost like BC and AD—only it's Before Lesher and After Lesher." Single-minded in his focus, Lesher was not interested in moderation in the pursuit of business power. He immediately began forging the Chamber into an instrument of battle. It resumed contributions to its political action committee (PAC), the Business-Industry Political Action Committee, whose status had been newly regularized by campaign finance law. It also organized a number of new initiatives. First, it set up an associated think tank, the National Chamber Foundation, which could produce reports and design proposed legislation. Second, it set up the National Chamber Litigation Center, which would lead the fight for business in the courts. Finally, it set up its own grassroots organization,

Citizens Choice, modeled after Ralph Nader's Public Citizen, which would mobilize members to contact congressmembers on issues of concern. These initiatives, alongside a determined membership campaign by Lesher, revitalized the group's flagging fortunes. In 1976, at the beginning of Lesher's campaign, the Chamber had 49,350 members. Just six years later, it had amassed 234,000.[36]

The Chamber never became as central to the policy process as the CED or the Business Roundtable. However, its tenacious, multifront war on activist government augmented the work of the Roundtable in important ways. The Chamber, after all, can claim a kind of popular character that is simply unavailable to the mandarins of the Business Roundtable. As Patrick Akard put it, when its "enormous grassroots potential is mobilized in support of pro-business policy initiatives formulated by the Roundtable and other corporate leaders, it is a powerful political force."[37]

The Business Offensive

In the second half of the 1970s, business flexed its new muscles. Though they had been able to count on Gerald Ford, who had replaced Nixon, to veto liberal legislation, in 1976 the Democrats took control of the White House with massive majorities in the House and Senate. Liberals and labor organizations assumed they would finally be able to pass the reforms Ford had blocked. They failed to see how the political terrain had changed.

The liberal-labor coalition had coalesced to focus on three priorities: consumer protection legislation, labor law reform, and a full employment bill. Consumer protection looked like the surest bet. However, the Consumer Issues Working Group, which coordinated action between the Roundtable, the NAM, and the Chamber, launched a massive campaign that peeled away Democratic House members. One congressman was candid about the reason he switched: "I'm afraid that the Chamber will run a candidate against me in the primary." Labor law reform ran aground on similar opposition. According to one Chamber lobbyist, the campaign against it "took on the dimensions of a holy war." Coordinating through the National Action Committee on Labor Law Reform, business organizations maintained impressive discipline, even in the face of some members who did not want to expend political capital over a fight that would worsen relations with their unions. Finally, the fight for a full employment bill, which had roots going back to the civil rights movement, was successful; the bill passed, but business had watered down the legislation so thoroughly that it had no impact at all on employment policy.[38]

By the second half of the Carter administration, business had turned the tide so thoroughly that it was ready to go on the offensive. Its main target was inflation. There was by now a consensus across the American corporate leadership that inflation was a result of workers having too much power and that halting inflation required breaking labor's back. To accomplish this, they turned to the state. In 1978, Jimmy Carter appointed Paul Volcker head of the Federal Reserve with the mission of getting inflation (which would reach 13 percent by the end of the decade) under control. Volcker was a conservative banker who was well connected in corporate planning circles, serving on the Trilateral Commission and the Council on Foreign Relations. By raising the reserve requirements for banks, Volcker pushed interest rates sky-high. The result was an intense contraction of economic activity that pushed unemployment from a dismal 6 percent in October, the month the Volcker Shock began, to a painful 7.8 percent by July. The effect on the American working class was devastating.[39]

The Volcker Shock destroyed many businesses. In the second quarter of 1980, business investment declined by a staggering 31.4 percent. Seventeen thousand companies failed. Yet what was extraordinary was the discipline capital showed in continuing to support high interest rates. In 1980, the CED's subcommittee on inflation held a meeting at which the subcommittee's chair, who also sat on the policy committee of the Roundtable, remarked, "I think there is widespread support for persistent, steady demand management in the business community. There is strong support there." The report produced by the subcommittee argued forthrightly that a recession was a price worth paying for combating inflation. In 1983, in the midst of the worst recession since the Great Depression, the Chamber and the NAM came out for Volcker's reappointment (they were opposed by the National Association of Homebuilders, who were being wrecked by high mortgage rates). Business was displaying remarkable unity on a project that inflicted severe short-term costs on many employers.[40]

When Reagan won in 1980 (with backing from a coalition that extended from Goldman Sachs to Bethlehem Steel), business's next priority was rewriting the tax code. As negotiations on Reagan's first major policy priority got underway, business pushed for a major cut in the corporate tax rate. At the same time, supply side ideologues like Jack Kemp pushed for a massive cut to personal income taxes. Though groups like the Business Roundtable were concerned about the possible deficit effects of such a munificent tax cut, they supported the entire package with the view that later spending cuts could make up for the lost revenue.[41]

The effort to pass Reagan's tax bill through a Democratic congress was impressive. The Chamber of Commerce launched a full-scale lobbying and public education campaign. White House staffers praised the group as "more active than perhaps any organization" in "fully endorsing every aspect of the President's program." An informal breakfast group for business lobbyists, the Carlton Group, became a major coordinator for the pressure campaign, with representatives from the Chamber, the Roundtable, and a host of other business organizations. Such coordination was necessary, the Chamber's manager of the effort noted, "to keep a united front within the business community so we don't start tearing the package apart."[42]

The tax bill passed. The effective tax rate on businesses plunged, from 33 percent to 16 percent. Yet almost as soon as the bill passed, cracks began to appear in the edifice of business unity. The skyrocketing deficits caused by the tax cuts opened up new fractures among the business community, which was divided between those who thought closing the deficit was most important and those who thought preserving the tax cuts was.

Crucially, this was a debate entirely among the business elite. As Patrick Akard remarks, "labor and progressive interests were nonparticipants in the policy process. The only question was which conservative faction would rule."[43]

Things Fall Apart

The deficits opened up by the 1981 tax bill quickly exposed the limits of business unity. Groups like the Business Roundtable and the NAM pushed for deficit reduction measures that would spare business, from military cuts to delaying or even rescinding personal income taxes. Both were policies the Reagan administration strongly opposed. When the administration pushed hard for a clawback of some of the business cuts, the Roundtable's policy committee was itself divided over whether to accept or oppose them. The Chamber of Commerce, meanwhile, opposed any tax increases, remaining fully committed to the supply side agenda even as Reagan himself abandoned it. This has often been attributed to Chamber head Richard Lesher's being, ideologically speaking, plus royaliste que le roi. Yet the organization's inability to find a compromise was itself a result of its attempt to function as a consensus-seeking organization of American capital. The Chamber's tax committee tried again and again to find a consensus plan for raising revenue, but every plan was rejected by large numbers of members. As the manager of the Chamber's tax policy center put it, "[A proposed compromise approach] attracted more opposition than either one of the others, so we dropped the whole thing. If we haven't got a strong consensus, we just don't move." The Chamber's sudden opposition to the administration, after having worked so closely with it on the 1981 tax cuts, stemmed not from ideological purity, but from the dilemmas an organization trying to forge a class-wide consensus now faced.[44]

In the absence of a unifying external threat, capitalist class unity became far more difficult to maintain. On the most basic level, organizations like the Chamber of Commerce had trouble selling membership with a friend of business like Reagan in the

White House. By the mid-eighties, Chamber membership was once again falling, dipping below 200,000 in 1985. One senior official explained the trouble, "For the last six and a half years, you've had a President in the White House who said he'd veto anything antibusiness. So why should business people bother to join?" With the various threats of the 1970s receding in the rearview mirror, the divisions and disorganization that characterized American business associations for most of the twentieth century once again began to assert themselves.[45]

As noted above, the Business Roundtable started experiencing severe internal divisions after the 1981 Reagan tax cuts blew a huge hole in the federal budget. In both the 1982 and 1986 tax bills, the organization was divided and unable to exert significant pressure to preserve the tax provisions most favorable to business. As one Reagan administration official said of the business lobby at the time, "They were brought down by the narrowness of their vision. Precisely because they defined themselves as representatives of single special interests, they failed to notice their collective power." Some issues, however, could still motivate decisive action—for example, new Federal Accounting Standards Board (FASB) regulations that would have forced companies to treat stock options for executives as real costs to the business, rather than essentially free perks. The Roundtable moved swiftly into action to block the changes, inviting the FASB's research director to a private meeting with the chair of the group's accounting principles taskforce. The head of the SEC later said he had to devote about a third of his time to this issue alone and was constantly "being threatened and cajoled by legions of businesspeople." The Roundtable had found an issue on which there was unanimity, but it was one that only confirmed how narrow and provincial corporate political action was becoming.[46]

Over the course of the 1990s, the Roundtable went into organizational decline. To be sure, there were some key victories, as when it organized vigorously for the World Trade Organization and other free trade agreements. But observers in Washington noted that its influence was not what it once was. In 1997, *Fortune* magazine ran a story on its decline entitled "The Fallen

Giant," which noted the group's troubles achieving consensus. Around the same time, the group's president wrote a memo urging a tripling of its dues to finance more aggressive campaigning. But the move backfired, costing the group nearly a third of its membership. At the same time, the organization found itself bullied by the GOP, who, with their new congressional majority after 1994, tried to corral the business lobby into exclusively backing Republicans.[47]

The New Rules of the Game

By the 1990s, the main business organizations were operating very differently from how they had in the late 1970s. Freed from the external threats that had generated their unity, they reverted to the kind of sectional and fragmented mobilization that had characterized business organizing for most of the twentieth century.

During this period, the Roundtable continued to press for business-friendly policies like tax cuts and social security privatization. But the issue that spurred large-scale mobilization was, once again, a narrow question of corporate governance. This time, it was a provision in the Dodd-Frank financial reform bill that would have made it easier for shareholders to elect different directors to a corporation's board. In response, the Roundtable flew into action. Castellani declared, "This is our highest priority. Literally all of our members have called about this." In the aftermath of the 2008 financial crisis, this mobilization wasn't enough to kill the provision. It passed as part of Dodd-Frank. However, the Roundtable and the Chamber of Commerce sued and succeeded in getting the rule removed. Social scientists later estimated that the Roundtable's success in protecting managerial autonomy against shareholder oversight wiped $70 billion off the value of public corporations. Once again, the Roundtable's political activity focused on the narrowest and most provincial aspects of policy.[48]

The Chamber of Commerce's evolution has been even more bizarre than the Roundtable's. As noted above, the Chamber also faced significant internal dissension over Reagan's deficits, and its consensus-seeking procedures prevented it from putting forward any plan for dealing with them. The political scientist Mark Smith provides a description of the Chamber's decision-making during this period:

> The organization probably could not survive without incorporating its members into decision-making. By involving its diverse membership in deliberations that set its positions, the Chamber can help avoid taking stands opposed by part of its constituency. The participation of members helps to ensure that the Chamber takes action only when there is a consensus within business. Even when decisions must be reached without large-scale consultation of the Chamber's constituency, the policy committees, board of directors, and staff use available information and precedents to find the common ground supported throughout the business community.

This kind of procedure put the Chamber at a disadvantage in the increasingly fractious world of American business.[49]

By the early 1990s, the Chamber's budget had fallen by more than 40 percent in real value, and its membership had declined significantly from the early 1980s. Its conduct during the fight over Bill Clinton's healthcare plan illuminates the multiple pressures the group was under. On the one hand, the Chamber hoped to influence Clinton's bill and declared its support for the project of healthcare reform early on. On the other hand, the GOP put pressure on them to fall in line behind Newt Gingrich's increasingly bellicose leadership. John Boehner told the Chamber's leadership it was "the Chamber's duty to categorically oppose everything that Clinton was in favor of." At the same time, the Chamber started to face competition from the National Federation of Independent Businesses (NFIB), a group claiming to represent small business. As G. William Domhoff has emphasized, the NFIB is not actually a business organization. It was founded as a for-profit company selling membership to businesses. While it reincorporated as a nonprofit in the late 1960s, the sales model still dominated the group. In the 1990s, 600 of its 800 employees were sales representatives tasked with signing up businesses for the group. Since the early 1990s, it had drawn extremely close to the Republican Party. Significant evidence suggests that the group exists mainly as a GOP-linked lobbying firm selling membership to small businesses, rather than an actual business association.[50]

It is thus indicative of the Chamber's weakness and disorganization that it began losing members in significant numbers to the NFIB in the 1990s. As one Chamber official later recalled, "We were getting creamed in the field by NFIB. It was as much a market share, competitive issue as anything else." Ultimately, as discussed in more detail in a subsequent chapter, the Chamber turned against the bill.[51]

When Richard Lesher retired in the late 1990s, he was replaced by Thomas Donohue, former head of the American Truckers Association and manager of the Chamber's astroturf organization, Citizen's Choice, in the 1970s. Donohue found a new model for the Chamber's work. He followed the example of Citizens for a Sound Economy (CSE), a group associated with the libertarian milieu around the Cato Institute and funded by Charles and David Koch. CSE had pioneered a business model in which the group's mobilizing capacities were effectively rented out to its donors. CSE could take corporate donations and then lobby for potentially unpopular causes under its name instead of the corporate donors. Under Donohue, the Chamber picked up this business model. Rather than attempting to forge a consensus among a diverse group of companies, the Chamber would offer its resources to the highest bidder. Operating nominally as a trade association, it would focus on shielding companies wishing to push unpopular causes that might damage their brands. Their donations to the Chamber would be secret, and the Chamber's lobbyists and attorneys would be the ones to get their hands dirty. Donohue was explicit about the purpose of this business model, boasting, "I want to give them all the deniability they need."[52]

This new business model was first piloted with the tobacco industry, who, as we will see, lurked behind many of the 1990s' most significant political developments. Facing pressure from Bill Clinton's FDA, the industry needed a new strategy for fighting back. It found its way to the Chamber in the fight over a new cigarette tax being discussed in Congress. The Chamber offered its services to derail the bill. Philip Morris poured over $200 thousand into the Chamber in 1998 alone. As the Chamber pumped out ads opposing the bill and supplied a constant stream of lobbyists to oppose it on Capitol Hill, other tobacco companies took note of its good work and started kicking in funds. The Senate blocked the bill, and a new model of business advocacy (one can no longer call it organization) was born.[53]

Over the next decade and a half, the Chamber would offer its reputation-laundering services to a number of different industries. When Congress considered new auto safety regulations in the wake of the Ford/Firestone recall in 2000, GM, Toyota, Ford, and Chrysler pumped over half a million dollars into lobbying to remove criminal penalties for auto executives from the legislation. Eleven pharmaceutical companies kicked in over a million dollars each for a campaign about prescription drug pricing. All of this paled, however, next to the tidal wave of cash the insurance industry sent towards the Chamber in 2009 and 2010. In 2009, the America's Health Insurance Plans, an insurance trade group, donated more than $85 million to the Chamber, which came to 42 percent of its funds that year. These funds allowed the insurance industry to play a double game, pledging support for reform efforts in public, all the while funding the Chamber's scorched-earth campaign against a public option or any meaningful regulations on the industry. Throughout all of this, Donohue continued to insist to journalists that donations to the Chamber were unrelated to its decisions to get involved in different political causes. The group was selling plausible deniability so rapidly, it seemed, it had forgotten to save any for itself.[54]

In the three decades that followed Reagan's administration, American business's form of political action changed drastically. The united fight to tear down the remnants of New Deal liberalism was over, and business had won. Its victory, however, undermined the very conditions that had made such unity possible. Now exercising an unquestioned dominance over American politics, business found itself rent by the kinds of divisions that had seemed insignificant in the 1970s. They became, once more, "a band of warring brothers." The political-economic changes that followed capital's victory undermined their ability for unity even further.

In this new environment, the leading organizations of American capital could no longer operate in the same way. They stopped trying to forge a class-wide perspective and stopped seeking consensus. Instead, they attached themselves to the most narrow and sectional concerns of business, whether that meant shielding the tobacco industry from liability or doing everything possible to preserve managerial autonomy.

For these sorts of endeavors, a Republican Party moving ever further to the right was a profitable partner. The Republican right could be counted on to fight against any real penalties for business malfeasance, to back the most brutal slashing of the tax code, and to fight for judges who would maintain a ceaseless hostility towards labor unions and regulations. What Richard Lachmann describes as the "autarkic" orientation of American capital fit perfectly with the party becoming more and more conservative.[55]

2

The Enfeebled Parties

From the perspective of many other capitalist democracies, American political parties don't really exist. They have no membership lists, their platforms are largely built after their candidates are nominated, and, perhaps most important, the parties themselves have very little control over the nomination process. Thus, it is not unheard-of for a Holocaust denier, for example, to win a Republican primary in a deep-blue district in which the party invests no resources or for a member of the LaRouche cult to win a Democratic nomination in a deep-red district. Though in such cases the party will often denounce the candidate, it has no power to prevent them from running on its ballot line.[1]

The insubstantiality of American parties is one half of the explanation for why the Republican Party has found itself driven by a series of conservative political entrepreneurs into a position where it is often in conflict with its historic benefactors in the business community. Lacking a party leadership capable of containing and channeling insurgent energies, the party has lurched rightward time and again since the 1980s. The results have ranged from the debacle of Newt Gingrich's government shutdown in the 1990s to the abortive corporate boycott of the GOP in the wake of the riot on January 6, 2021.

This weakness has both proximate and more distant causes. This chapter traces the longstanding roots of party weakness in the United States, as well as the specific trajectory of parties after World War II that resulted in their current hollowness.

Parties Without Principle

The authors of the American Constitution did not want political parties to exist in their new nation. Inheritors of the political thought of Georgian England, the founders were at best ambivalent about organized political opposition to the current government, seeing in such activity the seeds of civil war. Of course, in a political system based on mass suffrage, parties were an inevitability, and organized opposition soon cohered against George Washington's administration. Calling themselves the Democratic-Republicans, they built "the world's first modern party organization." The party united legislators with extra-governmental figures who coordinated party actions and work among constituents. Yet if the Democratic-Republicans built something like a modern party organization, the postrevolutionary period never saw a real party system. The Federalists never managed to build a corresponding infrastructure, largely decayed after their defeat in 1800, and by the mid-1810s the Democratic-Republicans simply absorbed the remnants of the Federalists, yielding a one-party system.[2]

In the 1820s, under the impact of the depression that began in 1819, the one-party system fractured, yielding the first mass parties in American history. Andrew Jackson, representing those who had been excluded under the ruling National Republicans (as they had renamed themselves after the Federalist infusion), partnered with the Albany politician Martin Van Buren to form the Democratic Party. Using patronage to reward supporters, the Democrats built a party with a mass base in the electorate and a more extensive officialdom to coordinate party activities than anything that had existed previously. Opponents of Jackson responded by building the Whig Party, which always remained an echo of the Democrats, but was also a mass party.[3]

These parties, which formed what scholars have come to call the Second Party System, were the first mass electoral parties in world history. Voter turnout approached 70 percent in these years. Yet for all of their organizational strength, they remained ideologically indistinct. This was by design. As Stephen Skowronek has written, the idea of two parties competing on a continental scale—that is, the idea of a national two-party system—was first conceived in America as a way to circumvent not only factionalism within the national government but also comprehensive political programs for the nation. Holistic policy programs would only have exacerbated sectional cleavages and threatened national unity ... Such parties would not articulate a clear policy linkage between citizens and government, but they would bind together a radically decentralized state and a faction-ridden nation.[4]

To be sure, there was no shortage of partisan conflict in these years—over issues ranging from internal improvements to the national bank. Yet for all the Sturm und Drang, the limits on ideological polarization are more impressive. First, neither party could articulate a clear position on slavery versus free labor. Both parties contained Northern and Southern wings, and when the issue of slavery became irrepressible in the wake of the Mexican–American War, divisions between sections within parties immediately became more important than divisions between parties. Second, to the extent that each party articulated a coherent worldview—the Democrats worried about the development of modern capitalism, while the Whigs worried about universal suffrage—the basis for disagreement steadily diminished over the 1840s, as both capitalist development and the expansion of the suffrage proved implacable processes. Finally, when it came to actual voting patterns, legislators voted less along party lines in the Second Party System than they did in the late nineteenth century, when the ideological divisions between the parties were even more hazy than they were before the Civil War. The parties in these years were organizationally strong, held together by alliances between various local elites, but were ideologically weak.[5]

This configuration would define American politics for most of the next century, with the exception of the Republican Party from the 1850s to the 1870s. Formed out of the collapse of the Whigs, the Republican Party combined the formidable organizational capabilities of the antebellum parties with an ideological crusade against the power of the slaveholders. Radicalized by developments like the Fugitive Slave Act, the Kansas-Nebraska Act, and the *Dred Scott* decision—all of which undermined the division between slave and free states—the Republican Party was built around the question of, as William Seward put it, "whether a slaveholding class exclusively shall govern America." Opposition to the slaveholders formed the keystone of Republican ideology and manifested on a policy level as total opposition to the admission of additional slave states. This opposition won Abraham Lincoln the White House, and his refusal to compromise on it, even in the face of secession, launched the Civil War. During the war and after, the Republican Party evolved into an ever-more-radical vehicle for crushing the slaveholders, embracing first the emancipation of slaves held by secessionists, then general emancipation, and then black male suffrage.[6]

After the war, however, the prewar pattern of organizational strength and ideological incoherence asserted itself with new force. What W. E. B. Du Bois called "the counter-revolution of property" purged the Republican Party of its emancipatory vision, leaving it denuded of the fervor it displayed before the war. The key force behind this transformation was flagging support for black suffrage. As working-class struggle rose in the North following the war, Northern capitalists began to question the prudence of governments based on the votes of property-less black men in the South. A coherent response to the rise of unions in the North necessitated an attack on "the dangerous class," both black and white, Northern and Southern. This response came in the form of articles such as "Socialism in North Carolina," written by E. L. Godkin, founder of the *Nation* and acting spokesman for New York City's bourgeoisie. According to Godkin, the South Carolina state government existed solely to "plunder the property owners," as the propertyless black majority voted tax after tax on the propertied whites. Godkin called for the state's whites to be "left to themselves," which would allow them to overthrow their black oppressors. For Godkin and the class for which he spoke, the example being set in the South, where propertyless men legislated against the interests of the propertied, was unacceptable in an era when the specter of socialism had begun to manifest. By 1880, the party had been largely purged of the spirit of "abolition-democracy." When

Gerritt Smith, a pioneer of antislavery politics and major funder of the early Republican Party, died, the *New York Times* commented that the "era of moral politics" had ended.[7]

The political system that resulted from this transformation was one in which the parties remained organizationally strong, but ideologically indistinct. The Democrats existed as a coalition between the Southern landowning class and immigrants in Northern cities. It was, in the words of one late nineteenth century critic, a "sort of Democratic happy family, like we see in the prairie dog villages, where owls, rattlesnakes, prairie-dogs, and lizards all live in the same hole." The Republican Party stood as the party of big business and native born workers. But in practice, both parties stood for the exclusion of workers' interests from the political system and distributed favors to various sectors of big business.[8]

By the early twentieth century, complaints about the lack of principle in American politics were sounding on both sides of the Atlantic. Woodrow Wilson, then a political scientist, argued that the muddled differences between the parties prevented elections from presenting a clear choice to the electorate, degrading the quality of democracy. In Germany, Max Weber agreed, noting that in the US, "the old conflicts over the proper interpretation of the Constitution have vanished and the parties are merely groups of careerists, changing their objective platforms at will to chase the support of the voters." There was wide agreement that the parties were in need of reform, though the remedy would do little to fix the anti-programmatic nature of American politics.[9]

Anti-party Politics

American politics entered a new era after the election of 1896. In that election, William McKinley defeated William Jennings Bryan by bringing almost the whole of American big business into the Republican camp. At the same time, Jim Crow was being built in the South, turning the region into a collection of one-party dictatorships propped up by terror. The resulting party system, referred to as either the Fourth Party System or the System of

1896, was one in which Democrats controlled the entire South, while Republicans controlled the majority of Northern states. On the presidential level, this meant that Republicans controlled the White House for twenty-eight of the next thirty-six years.[10]

The transformation of most states into one-party polities gave rise to a new political tendency among those seeking to contest the current regime. Rather than run in an election on the ballot of the opposing party, they instead mounted an attack on the parties themselves, in the hope of dislodging those currently in power. These prosaic power politics combined with a new skepticism towards democracy among the Northern upper class to produce a strong impetus for reform.[11]

Reform came in two basic types: reforms that limited what parties could do once they won an election and reforms that changed the way elections were conducted. One of the main complaints in the late nineteenth and early twentieth century concerned the spoils system initiated by the Jacksonians. By controlling the distribution of government employment, parties could secure considerable loyalty among their constituents. Civil service reform, which replaced political appointments with a merit-based system, was embraced as a weapon against the power of parties. As one reformer summed up, "The Merit System … will help to abolish partisanship." A similar reform intended to reduce corruption limited the scope of popular government by replacing mayors and city councils with unelected city managers and city commissions. Reformers hoped that reducing the rewards for winning elections in this manner would cause parties themselves to wither on the vine.[12]

The other kind of reform in this era concerned the conduct of elections. One initiative made certain elections nonpartisan in character, directly removing parties from the process. The most consequential and widespread reform, however, was the introduction of the direct primary. Parties in various states had used primary elections, rather than nominations by party officials, to fill ballot lines at different levels since the mid-nineteenth century. In the 1890s, primaries spread rapidly throughout the South as a way to circumvent the Fifteenth Amendment, since parties could exclude black voters from membership, even if the state could not prohibit them from voting in the general election. In the early twentieth century, however, progressive reformers began passing laws making primaries compulsory for all state offices. The first compulsory primary law was passed in Wisconsin in 1903. By 1917, fully three quarters of the states mandated them.[13]

None of these reforms destroyed the parties immediately, much to the chagrin of reformers. However, in the long term, they tended to undermine parties and electoral participation more generally. Nonpartisan elections reduced voter turnout by as much as 20 percent. Primaries, meanwhile, decreased partisan competition by encouraging challengers to a ruling party to wage their fight inside the party. When partisan competition declined, popular participation declined with it. Voting rates declined precipitously from the highs of the late nineteenth century, and by the 1920 election, when turnout in the presidential election fell below 50 percent, the vanishing voter became something of a national crisis, whose causes were extensively debated in the press.[14]

Parties themselves suffered a slower decline than voting, though soon enough it was recognized that they, too, were not what they once were. Already by the 1950s, political scientists could invoke the figure of "the old-time politician" who "speaks with tears in his eyes about the destruction of party organization" as a familiar stereotype. In places where parties were already weaker, like Michigan or California, nonpartisan elections all but destroyed local party organization. By the 1930s, some 60 percent of municipal employees were covered by civil service rules, greatly diminishing the ability of local parties to dispense patronage. By the early 1940s, it was clear that the era of the machines was ending, though some well-known examples, such as the Daley machine in Chicago, persisted for several more decades.[15]

The direct primary's effects took longer to be felt. In the short term, it certainly deprived parties of a number of important functions. Many of the key tasks of the party in the nineteenth century, from holding conventions to drafting a platform to building a balanced ticket, were eliminated by the primary. In the longer term, primaries facilitated the transformation from a party-centered system to a candidate-centered one, a process described well by V. O. Key:

The adoption of the direct primary opened the road for disruptive forces that gradually fractionalized the party organization. By permitting more effective direct appeals by individual politicians to the party membership, the primary system freed forces driving toward the disintegration of party organizations and facilitated the construction of factions and cliques attached to the ambitions of individual leaders.[16]

This effect would not be felt fully for decades after the primary's introduction, however. As Alan Ware has argued, the advent of television advertising exacerbated the party-weakening impact of the primary in two respects. First, it allowed candidates to take their case directly to voters without the intermediary of the party. Second, it reduced the dependence of candidates on the party by increasing the importance of money relative to labor in running a campaign. Labor was, after all, the resource in which parties had an indisputable comparative advantage. As television advertising allowed candidates to substitute money for labor in the work of reaching voters, candidates became more and more autonomous of parties. By the 1970s, the primary, together with new campaign technologies, was responsible for "the divergence of America's parties from those in other democracies during the twentieth century, and for the transformation of a polity that had been so party-centered for much of that democracy's history."[17]

Progressive-era reforms changed the structure and function of local American parties (national parties remained, up to the 1930s, basically nonexistent). They removed a number of key functions from the parties, constrained what parties could do, and choked off parties' access to the resources that sustained them. Ultimately the product of the anxieties of democracy in an industrial age, these reforms both made the American polity far less participatory and reduced the role of parties within it.

For all that progressive reforms changed, they did not alter the fundamentally ideologically incoherent character of American parties. If anything, they only intensified the incoherence. For example, both a Republican, Teddy Roosevelt, and a Democrat, Woodrow Wilson, exemplified presidential progressivism. The

System of 1896 itself, with its many one-party states across the country, tended to blur partisan differences even further than the Third-Party System did, since one-party politics was inevitably corrosive of ideological clarity. It was not until the New Deal that this system was overturned as parties became more ideologically coherent but organizationally weak. Ultimately, the efforts of partisans to create more ideologically coherent parties were crucial in completing the work of weakening party organizations —efforts that the progressive movement began.

The Struggle for Programmatic Politics

The New Deal ended the Fourth Party System, shattering one-party rule in the North and establishing the Democrats as the default party of government until the late 1960s. It did so by transforming first the Democrats and then the Republicans internally, changing them into different kinds of parties. New Deal reform incorporated the labor movement, particularly the wing represented by the Congress of Industrial Organizations, into the Democratic Party. The forces that produced social democracy elsewhere in the advanced capitalist world were thus organized into one party, and as one wing of that party, they attempted to create what Michael Kazin called "an American social democracy that dared not speak its name." Consequently, those opposed to the New Deal concentrated themselves in the Republican Party. For the first time since the immediate antebellum period, American politics began to be structured by clear and encompassing ideological divides between the parties.[18]

Yet the New Deal accomplished this realignment slowly. The period from the 1930s to the 1960s was one of transition. The Democrats contained both the forces of American social democracy, such as it was, and the most reactionary force in American politics: the agrarian ruling class of the Jim Crow South (in between them, and generally leading the party, were the postwar liberals). At the same time, the Republicans contained both the most intransigent, revanchist opponents of the New Deal, as well as a significant current of American business owners who sought accommodation with the institutional structure built by the Roosevelt administration.

This state of affairs, in which a more ideologically coherent party system was visible but still out of reach, provided the impetus for activists in both parties to attempt to complete the realignment. In the Democratic Party, liberals identified the Southern conservatives as their enemy early and, from the 1940s onward, tried to either run them out of the party, or, failing that, decisively disempower them. In the Republican Party, the battle was not quite so pitched, though conservative dissatisfaction with GOP moderates rose throughout the late 1940s and the Eisenhower administration. As with the Democrats, it would only be in the 1960s that conservative activists would succeed in defeating and marginalizing the party's liberal wing.

Yet these victories for the polarizers came at an unanticipated cost. The means by which activists in both parties sought to undermine their rivals and create more ideological coherence had the unanticipated effect of weakening the parties organizationally. Coming after the blows already struck by the progressives, these reforms resulted in parties that were shadows of their former selves. The activists had won ideologically consistent parties, but the parties were also much less able to act as independent entities. In the new era of political money that developed after the rise of campaigning via television, the parties found themselves buffeted as never before by shifting winds of donor funds. Though partisanship among the electorate intensified, the parties as organizations never recovered their former strength.

The New Deal and the American Party System

The New Deal decisively realigned American politics. The process was twofold. First, it reestablished political competition in the North, though the Democratic Party was clearly dominant. Second, and more importantly for the story of party enervation, it incorporated labor into the Democratic Party. In doing so, it created a social democratic pole in American party politics, albeit one congenitally deformed by its attachment to the Southern Democrats. The emergence of this pole is what began the process of realignment that culminated in a programmatically liberal Democratic Party and a programmatically conservative Republican Party.

Before the New Deal, American labor existed largely outside the party system. Employers' control of both parties was all but absolute. These were years when American labor law was governed by anti-strike and anti-boycott injunctions, hundreds of which were handed down by judges in the first three decades of the twentieth century. Neither the Democrats nor the Republicans evinced much interest in labor as a potential constituency. Labor unions, for their part, returned the indifference. There were a few small unions affiliated with the Socialist Party, and the Industrial Workers of the World wanted nothing to do with any party. The vast bulk of union members in the American Federation of Labor, meanwhile, practiced a politics of voluntarism that rejected active social policy. Taught by the hard experience of previous decades that they did not control the state, the leadership of the AFL distrusted any benefits not won by the action of their own members. While on the state and local level cracks in the façade of voluntarism had been apparent for decades, a wholesale rejection of it would only occur during the New Deal, ultimately yielding an entirely new wing of the union movement.[19]

Franklin Roosevelt did not run in 1932 as the candidate of labor. Though he had a record of backing various pieces of pro-labor legislation first as a state senator and then as governor of New York, Roosevelt had no strong attachment to the labor movement. His famous "Forgotten Man" speech of April 1932, which allowed him to decisively position his campaign as an alternative to Hooverism, made no mention of unions. His platform likewise failed to mention labor and promised a 25 percent cut in the federal budget. Though his campaign rested on his promise for a New Deal, voters went to the polls in 1932 with precious little idea of what that would entail.[20]

In the context of 25 percent unemployment, however, a promise is more than enough to carry a candidate to victory. Roosevelt won a sweeping victory in 1932, and his administration set to work bringing the New Deal to life. While various aspects of his relief programs, from public employment to agricultural policy, were important to Roosevelt's subsequent electoral triumphs, labor policy did more to determine subsequent political alignments than anything else. The crucial policy was section 7a of the National Industrial Recovery Act of 1933. The NIRA was the centerpiece of the administration's recovery efforts, and it revolved mainly around a series of agreements according to which business would self-regulate. Section 7a asserted organization and collective bargaining rights for labor. It had no enforcement mechanism, and its legal meaning was entirely unclear. To labor, however, the meaning was obvious. John L. Lewis, president of the United Mine Workers, declared, "We are convinced that there has been no legal instrument comparable with it since President Lincoln's Emancipation Proclamation." When workers flooded into unions in 1933 with, they believed, the president's blessing, the refusal of employers to recognize their unions resulted in a massive strike wave. This strike wave, in turn, forced the administration to clarify its interpretation of labor's rights through the National Labor Board. It was policymaking, as James A. Gross has observed, "on a crisis-by-crisis basis."[21]

Congressional liberals, led by Robert F. Wagner of New York, had been attempting to pass a more institutionally potent guarantee of the right to organize since shortly after the passage of the NIRA. When the Supreme Court declared the NIRA unconstitutional in May of 1935, they seized the opportunity. The National Labor Relations Act went significantly further than section 7a, specifying enforcement mechanisms and banning various forms of employer intimidation of union supporters. It was, quite simply, the furthest the US state had ever gone in favoring unions. Despite the unremitting hostility it encountered from most employers, it passed Congress with little opposition, receiving the votes of even a majority of Republicans. The reason for this was cogently explained years later by an aide of Wagner's, who recounted that after the Supreme Court's decision against the NIRA, the bill's opponents didn't think it was even necessary to organize against its passage, and "the opposition just folded up." Roosevelt, who himself had provided only lukewarm support for the bill, signed it in July. Over the next two years, the number of strikes exploded, and union membership grew rapidly.[22]

The electoral impact of the Roosevelt administration's embrace of reform can hardly be overstated. Between 1896 and 1932, the Republicans had won every presidential election but two (and Wilson's victory was only possible because of the splintering of the party between Taft and Roosevelt in 1912). Beginning in 1932, the Democrats won five elections in a row. Throughout the North, large demographic groups swung heavily towards the Democrats. The black vote, which had gone more than two thirds for Hoover, gave an astounding 76 percent to Roosevelt. Large class divides in voting appeared, as workers declared themselves for Roosevelt. By 1936, it was clear that the System of 1896 was dead and buried.[23]

Part of this realignment was the forging of a profound alliance between the labor movement and the Democratic Party. As mentioned above, unions grew rapidly in this period, under both the AFL and the new Congress of Industrial Organizations (CIO). The CIO, in particular, developed a close relationship with the Roosevelt administration. In 1936, its leadership formed Labor's Non-Partisan League (LNPL) with its "sole 1936 objective the re-election of President Franklin D. Roosevelt." Union leaders found themselves appointed to important positions within the administration and the Democratic Party. To be sure, labor was an important constituency, but it was never hegemonic in the party—which never became a party of labor in the manner of social democratic parties elsewhere. Liberals like Roosevelt and Harry Truman, neither of whom had a strong connection to unions, continued to lead the Democrats, and the reactionary Southern wing continued to be a crucial source of votes for anything the party hoped to accomplish. In spite of all of this, however, the New Deal succeeded in bringing together in the Democratic Party the forces that were attempting to build something like an American social democracy.[24]

By the end of World War II, the Democratic Party had been remade into something quite different from what it was under the Fourth Party System. It was now, unquestionably, the party of urban liberalism, which included both progressive intellectuals and much of the labor movement. Northern progressives, like Hiram Smith in California, the Minnesota Farmer-Laborites, and the Wisconsin followers of La Follette, had either switched their allegiance from Republicans to Democrats or merged their independent parties with the Democrats. The Republicans, meanwhile, continued to win the support of American business and augmented their ranks with plenty of conservative "Bourbon" Democrats, who became Republicans in reaction to the New Deal.[25]

The parties had become far more ideologically coherent, though there were limits to this process. The Democratic Party was clearly the party of reform, and the Republican Party opposed reform. Yet the ideological realignment that had occurred only threw into sharper relief the contradictions that remained. The Jim Crow South remained solidly Democratic, and in Congress, Southerners played an outsize role due to the advantages the seniority system bestowed upon politicians from one-party dictatorships. Similarly, the Republican Party still had a large wing that at best sought to tinker with the institutions of the New Deal, rather than raze them to the ground. In fact, from 1936 to 1960, all of the party's presidential nominees came from the party's moderate wing.[26]

These contradictions motivated activists in both parties to complete the process of realignment. Democrats tried to make their party into one of consistent programmatic liberalism, and the Republicans began to dedicate themselves mainly to overturning of the New Deal order.

The Democrats

Liberal dissatisfaction with the contradictions of the post–New Deal Democratic Party mounted quickly. These contradictions made themselves felt as early as 1937, when Southern conservatives turned against Roosevelt and voted with Republicans to stop further New Deal initiatives. In doing so, they formed a conservative coalition in Congress that proved difficult for liberals to overcome in the postwar decades. Alongside the Dixiecrats, the urban machines and state parties in the North were, more often than not, still wedded to a nonideological mode of politics and would need to be overcome in order for the realignment to be completed.[27]

Roosevelt himself was one of the earliest to voice his dissatisfaction. In the 1938 elections, he led an unprecedented effort to purge members of his party who had voted against him, intervening, unsuccessfully, in a number of primary races. During World War II, he wrote to Wendell Wilkie, his opponent in 1940 and a leading liberal Republican, suggesting that together they form a new liberal party. As he explained to an aide, "We ought to have two real parties, one liberal and the other conservative. As it is now each party is split by dissenters." Variants of this complaint sounded for the next two decades from a number of quarters, from Democratic congressmembers to the heterodox socialist Max Shachtman to Students for a Democratic Society in the early 1960s.[28]

Conflict began with the Dixiecrats in 1948. Harry Truman, who succeeded Roosevelt when the latter died in 1945, was worried about leftist third party candidate Henry Wallace, whose campaign attacked segregation directly. Spurred by liberal Democrats, the convention adopted a civil rights plank in its platform, which triggered a walkout by Southern delegates and inspired Strom Thurmond to run for president on a segregationist ticket. Yet the Dixiecrats returned to the fold after 1948, and the party's desultory efforts to discipline them were quickly abandoned. By the mid-1950s, the party's retreat on civil rights gave Eisenhower a chance to win back the black vote for the GOP.[29]

The party's liberals had more success in taking over state parties. In the North, many of these organizations were hollow shells, desiccated by their exclusion from power during the decades of Republican hegemony that followed 1896. To the extent the parties had any organizational life at all, it tended to be based around nonideological patronage politics. In the 1940s and 1950s, these organizations were taken over by liberals who sought to make them vehicles of programmatic liberalism. In North Dakota, the progressives in the Non-Partisan League, whose roots went back to the farm revolt in the 1910s, left their position in the Republican Party and took over the state's rump Democratic Party. A similar process took place in Wisconsin, where the state's progressives entered the Democratic Party after Robert La Follette Jr. was defeated in his Senate reelection campaign by Joseph McCarthy in 1946. Elsewhere the liberals either facilitated a merger between local left parties and the Democrats (Minnesota) or simply took over moribund Democratic organizations (Michigan). Many city machines went along with the New Deal, glad that its programs gave them another potential source of patronage. In the long run, however, federal entitlements tended to undermine those machines by weakening citizen dependence on the local party. By the 1960s, the machines were in decay, and most Northern Democratic organizations were in the hands of New Deal liberals.[30]

On the national level, the 1950s were a period of both frustration and innovation for liberal Democrats. Eisenhower did little to challenge the overall framework of the New Deal, running instead on his personal reputation, which blurred the ideological clarification liberals were hoping to achieve. Adlai Stevenson, the Democratic nominee in 1952 and 1956, was himself a moderate, leading the comedian Mort Sahl to quip that "Eisenhower stands for 'gradualism.' Stevenson stands for 'moderation.' Between these two extremes, the people must choose!" This was precisely the situation Democratic liberals hoped to remedy.[31]

The problem for the liberals was that the Democratic Party's congressional leadership was actively hostile to their project. Senate Majority Leader Lyndon Johnson and Speaker of the House Sam Rayburn were both dedicated foes of building a programmatically liberal party. As Johnson put it, "The biggest danger to American stability is the politics of principle, which brings out the masses in irrational fights for unlimited goals, for once the masses begin to move, then the whole thing begins to explode." With their ambitions largely blocked in Congress, the liberals instead focused on the presidential level. Many of the new liberals were devoted partisans of Adlai Stevenson, despite his moderate politics, as they were attracted to his style of intellectual, policy-focused campaigning. Their first organizational victory came with the election of Paul Butler as chair of the Democratic National Committee in 1954.[32]

Butler, a lawyer from Indiana who was active in the Democratic Party there, was strongly influenced by the criticisms political scientists had been making of the weaknesses and nonideological character of American parties. These criticisms had culminated in the American Political Science Association's 1950 report *Toward a More Responsible Two-Party System*, which advocated for biennial party conventions to shape party ideology independently of candidates, reforming the seniority system in Congress to empower party leadership, and strengthening the executive branch. From his position on the DNC, Butler could affect the first of these, and he proposed a biennial convention in 1953, before winning election to chair of committee. The rest of the committee rejected it as too expensive, and Butler turned instead to a group of Adlai Stevenson supporters who had begun meeting informally to develop Democratic Party policy proposals. In 1956, after Stevenson once again lost to Eisenhower, the DNC as a whole voted to make this group into an official body, the Democratic Advisory Council (DAC).[33]

The DAC took an aggressive posture after the Democrats' massive gains in the 1958 midterms, laying out the policy proposals it hoped would give the Democratic Party a clear ideological basis. On foreign policy, it was extremely hawkish, reflecting the influence of Dean Acheson and Paul Nitze. On economics, it advocated Keynesian policies, though its prescriptions here were hamstrung by persistent conflict between John Kenneth Galbraith and Leon Keyserling over taxes and deficits. Its boldest prescriptions were undoubtedly those on civil rights. Unburdened by the Southern politicians who controlled the committees, the DAC advocated strongly for civil rights legislation and criticized Eisenhower's failures to move more aggressively against Southern intransigence following *Brown v. Board of Education*. Though none of the DAC's proposals became policy in the 1950s due to Republican control of the White House and Johnson and Rayburn's control of Congress, they shaped the public perception of the Democratic Party's positions, and many veterans of the council went on to serve in the Kennedy and Johnson administrations.[34]

One of the DAC's proposals on the civil rights front involved reducing the number of senators necessary to end a filibuster. Over the course of the 1950s, this kind of proposal to reform congressional procedure became an increasingly important cause for the partisans of programmatic liberalism. Outside of Congress, civil rights groups attacked the filibusters and the committee system regularly. In 1951, the NAACP ranked filibuster reform on par with fighting employment discrimination. The following year the Leadership Conference on Civil Rights declared that until the filibuster was reformed, there would be "no hope for congressional action against the forces of bigotry."[35]

Supporters of reform assembled inside Congress as well. Following Eisenhower's reelection in 1956, two Democratic liberals in the House, Eugene McCarthy of Minnesota and Frank Thompson of New Jersey, released their "Democratic Manifesto," calling for congressional reform and endorsing a strong civil rights agenda. They were joined by over eighty other congressmembers, who began calling themselves McCarthy's Mavericks. Their counterparts in the Senate were young liberals like Hubert Humphrey and Paul Douglas, who were scorned by their party's Southern leadership for their insistent advocacy for civil rights. After the 1958 election sent large numbers of new Northern Democrats to both the House and Senate, McCarthy's Mavericks in the House formally organized themselves as the Democratic Study Group (DSG), which joined the DAC in pushing liberal policies and attacking Southern Democratic obstructionism. The two groups worked closely together in the run-up to the 1960 election, crafting a Democratic platform that advanced programmatic liberalism more strongly than ever before.[36]

Though Democratic liberals were optimistic in the late 1950s, the Kennedy administration was a disappointment. Kennedy, while stocking his administration with DAC veterans, wound the committee down, and replaced Paul Butler first with Henry Jackson, "the Senator from Boeing," and then with a Connecticut machine boss. Like Stevenson, with whom he was often contrasted, Kennedy's lofty rhetoric tended to conceal a rather limited political imagination. Nonetheless, events in the 1960s would accelerate the cause of party reform faster than the programmatic liberals of the 1950s had thought possible.[37]

The Reform Coalition Splits

The first was the rapid development of the civil rights insurgency in the South. The movement for desegregation, which had been largely stymied by the campaign of "massive resistance" in the late 1950s, finally broke through with the student sit-ins in the early 1960s. The tactics of direct action spread rapidly, and the movement's ability to disrupt Southern society quickly escalated. This disruption drove a wedge between Southern business owners, who, bearing the brunt of urban protest's consequences, pushed for compromise, and Dixiecrat politicians, who depended on black disenfranchisement and refused to compromise. As the "solid south" split, the Dixiecrats found their position weakened. Movement insurgents took advantage of this weakening to directly challenge the Dixiecrats' standing in the party, organizing the Mississippi Freedom Democratic Party in 1964 to replace the segregationist state's official Democratic delegation at the DNC. Though the challenge did not displace the Dixiecrats, it spurred the development of stricter DNC rules governing state parties, achieving some of the centralization for which the reform coalition in Congress had fought. Finally, in 1964 and 1965, the walls of Dixie crumbled as Johnson, responding to continued insurgency in the South, pushed the Civil Rights Act and then the Voting Rights Act through Congress, destroying the legal foundations of Jim Crow. With the rise of black voting in the South, Northern liberals looked forward to the replacement of Dixiecrats with Democratic politicians who would advance the party's goals of programmatic liberalism.[38]

With the Dixiecrats defeated, it seemed that the forces of programmatic liberalism had triumphed. Yet no sooner had the party resolved its sectional divide decisively in favor of Northern liberalism than Northern liberals found themselves bitterly divided over the American war in Vietnam. As Johnson escalated the American intervention following the Gulf of Tonkin Resolution in the summer of 1964, opposition to the war grew more public and widespread. Though the antiwar movement grew quickly in this period, it would take slightly longer for this opposition to find expression from Democratic politicians. By early 1966, however, discontent was mounting in Congress. It was centered in the Senate Foreign Relations Committee (SFRC), headed by William Fulbright, a Southern conservative who nonetheless by 1964 was already becoming disillusioned with Cold War foreign policy. Eugene McCarthy, who also served on the committee, helped organize a letter in late January of 1966 urging the administration to extend the pause in bombing North Vietnam that Johnson had begun on Christmas. The day the letter was published, McCarthy gave a speech in the Senate in which he said US involvement in Vietnam required "a real searching of the mind and soul of America." Shortly thereafter, Fulbright launched a series of hearings from the SFRC exposing official dissent against the administration's policy to a national audience.[39]

By 1968, the war had become the central issue fracturing the Democratic Party, resulting in primary challenges to Johnson. In 1967, Allard Lowenstein, who had been a leader of the Mississippi Freedom Democratic Party (MFDP), launched his "Dump Johnson" campaign. Speaking on campuses across the country and building a network of Democratic activists opposed to Johnson, Lowenstein had by 1967 mobilized enough discontent that the question of a candidate to challenge Johnson became paramount. After Robert F. Kennedy and George McGovern both refused, Eugene McCarthy stepped in, and in late November of 1967, he publicly declared his intention to challenge Johnson.[40]

Events moved quickly in the months that followed. In February, the Tet Offensive gave the lie to the Johnson administration's guarantees that the war was winding down. On March 12th, McCarthy won 42 percent of the vote in the New Hampshire primary, a result that put Johnson on notice that his renomination was in no way assured. Four days later, Robert F. Kennedy announced he would, after all, enter the race. At the end of the month, Johnson announced he would not be running for reelection.

Yet this was no assurance of victory for the war's opponents. Hubert Humphrey, who had served as Johnson's Vice President, announced his candidacy in late April, and the wing of the party that supported Johnson quickly assembled behind him. This was too late to enter any of the party's primaries, but in 1968, only seventeen states held Democratic primaries, and these primaries allocated only 38 percent of the national convention's delegates. Humphrey could win without running in a single primary.[41]

This fact, more than any other, spurred antiwar Democrats to reform the party's structure at the 1968 convention. McCarthy and Kennedy supporters pointed to the various undemocratic means that allowed state party officials to dominate the selection of delegates. Drawing on the precedent of the MFDP's challenge to the Mississippi delegation, they argued that delegates selected against the will of Democratic voters were illegitimate. As a result, fully 40 percent of the delegates at the Chicago convention were subject to credential challenges. While antiwar protesters were beaten bloody in the streets outside the convention by Mayor Richard Daley's police force, McCarthy and Kennedy delegates inside the convention fought for antiwar planks in the platform, as well as for a restructuring of the party that would prevent the party officialdom from overriding the will of primary voters. On the former, they lost, as delegates closed ranks behind Humphrey's desire to stay the course Johnson had set (in doing so, they very likely delivered the presidency to Richard Nixon). On party reform, however, Humphrey and his allies saw an opportunity for compromise. So long as the demand for reform was oriented towards *future* elections, Humphrey was happy to give it his blessing in the interest of shoring up party unity.[42]

New Politics

Two commissions emerged from the convention with the mandate to pursue party reform. The first was the Commission on Rules, which would examine the conduct of conventions themselves and was headed by James O'Hara, a Michigan Democrat with close ties to Humphrey and organized labor. The Commission on Party Structure and Delegate Selection, headed by George McGovern (and, after McGovern entered the 1972 presidential race, Donald Fraser), had a far wider mandate, encompassing the overall structure of the party and the rules by which delegates to the convention would be selected. This latter commission would come to be an organizational base for the New Politics movement, which took up the task of producing a more programmatically liberal Democratic Party after 1968.[43]

The reformers moved quickly following Humphrey's narrow loss to Nixon. Though the AFL-CIO, headed by George Meany, announced its boycott of the McGovern-Fraser Commission early in 1969, opposition in the party as a whole was muted. The reason was quite simply that in most of the country, there was no organized system governing party structure and delegate selection. Procedures existed only because they had in the past. As such, opponents of reform had little ground to stand on. Reformers were able to seize the initiative and, over the next few years, presented a number of proposals for restructuring the party. First, they proposed affirmative action in delegate selection to increase the representation of women and racial minorities at the convention. Second, they proposed forbidding a number of non-primary mechanisms of delegate selection that privileged the party officialdom. Third, they proposed, for the first time, a charter for the Democratic Party that would describe the party's purpose and structure. Fourth, they proposed a new biennial conference to set the party platform (which, as we saw, was an idea that went back to the reformers of the early 1950s). Finally, they proposed a dues-paying membership to help pay for the new party activities. This membership, in turn, would be able to define the party politically through the new institutions.[44]

The first round of proposals, which concerned delegate selection and were issued in the McGovern-Fraser Commission's 1970 report *Mandate for Change*, were rapidly enacted. State parties shifted to primaries in large numbers. Just as primaries for state and local offices were made mandatory during the Progressive Era, twenty-two states changed their laws to bring their parties' delegate selection procedures in line with the commission's recommendations. The rest of the reform agenda, however, encountered fierce resistance.[45]

This resistance occupies an ironic place in the historiography of New Politics reforms, which scholars from very early on began disparaging as responsible for the death of American parties. In this, historians have tended to mirror the perspective of the opponents of reform, or counter-reformers, as Adam Hilton as called them. Yet at the time, it was widely recognized by both reformers and their opponents that the goal of the New Politics movement was to create a *stronger* party, in the vein of the ambitions of the DAC and DSG in the 1950s. Their goal was, in the words of one advocate, to establish a party that "would welcome and recruit members on the basis of one test and one test alone—belief in the principles and goals of the party as defined in the national platform." The opponents of reform were similarly clear-eyed about the goals of the reformers, accusing them of wanting to "centralize, ideologize, and 'Europeanize' the party in ways that run against the grain of American political tradition and the unique coalitional character of the Democratic Party." Both sides agreed that it was the New Politics tendency that wanted a stronger, more ideologically coherent party.[46]

Indeed, it was not the New Politics reforms themselves that resulted in a much weaker party but the defeat of the full New Politics agenda by the counterreformers. Mobilized primarily through the Coalition for a Democratic Majority (CDM), which was closely associated with the AFL-CIO officialdom, the counterreformers assailed the New Politics agenda as responsible for George McGovern's devastating defeat in 1972. They were able to defeat or defang all of the party structure proposals that emerged out of the McGovern-Fraser Commission. They did not, however, roll back the delegate selection reforms. The result was something quite different from what New Politics reformers sought. Convention delegates were now awarded on the basis of direct primaries. However, the structure that the reformers hoped would give shape to the competition between candidates including a party platform and defined and committed party membership was never instituted. The *New York Times* recognized that the defeat of this vision was "testimony to anti-party power in national politics—to the primacy of candidates over structure."[47]

A weaker party was the result of the defeat of reform. With primaries now the unquestioned vehicle for nomination to office and with no structure defining party membership or goals, political contests inevitably became more candidate centered. Collective decision-making through the apparatus of the party declined even further. Moreover, though these reforms were made by Democrats, their effects were not limited to Democrats. As mentioned above, the reform recommendations led a large number of states to change their laws. As a consequence, primaries became the basis of the Republican nomination as well. The weakening of the parties that the progressives began at the state and local level was completed at the presidential level.[48]

At the same time that the fight over the presidential nomination and party structure was happening, Democrats (though often with Republican help) in Congress were making important changes to congressional procedure that would—once again against the intentions of their authors—produce weaker parties. Events from 1964 onward had concentrated the attention of reformers on the presidency. But the congressional rules that had vexed liberals in the 1950s were, by and large, unchanged. Moreover, many of the Dixiecrats still sat in Congress, protected by incumbency advantages even as black voting rates climbed. While Strom Thurmond famously left Democrats for the party of Barry Goldwater in 1964, his was not the modal trajectory for his species of politician. James Eastland remained a Democratic senator until 1978, while Herman Talmadge served until 1981. In the House, John Conyers tried and failed in 1971 to strip the Mississippi Democrats of seniority, given that they remained members of a segregated Mississippi Democratic Party that was not recognized by the national committee. Discontent with seniority mounted among liberals. As Allard Lowenstein, elected to the House in 1968, quipped, "Even societies that worship their ancestors don't automatically put their ancestors in charge of the Armed Services Committee."[49]

The changes to seniority and committee responsibilities that were subsequently made had significant consequences for the structure of the parties and the practice of congressional politics. In early 1971, both the Democratic and Republican House Caucuses voted to allow committee chairs to be appointed on bases other than seniority, and the Democrats went further, allowing a caucus-wide vote on the appointment if ten or more caucus members demanded it. In 1973, the Democrats made such caucus-wide votes on chair appointments automatic, and in 1975, three Democratic House committee chairs were removed by caucus vote and replaced with more junior members. In the

Senate, Republicans overthrew the seniority principle in 1973, and the Democrats in 1975. As a result of these reforms, there was now widespread competition among officeholders for committee assignment and leadership.[50]

By the end of the 1970s, then, many of the goals of those reformers who sought to complete the New Deal realignment in the 1950s had been achieved. Seniority had been dethroned in both the House and the Senate, and control over the presidential nominating process had been thoroughly expropriated from the remaining machines. Yet the crises of the 1960s had splintered the reform coalition into a camp that embraced the social movements of that decade and one that recoiled from them. As the former pursued the cause of party reform more vigorously than ever, the latter became counterreformers. Where labor liberals had been the most outspoken advocates of reform in the 1950s, in the 1970s the Democrats closest to the AFL-CIO were the most implacable enemies of reform, denouncing the very goal of creating ideologically sorted, responsible parties. Reformers were able to win the extension of the primary election but were unable to pursue any of their designs for restructuring the party. The result of this failure, and of the congressional restructuring in the 1970s, created parties that were less institutionally coherent than ever. Most crucially, as will be discussed later in this chapter, the arms race of campaign fundraising that erupted in the 1970s gave new content to these reforms, turning them into mechanisms by which political money could exert more direct control over the parties than ever before.

The Republicans

It may seem counterintuitive that the Republican Party only slowly became the party dedicated to undoing the New Deal order. After all, devotees of the free market were hardly uncommon in the party of McKinley and Mellon. Yet the scale of Republican electoral defeats in 1932 and 1934 made clear that before the party could do anything about the New Deal, it needed to be able to beat Roosevelt. As a result, Republican moderates, who advocated tinkering with but not overthrowing the New Deal, led the party, particularly at the presidential level, for the next thirty years. In fact, until Ronald Reagan's victory in 1980, it remained unclear whether the conservatives would succeed in redefining the party. From the 1930s onward, they waged a battle to displace the moderates. In doing so, they also transformed the party organizationally, forging the service party model, in which a party provides services to candidates, rather than determining policy. This new model would soon be taken on by the Democrats as well, further hollowing out the parties.

The electoral defeats first in 1932 and then 1934 were chastening for the much-reduced ranks of Republican officeholders. Many quickly judged discretion the better part of valor and declined to challenge the Roosevelt administration. Senator Wallace White of Maine spoke for this group when he concluded "I suppose prudence dictates that one should not attempt to swim against the tide." The RNC was more pugnacious and attempted to rally the party around all-out opposition to the New Deal, only to be publicly rebuked by the congressional party. Approaching the 1936 elections, former President Hoover attempted to consolidate a more oppositional stance in the party, with himself as its standard bearer. Unfortunately for Hoover, however, his natural allies in the party—the old guard Eastern conservatives—felt that the secret to Republican rejuvenation lay in the nomination of a Midwesterner. Alfred Landon, governor of Kansas, fit the bill, having achieved some of the very few Republican successes on the gubernatorial level in the age of Roosevelt. Landon was himself an old Bull Moose progressive, and was, so his backers hoped, capable of straddling the Eastern conservative and Western progressive wings of the party.[51]

Landon's campaign reflected the divided Republican Party, hobbling what would have been a difficult race regardless. On the one hand, Landon attempted to differentiate himself from Hooverism. "Four more years of the same policies that we have had will wreck our parliamentary government, and four more years of the old policies will do the same job also," he argued. He preferred to criticize inefficiency and impropriety in the administration rather than the administration's fundamental goals. At the same time, however, behind the scenes his campaign was suffused with reactionaries. Ogden Mills, who had served as Hoover's secretary of the treasury and represented the party's conservative old guard, was the primary force in shaping Landon's policy proposals. The American Liberty League, which had been founded by anti-Roosevelt Democrats and would come to be synonymous with business-led reaction in the thirties, was ubiquitous in campaign staffing and financing. This proved something of a blessing for Roosevelt, whose campaign seized on the league as evidence of an elite conspiracy against the New Deal and delighted in excoriating it. As the Democrats painted the Landon campaign as a mere puppet of the league, the Republicans began shamefacedly distancing themselves from it, and by the fall of 1936 Landon supporters were calling for the league to dissolve, the only way they could see to rid themselves of the albatross it had become. None of this was sufficient, of course, and Landon went down to even more ignominious defeat than had Hoover. Immediately after the election, Gallup polled voters on whether the Republican Party was dead. Twenty-seven percent said yes.[52]

Congressional conservatism, however, showed itself to be more vital than the fortunes of the GOP would suggest. In 1937, the advance of the New Deal policy agenda had seriously strained the Democratic coalition. Roosevelt's court-packing plan, introduced in early 1937, led to a congressional revolt that united Southern Democrats with Republicans. Southern Democrats were also, by this point, determined to resist any further New Deal labor legislation and joined Republicans again to oppose the Fair Labor Standards Act in 1937. From this moment forward, the Southern congressmembers were implacable enemies of New Deal labor reforms and soon joined Republicans in opposing other aspects of the administration's agenda. Republican electoral fortunes soon reversed as well, with the 1938 midterms delivering much-needed rejuvenation to Republican ranks.[53]

Yet while conservatives in Congress found greater success in blocking Roosevelt's agenda after 1936, the fact that they could only do so in a bipartisan coalition retarded the progress GOP conservatives hoped to make in redefining their party. Moreover, outside of Congress, GOP governors were proving far less steadfast in resisting Roosevelt. On the presidential level, the picture was no clearer. The 1938 elections had put forward two new figures contending for leadership of the party. The first was Robert A. Taft of Ohio, son of President William Howard Taft. Taft represented the old Midwestern business Republicanism that was so dominant during the 1920s. A cunning political operator, Taft quickly displaced Hoover as the leading spokesperson for the party's conservatives. The second figure was Thomas Dewey, whose narrow loss to Herbert Lehmann in the 1938 New York gubernatorial election made him an attractive figure to Republicans anxious to win moderate voters. Dewey, however, called himself a "New Deal Republican" and held that "nine-tenths of the New Deal legislation was sound and proper." The regional split in the Republican Party had evolved since 1936. Then, Western progressives contested with Eastern conservatives. The ascent of Dewey and Taft revealed a different configuration. Now old guard Republicanism was anchored in the Midwest, and the Eastern Republican interests had become the more moderate wing of the party.[54]

Events in Europe would wrong-foot both Taft and Dewey, elevating instead a man the GOP hoped could embody the best of both of them: Wendell Willkie. The march to war in Europe discredited both Taft, an ardent isolationist, and Dewey, whose highest elected office, Manhattan District Attorney, had left him bereft of foreign policy gravitas. As 1940 neared, attention instead concentrated on Wendell Willkie. Like Taft, he was a Midwesterner, originally from Indiana. Like Dewey, he had few connections to the GOP old guard. Indeed, Willkie had been a Democrat, only switching parties in 1940, though his position as a utility executive had brought him into conflict with the Roosevelt administration for years previously. By the late 1930s, he was well known both for his criticisms of Roosevelt and for his ties to Wall Street. Willkie had deep connections to Eastern financial interests, particularly the House of Morgan (the last presidential candidate of whom this was true). These interests proved the focal point of Republican opposition to his rise. An RNC member close to Hoover complained to the latter that "a certain group of extreme internationalists centered in the lower part of New York are ... bringing all pressure possible to stampede the convention for Willkie." One North Dakota representative denounced Willkie on the House floor, declaring the GOP needed to be protected from "the machinations and attempts of J. P. Morgan and the other New York utility bankers in forcing Wendell Willkie on the Republican Party." Yet Willkie's support in the party was broad, ranging from elites like the head of the National Association of Manufacturers to grassroots Republicans, who organized thousands of Willkie clubs in advance of the convention.[55]

Willkie's subsequent campaign against Roosevelt attempted, like Landon before him, to oppose the administration selectively and constructively. He endorsed New Deal social programs, supported the unions, and offered a more enthusiastic embrace of civil rights for black Americans than Roosevelt had managed. On foreign policy, his fundamental internationalism made it difficult for him to differentiate himself from Roosevelt, and his pronouncements were inconsistent. Willkie would go on to lose the election to Roosevelt, just as his predecessors Landon and Hoover had. However, where Hoover won about sixteen million votes, and Landon seventeen million, Willkie managed a respectable twenty-two million. Significantly, he won a slim majority of votes outside the South.[56]

This result only deepened the conflict in the party between moderates and conservatives. Throughout the campaign, Taft and his allies were infuriated by Willkie's endorsements of New Deal programs and his internationalism. Moreover, Republican party officials looked on the Willkie clubs with disdain, seeing them (quite rightly) as an attempt to bypass the party. After the election, Willkie himself moved leftwards, becoming more critical of business and less critical of the New Deal. When Alfred P. Sloan of General Motors complained to Willkie in 1942 about Willkie's vocal support of unions, Willkie responded that opposing collective bargaining was trying "to live in a world gone forever." Similarly, Willkie dedicated himself to scourging the isolationists in the GOP, even after the latter group was fortified by their success in the 1942 elections. Among Republican members of Congress, Willkie was despised. Taft told a correspondent that "if Willkie were elected we would simply have another New

Deal, perhaps more difficult to combat than the Roosevelt New Deal today."[57]

The conflict Willkie stoked in the party ironically fostered party unity in the 1944 elections. The previous year, Harrison Spangler, chair of the RNC and an old Willkie foe, assembled a meeting at Mackinac Island, Michigan, to forge some kind of consensus between the party's warring wings. The result was a hybrid declaration. On foreign policy, it was far closer to Willkie's internationalism than Taft's isolationism. The domestic portion, however, was largely shaped by Taft, though it did crucially endorse collective bargaining. This compromise allowed party leaders like Landon and Hoover to coalesce around Thomas Dewey as the candidate to stop Willkie. Accepting his position as a centrist in the party, Dewey dropped the rhetoric of "New Deal Republicanism" and saddled Roosevelt with responsibility for "seven years of New Deal depression." At the same time, Dewey's foreign policy reflected the internationalism of the Mackinac Island conference, and he continued to endorse federal social security and minimum wage legislation, much to the chagrin of Taft and the conservatives. Unlike Willkie, Dewey ran a vituperative campaign against Roosevelt, accusing him of being a tool of the Communist Party. But his platform bore unmistakable evidence of the influence Willkie had on Republican politics. The *New York Times* summarized the campaign:

> the outstanding characteristic was ... the promise by both parties of all good things to come from a benign and endlessly generous government ... Social Security was to be expanded greatly ... Health insurance and medical care were to be provided on a large scale, without cost to anybody ... Industrial wages were to be kept high ... On these and other similar points the two platforms written at Chicago did their thumping best to outbid each other."[58]

Dewey's loss to Roosevelt did nothing to bridge the political gap that existed between the wings of the Republican Party, though both sides recognized the need for unity if they were to have any hope of returning to power. Dewey came out of the election convinced that the party needed to moderate even further, and he set to work trying to remake the party in his image for a 1948 run. Opposed by the congressional party, he secured the office of RNC chair for one of his supporters, Herbert Brownell. Brownell undertook a number of organizational reforms of the party intended to bolster its competitiveness, but some of his most consequential work was ideological. Rather than focusing on policy issues, Brownwell concentrated Republican fire on issues of corruption, accusing the Democrats of buying votes with fiscal programs. His argument was that the GOP could "manage the New Deal programs more efficiently and bring them to their full potential." However, when congressional Republicans did well in the 1946 midterms, winning control of both the House and Senate, Taft claimed that his revanchist politics had received a mandate, gloating that "people finally were brought to realize what the New Deal was trying to do in regulating their daily lives." In the subsequent Eightieth Congress, the conservative coalition won some key victories, most notably the Taft-Hartley Act, which dramatically curtailed the power of unions.[59]

Taft's victories in Congress, however, made him complacent about 1948. Dewey had won the governorship of New York in 1942 and had used his position to build a formidable network of support inside the GOP. His head of fundraising, aviation entrepreneur turned New York corporate magnate Harold Talbott, helped Dewey corral business support. Taft was oblivious to all of this and imagined the convention would anoint him with little controversy. Instead, Dewey, buoyed by support from Republican governors who followed his much more moderate stance towards social programs, secured enough delegates before the convention began to win the nomination on the third ballot. California governor Earl Warren, who was even more liberal than Dewey, was nominated for vice president. With a moderate, non-controversial campaign and the Democratic Party facing both a right-wing defection from the Dixiecrats and a left-wing defection from Henry Wallace's Progressive Party, Dewey was confident he would be the first Republican to take the presidency in two decades.[60]

Truman's surprise triumph ended Dewey's reign as leader of the GOP and deepened the party's crisis of faith. At the first RNC meeting after the election, one moderate committee member declared, "we are not required by consistency to commit political harikari by an over-zealous and ceremonious insistence upon the doctrines of *laissez faire*." Dewey and his camp blamed the conservative record of the Eightieth Congress for his defeat, and indeed, labor unions were successful in punishing supporters of Taft-Hartley.[61]

Immediately after Dewey's defeat, a number of business figures formed a network dedicated to making General Dwight Eisenhower the Republican nominee in 1952. Eisenhower was deeply ensconced in the milieu of Eastern business that served as the bulwark for Republican internationalism. His brother, Milton, was close to the circles that founded the Committee for Economic Development in the 1940s and Eisenhower himself served as a trustee of the group from 1950 to 1952. His appointment as president of Columbia University in 1947 came largely as a result of the efforts of Columbia trustee and IBM executive Thomas J. Watson. Already in 1949, business leaders in these circles were pushing Eisenhower towards the presidency. A key vehicle for the effort was the American Assembly, a kind of public discussion forum Eisenhower established as president of Columbia that brought him into regular contact with the heads of the some of the country's largest corporations. Harry Bullis, the chair of General Mills, told Eisenhower after a dinner supporting the assembly, "You not only sold us on your Columbia project, but you made a sale of far greater potentialities—one that only you can 'close' when the proper time comes." Dewey himself was a leading figure in this effort, telling Eisenhower that only a figure unconnected to the Republican Party's unpopular policies was capable of saving the country from socialism. In 1951, a group of business leaders closely linked to the CED launched Citizens for Eisenhower, a public campaign to make him the Republican candidate. With this network, Eisenhower easily brushed Taft aside at the 1952 Republican National Convention.[62]

In 1952, the Republicans finally won back the presidency after more than twenty years as the opposition. Yet as the party retook the executive branch, its ideological position had grown less clear. The Eastern internationalist wing of the party, who had announced their presence with the Willkie campaign in 1940, had grown more powerful. Eisenhower's "modern Republicanism" aimed, in the words of one historian, to "rationalize and reform the New Deal rather than repeal it." In the House, Republicans elected during Eisenhower's tenure were generally more moderate than their predecessors. In the Senate, moderates like Ralph Flanders and Jacob Javits were prominent voices for modern Republicanism.[63]

If Eisenhower's presidency represented the dominance of the Eastern internationalist wing of the party, it also catalyzed the efforts of conservatives to overthrow that dominance and convert the GOP into the party of war against the New Deal. William Rusher, publisher of *National Review*, once recounted that "modern American conservatism largely organized itself during, and in explicit opposition to, the Eisenhower Administration." Though Taft had been the voice of the party's right wing since the mid-1940s and was for overturning the New Deal completely, he was a pragmatic politician who, however much he seethed about the Eastern internationalists elevating Dewey or Eisenhower over him, accepted a loss as a loss and tried to curry as much influence with the winners as possible. Already in the late 1940s, however, some rebellious Taftites were going further than their leader. In 1949, a Chicago Taft delegate, Fred Virkus, established the National Republican Roundup Committee (NRRC) as a kind of conservative lobbying group. It called for total rejection of the New Deal and a reaffirmation of 1920s Republicanism. Perhaps most notably, it rejected civil rights legislation completely, breaking with a Republican tradition that even Taft upheld.[64]

In the 1950s, the dream of melding conservative Southern Democrats and conservative Republicans into a single political vehicle became the dominant vision of Republican realigners. The flirtation between reactionary Republicans and Southern white supremacists went back to the days of the Liberty League, when Irénée Du Pont more or less openly sought an alliance with the Ku Klux Klan against the New Deal. These initiatives had amounted to little, despite the collaboration between Southern Democrats and conservative Republicans in Congress. GOP conservatives drew closer to Southern conservatives during

World War II, when the Roosevelt administration established the Fair Employment Practices Committee to open defense industry employment to black workers. Taftites opposed the FEPC, while Dewey supported it. By the late 1940s, conservatives were willing to go even further than opposing the FEPC and opposed any federal civil rights legislation.[65]

One of the first to travel this road was South Dakota Senator Karl Mundt. Mundt had made his name serving on the House Un-American Activities Committee during the 1940s and in 1949 became a Senator just as Joe McCarthy's crusade was getting underway. In 1949 he went on a speaking tour of the South, making the case that an alliance between Southern conservatives and Northern Republicans was necessary to stop the advance of socialism in the United States. Mundt was fully cognizant that any such alliance would depend on the Republicans dropping all advocacy of federal civil rights legislation, and he recommended the platform remove "any of the planks which are understandably repugnant to the [white] people of the South." His speeches received a rapturous response from Southern audiences, with one newspaper describing "not mere polite applause, mind you, but earsplitting level yells." By 1951, Mundt had founded a new organization, the Committee to Explore Political Realignment. Mundt's plan was for the Republicans to move their convention to after the Democrats' and respond to the Democratic nomination of a presumed liberal with a conservative Republican at the top of the ticket and a conservative Southern Democrat for vice president. Mundt was, however, unable to convince the party to follow his plans, and Eisenhower's nomination of Earl Warren to the Supreme Court put an end to his realignment ambitions for the time being.[66]

This, among other betrayals of conservatism by Eisenhower, led to a flurry of organizing on the right. The founding of *National Review* in 1955, the John Birch Society in 1958, and the even more right-wing Liberty Lobby in 1957 all stemmed from conservatives enraged at the direction of the GOP. One of the most influential figures in this milieu was Clarence Manion, host of the right-wing radio show, *The Manion Forum of Opinion*. Manion had been a Wilsonian Democrat, and then a Taftite Republican, but when Earl Warren handed down *Brown v. Board of Education* in 1954, he became convinced some stiffer medicine was needed. He found it in Orval Faubus, the Arkansas governor whose resistance to integration (and defiance of Eisenhower) made him a hero of Southern reaction. Through contacts with some of Faubus's advisors, Manion became convinced that Faubus could make a run for president that would unify conservatives North and South. The plan was for Faubus to enter Democratic primaries in the South and for a similarly conservative Republican to enter that party's primaries in the North. When both lost at the convention, they would unite to form a new, thoroughly right-wing party. For Faubus's Northern counterpart, Manion proposed Arizona Senator Barry Goldwater.[67]

The story of Barry Goldwater's role in the Republican Party's move to the right has been told many times, and only the broad strokes need concern us here. The prickly Arizona libertarian became, somewhat against his will, the avatar for conservative dissatisfaction with modern Republicanism. Through no small amount of skullduggery, his supporters managed in 1964 to make him the Republican candidate, whereupon he was thoroughly crushed by Lyndon Johnson in the general election. Nonetheless, his campaign acted as a sort of coming out party for the increasingly restive party and set the stage for Ronald Reagan, Newt Gingrich, and more.[68]

While the role Goldwater's campaign played in creating a polarized party system is undoubtedly significant, another result of his campaign, less widely appreciated, is the organizational transformation of the Republican Party. The roots of this transformation go back to the compromise struck between the party's right and left (left being, of course, a relative term here) wings. Goldwater had appointed an aide of his, Dean Burch, as chair of the RNC after his nomination in 1964. After the campaign's inglorious performance, however, pressure mounted for Burch to leave. Moderate Republicans, in particular, saw Goldwater's loss as an opportunity to reassert control of the presidential party. Though Goldwater resisted such an obvious move against him and his allies, the campaign against Burch was unrelenting. In December, the Republican Governors Association, long a redoubt of the moderates, issued a unanimous statement calling for a new direction at the RNC. Though it did not name Burch directly, its demand was clear. By January, Goldwater had caved, and Burch announced he would resign in April.[69]

During the campaign to oust Burch, Republican moderates had quickly coalesced around Ray Bliss of Ohio as their favored replacement. Bliss was not a moderate. He was an old Taftite who had led the Ohio party's rejuvenation after its slaughter in the 1948 backlash to Taft-Hartley. However, Bliss was committed to nonideological leadership of the RNC. In Ohio, he had run the party with the slogan "Keep issues out of campaigns." Bliss was devoted to a service model of political parties, in which parties existed primarily to provide campaign services (everything from voter outreach to messaging advice to fundraising) to candidates. In this model, the politics of the party weren't really the party's concern. That would be determined by the candidates who won nomination. The party's job was to help those candidates win. Because of this, Bliss was seen as a compromise candidate for the RNC, one who would take no part in the factional warfare that had been intensifying in the party since the second Eisenhower administration.[70]

Bliss's reconstruction of the RNC around the service party model had two effects. First, even though Bliss himself was resolutely nonideological in his leadership, during his tenure the presidential party no longer opposed the right, which was thereby bolstered. Since Willkie, the presidential party had been a stronghold of the moderates. Even Richard Nixon, who had been added to Eisenhower's ticket as a sop to the right, had won the nomination in 1960 through a deal with Nelson Rockefeller, bête noire of the conservatives. However, because Bliss was opposed to the RNC taking sides, his time as chair effectively removed an important institutional source of opposition to the right. As Brian M. Conley, the leading scholar of Bliss's role in the party put it, "unity came at the cost of any possible change in direction from the rightward policy course set by the 1964 election."[71]

The second effect was to further hollow out the party. With the decline of patronage and the rise of primaries in the first half of the twentieth centuries, many of the traditional prerogatives of political parties had been lost. The service party model was both an adaptation to this loss and a deepening of it. The rise of television and radio had already altered the production function of successful campaigns, prioritizing money over labor as an input. The service party model adapted to this by turning the party into an institution dedicated to raising money. Similarly, it enhanced the trend of subordinating the party to candidates. Though the service party model resulted in a professionalization of many party activities, it also narrowed the scope of those activities. In following Bliss's model, the party now played less of a role in making decisions than ever.

Ray Bliss's great triumph came with the election of Richard Nixon in 1968. However, Nixon himself, never known for his displays of gratitude, pushed Bliss out almost immediately after being elected. The reason was less ideological than megalomaniacal; Nixon wanted a party totally subordinate to his whims, and Bliss was not willing to submit. Eventually, Nixon simply began circumventing the party altogether. He created the infamous Committee to Re-Elect the President (CREEP) to place campaign fundraising under his control and initiated the "Townhouse Project" to fundraise for candidates he believed would be his allies in Congress. Ironically, though Nixon has often been identified as the president of backlash par excellence, and thus as the decisive figure in the turn to the right in the United States, his undermining of the RNC and the party more generally actually disrupted the right's power in the party. Where the party under Bliss refused to disrupt the conservative advance, under Nixon, all party positions had to conform to his personal predilections, regardless of whether they accorded with conservative ideology. When Nixon governed contrary to conservative preferences, as he did on everything from relations with China to regulatory policy, conservatives found themselves out in the cold. As a result, by 1971, a large number of prominent conservatives announced they had suspended support for his administration. A few years later, by the time of the Ford Administration, William Rusher and others were counseling conservatives to abandon the Republican Party altogether and start a new third party.[72]

Watergate, which was itself a product of Nixon's efforts to circumvent the party apparatus, put an end to Nixon's dominance of the GOP. In doing so, it also revitalized the service party model. After Jimmy Carter's election in 1976, the position of RNC chair went to Bill Brock, a conservative who had come up in the factional knife-fighting of the Young Republicans in the 1950s. Brock expanded greatly on the kinds of organizational initiatives Bliss had developed in the 1960s, further developing the party's fundraising prowess and communication capacities. At the same time, Brock took a step away from the service party model, involving the RNC much more directly in ideological questions. Under his leadership, the RNC was active in promoting conservative politics through its publications and messaging. Yet this proved only a temporary deviation from the service model. When Ronald Reagan won the presidency in 1980, the RNC chairs under his leadership refocused once more on the party model established by Bliss.[73]

Just as the New Politics reforms of the Democratic Party influenced the Republicans, so too did the service model spread to the Democrats. After McGovern's loss, DNC chair Bob Strauss followed the advice of subordinates who urged him to copy Bliss's model of providing professionalized services to candidates. As the out-party under Reagan, the Democrats went even further down this road and "shifted the headquarters toward fund-raising and providing campaign services." Under DNC chair Paul Kirk, the goal was to stop "advancing the Democratic *Party* as the central focus of factional electoral politics, and use the party headquarters to support Democratic candidates and support a more *campaign*-centered politics, enabling each candidate and campaign organization to proceed however it liked." By the 1980s, both parties had reoriented their operations. They were no longer, by and large, in the business of setting policy or choosing candidates. Instead, they existed to provide services to candidates.[74]

The story of how the Republican Party transformed after the New Deal is remarkably similar to the story of how the Democratic Party transformed. Both parties went through a protracted period of conflict between the 1930s and the 1960s, in which large factions of each opposed the attempt to define their party through a clear stance on the legacy of the New Deal. In the Democratic Party, it was the Dixiecrats of the South who resisted making their party into an organization dedicated to the politics that characterized the New Deal. In the Republican Party, it was the Eastern internationalists—first to flex their power during the Willkie campaign—who persistently blocked the Taftites' ambitions to turn their party into a weapon against the New Deal. Compromises between the two wings of each party ultimately had the effect of hollowing out their institutional capacities. The Democrats' adoption of the New Politics reforms, using primaries to select delegates, and their failure to adopt more ambitious reforms to restructure the party, effectively denied the institution a role in shaping its politics. The Republicans' service party model, which came as a kind of uneasy truce between the moderates and conservatives, had much the same effect. Both sets of reforms then cross-pollinated between the parties, and by the mid-1980s, both parties were playing a different, more diminished role in American politics than they had two decades earlier.

Campaign Finance Reform: Altering the Organizational Ecosystem

The final institutional transformation responsible for hollowing out American parties was campaign finance legislation. In the 1970s, the Democrats, motivated both by sincere desire for reform and by their own financial problems, passed the Federal Election Campaign Act (FECA), which required the disclosure of donations by campaign contributors and also placed limits on media spending by campaigns. Before FECA, American campaign finance law was disorganized at best. PACs, which had been operating since the 1940s, were still of undecided legality in the early 1970s. The institutional relationships between candidates, campaigns, parties, and supporters were unclear and ad hoc. FECA—with the help of subsequent legislation and interpretation by the Supreme Court—changed all of this, creating the legal infrastructure of modern campaign finance. It clarified relations between PACs and campaigns, established donor limits, and laid out clear rules for campaign financing. These rules had two key effects on parties. First, they established candidate committees as primordial fundraising entities in a campaign, sidelining parties themselves. Second, they legitimized PACs, contributing to the explosive growth of extra-party institutions involved in elections. Coming after Progressive-era reform and the unintended consequences of the party polarizers, campaign finance reform was the final act in the diminishing of American parties.

The immediate impetus for campaign finance reform in the early 1970s was the fiscal crisis of the Democratic Party. Lyndon Johnson bore most of the responsibility for this crisis. Johnson had worked to systematically circumvent the DNC in his administration, starving it of resources and dismantling much of its organization. In a manner similar to Richard Nixon, he sought to concentrate power in himself, not his party. Johnson took over a vehicle Kennedy had established, called the President's Club, and used it to gather contributions that normally would have gone to the party. Essentially a ticket to presidential social events, the President's Club quickly developed into a serious competitor with both the DNC and state parties for funds. Lacking the resources, the DNC began to cut initiatives, most notably its voter registration program. After the 1966 elections, in which the Democrats incurred serious losses, some of Johnson's advisors urged him to rebuild the DNC. He ignored them. One committee member from California lamented, "The Democratic National Committee is basically a shell." By the time Hubert Humphrey picked up the torch from Johnson, the party was broke and demobilized, only getting around to printing buttons in September. If not for the massive effort of the AFL-CIO, Humphrey barely would have had a campaign at all. As a result, by the early 1970s, the DNC was deeply in debt and lacking the fundraising advantages of incumbency. One AFL-CIO lobbyist predicted that, without publicly funded elections, "the Democratic Party will be in desperate shape."[75]

Accordingly, the Democrats had tried to pass campaign finance reform beginning in 1970. The reforms focused on a few key issues. First, they included requirements that donations to campaigns be publicly disclosed. Second, they included requirements that broadcasters sell advertising to candidates at reduced rates, to control campaign costs. Third, the reform legislation established public funding for presidential elections, with the hope that it could soon be extended to Congress. Fourth, it included contribution limits for individuals and limits for what individuals could spend on their own campaign or what independent organizations (such as PACs) could spend on a campaign. All of this was included in the Federal Election Campaign Act (FECA) and its subsequent amendments. At the same time that this legislation was being passed, the Supreme Court ruled that PACs were a legal part of the campaign finance ecosystem. Subsequently, the court also struck down FECA's limits on what individuals could spend on their campaigns and what independent organizations could spend.[76]

The legal infrastructure developed by FECA only enhanced the increasingly candidate-centered nature of American politics. As Morris Fiorina wrote, "it virtually requires the candidate to set up a finance committee separate from the national party." Both state and national parties' donations to candidate committees were limited to only $5,000 a year per committee, ensuring that candidate committees, and not parties, would be the key fiscal nexus for campaigns. These limits also accelerated the organizational decay of local parties. The law's "immediate effect was to discourage state and local party organizations from fully participating in federal elections." This legal regime effectively forced parties to adopt the service model, since providing campaign services to candidates was one of the few functions parties could still reliably perform.[77]

Even more consequentially, the campaign finance laws of the 1970s contributed to the explosive growth of extra-party organizations participating in elections. Though unions were deeply committed to the preservation of PACs in the 1970s, the long-term impact of PACs has clearly benefited business more than labor. Before the 1970s, corporations had little use for PACs, since the laxity of American campaign finance law meant that they could easily donate directly to politicians they supported without organizational intermediaries. However, the much stricter financial oversight regime created in the 1970s, together with the corporate community's organizational offensive in that decade, contributed to an explosive growth of business PACs. Before 1970 the number of corporate PACs never exceeded fifty, but by the mid-1980s there were over 1,200. Moreover, already by the second half of the 1970s these PACs were outperforming labor PACs in fundraising. One estimate of business and labor PAC performance found that "business and business-related groups outraised and outdisbursed labor groups by almost two to one by 1978."[78]

The rapid proliferation of PACs, corporate or otherwise, in the 1970s added a new challenger to parties in the organizational ecology of American politics. With alternative sources of funds, candidates had less reason to worry that bucking their party line would result in their losing bids for reelection. PACs also competed with parties as entities structuring political competition. Ronald Reagan's first RNC chair, Richard Richards, was in constant conflict with conservative PACs, who often intervened in elections specifically against the wishes of the party. After just two years in the role, Richards was replaced as RNC chair, and afterwards, "no formal party leader would follow in Richards's footsteps in taking independent groups to task." Going forward, parties and their leaderships would have to learn to live with PACs and adjust their own roles accordingly.[79]

By the 1980s, campaign finance law had reduced the role of parties even further than the earlier progressive reforms had. Coming on top of the rise of the service party and the institutionalization of presidential primaries, these legal changes reduced parties to a condition that was unrecognizable from the perspective of the early twentieth century. Candidates could now run on a party line independent of the party organization; and increasingly they did not even have to rely on that organization to win a general election. To the extent that the parties have survived, it has been by redefining their role and function in the new environment.

Parties as Bit Players

The new environment parties faced after the reforms of the 1970s consisted primarily of two new factors. First, the parties themselves were organizationally hamstrung by the various legal changes of the decade. Second, the cost of campaigning was escalating vertiginously, and new institutions were increasingly important as suppliers of funds to candidates. Parties adapted, but their adaptations ultimately reduced the decision-making capacity of parties as institutions, leaving them "empty vessels."[80]

The money flooding into Congress interacted with congressional rules reforms in ways that profoundly changed American politics. Now that committee leadership, the most important route to power in Congress, was an open contest, candidates' quests for support from their colleagues led them to the most obvious commodity that could be traded for that support: money. Candidates began fundraising with the goal of redistributing money to their colleagues, thereby winning their support for key committee and caucus leadership positions.[81]

As with so much else in this story, Democrats led the way. In 1977, when Tip O'Neill assumed his position as Speaker of the House, the race to serve under him as majority leader was conducted, for the first time, on the basis of who could redistribute most to their colleagues. Jim Wright of Texas won, setting himself up to become Speaker after O'Neill's retirement a decade later. Two years later, Henry Waxman of California, a two-term representative, ascended to the chair of the Health and Environment Subcommittee of the Energy and Commerce Committee (on which he ranked fourth in seniority) by redistributing money to his colleagues. He founded a new PAC, the Friends of Henry Waxman and directed $24,000 to his colleagues on the committee, who rewarded him with their votes. Seniority was, at long last, dead.[82]

Others soon followed Waxman's example. In 1988, there were forty-five such "leadership PACs," which existed to redistribute money among congressmembers. By 2000, there were 141. One new congressmember who proved a keen student of Waxman's approach was the representative from suburban Atlanta, Newt

Gingrich. By 1998, freshmen congressmembers were launching leadership PACs before they had even been sworn into office.[83]

Soon, not just committee leadership, but caucus leadership itself was being determined by the money race. As campaign costs have risen, congressional ability to redistribute money to needy campaigns has become a key criterion for caucus leadership. Since the 1990s, party leaders have been distinguished by giving vastly more money to their colleagues than non-leaders (though the amount distributed by non-leaders has greatly risen as well). Nancy Pelosi's reign in the House was built largely on this foundation. She is, as Ian Shapiro and Frances McCall Rosenbluth note, "the most effective Democratic fund-raiser the House had ever seen." In 2008, Pelosi pledged to raise $25 million for the Democratic Congressional Campaign Committee, more than the other eight House Democratic leaders combined. Despite leading her party to defeats in the 2004, 2010, 2012, 2014, and 2016 elections, Pelosi remained the head of the House Democratic Party by virtue of her immense fundraising prowess.[84]

In the 1970s, scholars began to notice the weakening of the parties. Some of this attention was driven by a partisan opposition to the reforms. Jeane Kirkpatrick of the Coalition for a Democratic Majority (and later the Reagan administration) published a book on party reform with the melodramatic title *Dismantling the Parties*. But the dynamics in question were clear, and in the seventies and eighties the reigning consensus in American political science was that American parties were weak.

As Coco Chanel remarked, fashions change, but style is forever. Academic fashions change faster than most, and by the 1990s, a new orthodoxy had emerged around the resurgence of American parties. The parties, scholars observed, were flush with money, and surveys of state and local parties revealed they were busier than ever. With a palpable sense of relief, political scientists proclaimed that the parties had recovered.[85]

Yet the more perspicacious among them noticed that parties now played a different role in American political life than they once had. On the state level, parties were now decisively subordinate to candidates, whose nomination was not controlled by party organizations and who did not even rely on parties for fundraising or campaigning. Instead, state parties exist mainly to "provide linkage with the increasingly well-funded national organizations." As one scholar summed up the new role of state parties, they are "no longer performing all or even most of the roles of recruitment, nomination, electoral support, and party discipline of elected officials. The activities of the formal state party organizations are more supplemental than controlling." On the national level, the story is much the same. Parties now exist primarily as networks of funders, external organizations, and campaign service vendors. Their role is to act as "intermediaries between the candidates and the private market of campaign services."[86]

The place of American parties in our polity has been transformed. They are, in the words of two prominent scholars, "hollow parties, neither organizationally robust beyond their roles raising money nor meaningfully felt as a real tangible presence in the lives of voters or in the work of engaged activists." Lacking their own institutional dynamism, they exist mainly as conduits through which political money can flow from source to destination.[87]

By the end of the twentieth century, then, American parties had fallen into a new configuration—they were ideologically coherent, but institutionally feeble. The parties were now more ideologically sorted than any other period in American history, with Democratic and Republican parties clearly distinguished by contrasting party platforms and with increasingly little overlap between the political positions of partisans in Congress. The polarizers who sought parties that would take clear, opposing positions on the issues of the day were ultimately successful. Yet the polarizers' battles inside of their parties had the unanticipated consequence of advancing the hollowing out of the parties that had begun in the Progressive Era. By the time that the parties were thoroughly ideologically polarized, they were less capable than ever of acting independently to structure American politics.[88]

As a consequence, the enfeebled Republican Party can exert little counterpressure against extreme candidates who run for nomination on its ballot line, particularly if they are well financed. Sometimes, as in the case of a Holocaust denier running in a deep-blue district, the only result is half a news cycle of bad press. In other contexts, however, it has cost the party wins. In 2010, Christine O'Donnell, a Tea Party activist only loosely tethered to reality, beat the former Republican Governor of Delaware in a primary, and proceeded to lose the general election by more than fifteen points. In 2012, Tea Party Senate candidates in Indiana and Missouri handily won primaries against more establishment candidates and proceeded to lose winnable general elections, making a Republican seizure of the Senate that year all but impossible. Though these candidacies were opposed by many in the party leadership, they possessed no organizational resources with which to derail them.

This weakness has yielded a pattern in which insurgents against the party leadership arise, generally in Congress, and initiate a period of conflict with the party leadership. Eventually the insurgents win, becoming the party leadership themselves. However, because the party apparatus they have won is so weak, they are unable to stave off challenges from a new round of insurgents, who begin the cycle again.

3

The Republican Revolution

For decades now, the Republican Party has been in a constant process of reinvention. In the 1960s, supporters of Barry Goldwater sought to remake the party of Eisenhower and Nixon into a decisively right-wing organization. In the early 1970s, the New Right of politicos, like Paul Weyrich and Terry Dolan, worked to turn the Republicans into the party of counterrevolution. In the 1980s, Ronald Reagan's presidency inaugurated an aggressive new style of conservative governance.

Observers of the party have, at various times, pointed to all of these as nodal points in the party's history. Building on the account of transformations in the party system and in the organization of the capitalist class in previous chapters, this chapter takes a different view. It argues instead that the 1990s were the pivotal moment and that Newt Gingrich was a more important figure in this process than Ronald Reagan. While it's undoubtedly true that conservative activists in previous decades were transforming the party, this chapter argues that the late 1990s were a crucial moment during which the Republican Party broke violently with the preferences of most of big business in the waging of its long-running war against Bill Clinton. At this moment, the party was not merely becoming more conservative. Rather, its pursuit of conservative partisan warfare against a president who had cannily built a massive corporate coalition behind his administration pointed towards a new relationship between the GOP and many of the boardrooms of corporate America. Where once the party had been a loyal supplicant to corporate preferences, its fealty to groups like the Chamber of Commerce and the Business Roundtable would now be far less dependable.

The Newt Right

Newt Gingrich was never shy about his plans to transform the Republican Party. From the early 1980s until his resignation from the House in 1999, Gingrich trumpeted his plans to remake the party along conservative ideological lines. The Republican Revolution of 1994, when the GOP, led by Gingrich, won a majority in the House of Representatives for the first time since 1952, was undoubtedly the high point of this process, and Gingrich would eagerly claim it as vindication of his project. Two aspects of Gingrich's quest remain underappreciated, however. The first is the degree to which Gingrich's ascent in the party during the 1980s was the result of conflicts with the Reagan administration itself, which Gingrich persistently accused of being insufficiently conservative. These conflicts reveal the extent to which previous conservative polarizers had, even by the end of the Reagan administration, failed to transform the party to the extent they had hoped. Second, Gingrich's rise to leadership, and the rise of similarly conservative allies in the 1990s, was predicated on his ability to raise money and redistribute it around his party. Recognizing how the rules of the game were changing in the wake of party disorganization and the revolution in campaign financing, Gingrich built a fundraising machine that won him the loyalty of a huge number of GOP representatives, who would become eager devotees of his vision of the Republican Party as an instrument of all-out war against liberalism.

The Vietcong of the Republican Party

A former college professor, Gingrich had run for Congress in Georgia twice as a Rockefeller Republican in the mid-1970s, before finally winning in 1978. From the beginning, his ambitions exhibited the borderline megalomania that would define his career. "My job description as I have defined it," he told his staff, "is to save Western civilization." As a freshman representative, he made himself unusually conspicuous, forging a close relationship with the head of the National Republican Congressional Committee, Guy Vander Jagt, and even managing to convince presidential candidate Ronald Reagan to attend an event encouraging Republican candidates to pledge themselves to conservative policy proposals.[1]

Gingrich remained merely a noisier than average junior congressmember until the 1982 midterms, when he began making moves to shake up the party. Two events spurred him to action. First, Reagan had signed a Democratic tax bill that hiked taxes to repair some of the deficits caused by Reagan's earlier tax bill. Gingrich was furious with Reagan and with his congressional colleagues who supported the bill, accusing them of having abandoned their principles. Second, in the 1982 midterms, the Republicans suffered heavy losses in the House, paying the price for Reagan and Volcker's austerity monetary policy. Convinced of the need for a new approach to Republican politics, Gingrich started a new group, the Conservative Opportunity Society (COS). It would be modeled, ironically enough, after the Democratic Study Group of the 1950s and 1960s, which had played such an important role in allowing liberals to consolidate their position in the Democratic Party. However, as a pressure group in the Republican Party, which had been a minority in the House since the 1950s (leading political scientists to discuss the "permanent Republican minority"), it would have to operate a little differently than the DSG. As one political consultant wrote to Gingrich, the COS would have to be like the Vietcong, striking as "a revolutionary guerrilla movement."[2]

Appropriately enough, Gingrich's Svengali during this period was a man who had some familiarity with Vietnam's National Liberation Front: Richard Nixon. Gingrich and his first wife had met with Nixon in New York, where the disgraced ex-president told Gingrich that "the House Republicans were boring and had always been boring" and that if Gingrich wanted to build a majority, he would have to "fill the place with ideas."[3]

Rather than focusing on ideas, however, Gingrich and the COS decided to use procedural politics to build a more adversarial culture in the House. Long-accustomed to being in the minority, most House Republicans had habituated themselves to advancing their priorities through more or less cordial negotiations with the Democratic majority. Gingrich sought to break this culture. He and the COS settled on special order speeches, which are speeches that any House member can give at the end of the legislative day, when most members have already left. Gingrich wanted to use these speeches to attack the Democrats in viciously partisan terms, arguing that they would be "like Chinese water torture" to the majority. When the Speaker of the House Tip O'Neill, outraged at Gingrich's breach of the implicit rules of House conduct, ordered C-SPAN's cameras to turn and reveal that all of these angry speeches were being delivered to an empty chamber, the COS turned their attacks on him, baiting him into a personal attack on Gingrich for which he was rebuked by the House. Eventually, Gingrich was able to use this kind of procedural guerrilla warfare to bring down Jim Wright, the Democratic Speaker of the House who had succeeded O'Neill. When he succeeded in this campaign, which he had mounted against the wishes of the Republican congressional leadership, Gingrich's ascension to a top position in the conference became a fait accompli.[4]

As Gingrich embarked on his long march against the Democratic majority in the House, he was also fighting on another front, against his own party. Despite Reagan's beatification by conservatives in the 1990s, during his administration, the right was rife with discontent over his failure to advance their goals. Gingrich and the COS were at the center of this discontent. During the fight over Reagan's 1982 tax bill, Gingrich pronounced it the "opening round of a fight over the soul and future of the Republican Party." Clearly, Gingrich did not see himself and the president as on the same side of that fight. In 1984, Gingrich refused to support Reagan's budget, accusing it of "feeding the liberal welfare state instead of changing it." Writing to White House budget director David Stockman (himself a free market zealot of no small distinction), Gingrich accused the latter of "becoming the greatest obstacle to a successful revolution" and "blur[ring] the distinction between the revolutionary effort, the creative Opportunity Society and the Liberal Welfare State Establishment." When Reagan announced a summit with Mikhail Gorbachev in 1985, Gingrich implicitly accused the president of appeasement, declaring it "the most dangerous summit for the West since Adolf Hitler met with Chamberlain in 1938 at

Munich." On social policy as well, Gingrich was disappointed with Reagan's seduction by liberalism, and he joined a number of other congressmembers in writing the administration a letter declaring it "appalling" that children with AIDS were "not only encouraged to attend school but to do so anonymously so that other children are precluded from taking appropriate precautions." For Gingrich, during the 1980s, the problem was precisely that there *wasn't* a Reagan Revolution.[5]

Funding a Revolution

Even a guerrilla army needs money. Gingrich understood, like no one else in the Republican Party, that American politics had been transformed during the 1970s and that money played a bigger role in politics than ever before. Around the same time, he founded the COS, Gingrich also founded a PAC, which called the Conservatives for Hope and Opportunity PAC (CHOPAC), to allow him to begin exerting financial influence on his party. CHOPAC was never able to accomplish very much, however, partially as a result of its structure. PACs were only allowed to receive $5,000 per donor. Given that Gingrich was hoping to raise money from some of the richest people in the country, this was an extremely inefficient way to harvest their money. CHOPAC folded in 1988, having distributed only about $200,000 over the course of its existence.[6]

Gingrich would discover the solution to this problem in 1985, when he attended a fundraiser for Delaware governor Pete Du Pont's GOPAC. Du Pont had founded GOPAC in 1978 to train Republican candidates for state-level office in the hopes of improving Republican candidate quality. Gingrich later described his first encounter with GOPAC: "There was a high dollar fundraiser in 1985 and I walked in and saw the amount of wealthy friends that Du Pont had. I saw so much potential that this organization and this wealth could provide." In 1986, Du Pont, attempting an ill-fated presidential run, handed the organization over to Gingrich.[7]

Gingrich used the organization to accomplish two things. First, he used it to ideologically train the foot soldiers of his revolution. As he himself would later aver (as we shall see, quite disingenuously), "In 1985 and 1986 I studied and saw that the party needed a training institution, not a funding institution." Gingrich began using GOPAC to produce and distribute audio tapes, often of Gingrich himself, laying out talking points for GOP candidates on the issues of the day, as well as on broader philosophical questions. The tapes were, in one sense, a manifestation of Gingrich's megalomania and his tendency to imagine his role as analogous to business gurus like Peter Drucker and W. Edwards Deming, thought leaders for mid-century employers. Yet they were undoubtedly effective as well. State-level candidates spent many hours in the car driving from event to event, and many reported, even years later, having been inspired by Gingrich's exhortations.[8]

Though this ideological work has tended to occupy the attention of students of Gingrich's career, its importance is eclipsed by GOPAC's role in fundraising.[9] Gingrich quickly realized that GOPAC had some advantages over CHOPAC. Most centrally, since its goal was not to fund the campaigns of candidates for federal office, it was not registered with the Federal Elections Commission. Instead, it fell under the governance of the state of Delaware, then as now, a state very forgiving of the activities of the financially well endowed. GOPAC's status as a state entity, rather than a federal one, allowed it to escape both FEC PAC contribution limits and FEC disclosure requirements. GOPAC could take as much money as donors would give, and it didn't have to tell anyone.[10]

Donors quickly flocked to GOPAC. By 1990 the group was receiving donations from Republican stalwarts like Terry Kohler and George Gilder that surpassed a hundred thousand dollars—over twenty times the amount an individual could donate to a federal PAC. Gingrich used this money to both distribute his audio tapes and promote his own political leadership. During his campaign against Speaker Wright, for example, GOPAC distributed his broadsides to tens of thousands of the group's contributors, allowing him to build a constituency for his campaign that circumvented the party's congressional leadership. Effectively, Gingrich had found a way to solicit unlimited donations to bolster his own political leadership.[11]

The most crucial role for GOPAC, however, was as a node between a network of donors on one side and of politicians on the other. Though GOPAC itself was forbidden from making contributions to candidates for federal office, it could use its money to host events where donors met such candidates and to publicize candidates it felt its donors may be interested in learning about. One GOPAC contributor was remarkably frank about the process involved, describing how GOPAC staff would "call occasionally and say, 'We need a little help here,' or send a note and tell you, 'If you could possibly help this one … There is a very fine person running for Congress, and if you could possibly see a way to help with a donation, and of course that would go directly to the candidate, because your GOPAC money goes directly to the states, for state offices." Bob Ehrlich, a representative from Maryland elected during the Republican Revolution of 1994, proudly told a reporter, "It was fantastic … [Gingrich] came in for me and helped us raise a lot of money. We raised a quick $25,000, $30,000 … and we received big checks from Republicans around the country. That money was very, very important." In this way, Gingrich built GOPAC into a financial juggernaut, making himself indispensable to Republican candidates in need of ever-more campaign cash. By the 1990s, GOPAC would resemble, in the words of two political scientists, "a shadow NRCC."[12]

By early 1989, Gingrich had amassed enough support in the Republican conference to be elected minority whip, the second most powerful Republican post in the chamber. Working closely with NRCC head Bill Paxon, Gingrich began generalizing his fundraising practices across the entire conference. After Bill Clinton's election in 1992, these efforts reached a frenzy. Gingrich and Paxon let it be known that all members were expected to fundraise not only for themselves but for the RNC and NRCC as well. One member complained that he didn't know how to fundraise for the campaign committees. Gingrich, ever the pedagogue, replied, "I'll teach you." The member was sent to the RNC headquarters to work the phones and came back shortly afterwards boasting, "'I just raised $50,000 over at the RNC!" The fruits of this project were impressive. In 1992, only twelve Republican congressmembers raised money for the NRCC, contributing a grand total $50,000. By the 1994 election cycle, Gingrich was pushing Republicans to donate to each other's campaigns via leadership PACs, suggesting every member of Congress should give at least $148,000 in each election. Over one hundred members kicked in, sending over one million dollars to the NRCC. Members began also redistributing money amongst themselves, with incumbents in safe seats directing their money to challengers, drastically raising the marginal impact of each dollar raised on the party's chances to retake the House. By the last few weeks of the race, Gingrich and Paxon had managed to erase the Democrats' incumbency advantage in fundraising, and the Republicans reported to the FEC decisive advantages in both soft-money donations to the parties as well as fundraising for challengers. This money is what made the Republican Revolution of 1994 possible.[13]

GOPAC allowed Gingrich to play a crucial role in the House. The reforms of the 1970s decisively weakened the committee system and, in theory, empowered the party leadership to more effectively direct the chamber. Yet the rapid escalation of campaign costs in the 1970s changed the role of party leadership drastically. Fundraising was quickly becoming as important as the ability to move a bill along. Among the Democrats, this new principle was being discovered by representatives like Henry Waxman and Tony Coelho. On the other side of the aisle, Gingrich built a following among Republican members that assured that, by 1994, most of the new majority was personally indebted to Gingrich's largess for their victories. The road to power now needed to be paved in gold.[14]

After Gingrich's victory in 1994, there was a frenzied rush of donations to GOPAC, which raised more in the first six months of 1995, a nonelection year, than it had in all of 1994. GOPAC, however, would soon run into legal problems with the FEC and declined in importance. Now Speaker of the House, Gingrich had whole new set of institutions to remold into engines of fundraising. Upon assuming his speakership, Gingrich began reshaping the rules of the House to institutionalize his regime of money-driven politics. He proposed an audacious package of rule changes that centralized power in himself and other conference leaders, increasing the leadership's ability to control committee appointments. Yet what has frequently escaped notice is the way that fundraising was integrated into this project. After winning his majority, Gingrich's power to appoint committee members and leaders was used to reward members who met party fundraising goals. Departing from seniority more drastically than any congressional leadership since the Democratic rebellion in 1974, Gingrich appointed Robert Livingston, Henry Hyde, and Thomas Bliley to committee chairs above more senior members. All three men had distinguished themselves by fundraising for the NRCC and redistributing their funds to other candidates in 1994. This system rapidly evolved into one that, as Thomas Ferguson has noted, "amounted to posted prices" for committee positions. Already by 1998, Gingrich, along with NRCC chair John Linder, was threatening subcommittee chairs; unless they coughed up the requisite $100,000 each, they would lose their positions. One of the delinquent congressmembers summed the system up in a glum apophasis, "I hope [Gingrich and Linder] are not implying that the chairmanships are for sale—in effect, those who ante the most get the chairmanships."[15]

This system would quickly be copied by the Democrats. By the twenty-first century, committee assignments were more or less subject to auction, euphemized as "party dues." Committees were ranked A, B, or C based on their level of importance, and appointment to more important committees cost more money. In the 2013–2014 election cycle, Republicans chairing A committees were expected to contribute $990,000 to the NRCC. On the Democratic side, these appointments cost $1.5 million. Quantitative research on congressional career paths has confirmed that this kind of party fundraising, along with contributions to other members, is now decisive for attaining leadership in Congress.[16]

Newt Gingrich didn't merely lead a Republican Revolution. He built a new regime for both political parties, one fully adjusted to the legal and economic realities of the post-reform period.

Comrades and Enemies

As Gingrich was changing how parties operate, he was also transforming the character of the Republican Party. From his days with the COS onwards, Gingrich built a cadre of Republicans committed to both his mode of fundraising and his bellicose brand of conservative politics. Though Gingrich himself would reign for only a short period, retiring in disgrace in 1999 in the midst of GOP rebellion as well as an ethics investigation, the cohorts of politicians he trained would continue to lead American politics up until the present.

Gingrich's progeny in the Republican Party can be divided into two cohorts. First, there were the Republicans elected to the House alongside him in the late 1970s and the 1980s. These figures would either form part of Gingrich's leadership team after 1994 or, in some cases, move on to the Senate, to which they exported his new brand of pugnacious parliamentarism. Second, there were the Republicans elected in 1992 and 1994, who, almost to a person, looked to Gingrich as a leader, copying both his partisan warfare and his fundraising practices. Politicians from both groups were centrally involved in pushing Gingrich out of leadership in the late 1990s, as the Republican Revolution devoured its own.

The House Republican Conference in the 1980s contained a number of members who shared Gingrich's desire for a more thoroughly conservative and confrontational GOP, but they lacked his entrepreneurial gifts. Some of these, like Vin Weber of Minnesota, would become Gingrich lackeys in the COS. Others, like Trent Lott, would work closely with Gingrich to advance common political goals and then leave his orbit to make their own political ascents.

The most important figures to come out of this cohort, however, were those who became part of Gingrich's congressional leadership team after 1994: Tom DeLay, Dick Armey, Dennis Hastert, and John Boehner. All of these men distinguished themselves both with their adherence to hard right conservatism and their ability to redistribute money around the House.

DeLay in particular showed himself to be *plus royaliste que le roi* in this regard. Originally an exterminator from Texas, Delay got into politics when the EPA moved to regulate one of his favorite pesticides. He won election to the House in 1984. At first, he was not particularly close to Gingrich. In fact, he and

Hastert both had worked for the election of Edward Madigan to the position of minority whip in 1989, a contest that would be lost to Gingrich. But when the next leadership elections came around in 1992, DeLay proved himself an apt student. As Dick Armey became head of the House Republican Conference, the number-three GOP position in the chamber, DeLay won the position of conference secretary. His opponent in the race attributed DeLay's victory to his ability to move money, lamenting that "I wasn't very good at fundraising for myself … I was always uneasy about PAC money, for example … and Tom had no such inhibitions." Two years later, DeLay actually beat Gingrich's preferred candidate for the majority whip position. He did so by putting together a donor slush fund he would help redistribute to other congressmembers. As one lobbyist working with DeLay put it, "We'd rustle up checks for the guy and make sure Tom got the credit … So when new members voted for majority whip, they'd say, 'I wouldn't be here if it wasn't for Tom DeLay.'" DeLay helped channel over two million dollars in donations in this way, allowing him to overcome Gingrich's own efforts to support his preferred candidate. As a result, fifty-two of the seventy-three freshmen GOP representatives elected in 1994 backed DeLay in the whip race.[17]

With DeLay's victory, a new House Republican leadership team was complete. Gingrich served as Speaker, Armey as majority leader, DeLay as whip, Boehner as head of the Republican conference, and Hastert as deputy whip. The team wasted little time in establishing new fundraising routines. Armey, DeLay, and Boehner all launched leadership PACs of their own in 1995, and Gingrich launched a new federal candidate PAC, "Monday Morning." Some efforts were so brazen as to cause embarrassment, as when John Boehner handed out checks from the tobacco industry to representatives on the floor of the House. Facing potential new regulation, the industry would donate over half a million dollars to GOP representatives in the first six months of 1995 alone.[18]

Yet even as the model of politics Gingrich developed was spreading, it was undermining his efforts to centralize power in the House. The creation of new leadership PACs and new networks of funders and candidates reduced members' dependence on Gingrich and provided the basis for challenges to his leadership. From early on, many of the representatives elected in 1992 and 1994 mounted their own challenges to Gingrich from the right. In so doing, they initiated a pattern that has existed in the party since; the insurgents of one era (such as Gingrich) become the establishment in the next.

Tensions between Gingrich and the new representatives began practically as soon as they came to office. The freshmen wanted to continue Gingrich's guerilla warfare tactics, while Gingrich, now effectively in command of regulars, pursued a different strategy. Tensions escalated drastically after Gingrich's defeat in the 1995 and 1996 government shutdowns. Perceived as humbled by Clinton, Gingrich lost the respect of many of his most zealous followers. The nomination and subsequent defeat of moderate Bob Dole in 1996 and election of a number of moderate Republican representatives that year further convinced the party's right that drastic action was necessary. In March of 1997, eleven of their number moved to block a bill funding Congress that Gingrich had brought to the floor. One member of the class of '92 published an editorial calling Gingrich "roadkill on the highway of American politics"; he was now part of the establishment rather than the insurgency. By that summer, DeLay, Armey, and Boehner launched an abortive attempt to replace Gingrich as Speaker. Betrayed by one of their confederates, they publicly apologizes to the conference but retained their positions.[19]

Even as Gingrich transformed the operation of the House, that very operation rendered his own leadership less stable. For all the attention scholars have given to Gingrich's efforts to centralize power in the speakership, few have remarked on how that endeavor was undone by the spread of the kinds of fundraising and redistributing that brought him to power in the first place. The Republicans who won office in 1992 and 1994 were Gingrich's followers, to be sure. But that very fact meant that their loyalty to Gingrich was based only on his ability to supply funds when others could not. When Gingrich was no longer their exclusive only source of money, they were free to turn on him—and they did. As Lindsey Graham, of the class of '92, later recalled,

"Ain't nothing was off-limits, buddy. You could feed us, wash us, and comb us, but we'd still bite."[20]

The Political Economy of the Republican Revolution

As the Republican conference remade itself in Gingrich's image in the first half of the 1990s, it also engaged in a series of critical policy battles with the Clinton administration. These battles would reshape American institutions and set new patterns for how future conflicts would unfold. Three in particular stand out. First, in 1993 the GOP led a successful battle to defeat Clinton's healthcare reform plan. Second, in 1995, Gingrich's new majority attempted to force major budget cuts on the administration, ultimately triggering two government shutdowns. While the administration did embrace the goal of a balanced budget, the shutdowns damaged the Republicans generally, and Gingrich in particular, helping to set the stage for Clinton's reelection. Finally, in 1996, the House Republicans had assembled a veto-proof majority for welfare reform, forcing Clinton to sign a bill limiting lifetime welfare eligibility and imposing strict work requirements.

These policy battles certainly showcased a newly combative and ultra-conservative Republican Party. Yet what is striking about these episodes is that, in each case, the Republican Party was actually moving closely in accord with the main body of American employers. The congressional right of the early 1990s was not engaged in the kind of conflicts with business that became so prominent during the Tea Party and Trump years. Instead, even at its most confrontational, the party was pursuing goals that won wide assent in corporate boardrooms. It was only later, during the impeachment saga, that the party began to step decisively outside of the corporate consensus.

The Corporate Coalition Against Healthcare Reform
Bill Clinton's defeat in the healthcare reform battle was a key moment in his first administration. Even before the Republicans had taken the House, the fight showed that the new leadership of the party would be far more bellicose towards the Democrats

than it had been in the past. Indeed, the ferocity of the congressional Republicans has led some scholars to conclude that the plan's defeat was a case of the tail wagging the dog; corporate leaders were, in the words of one writer, "mau-maued by the hard right." According to this argument, while corporations would have benefited from Clinton's bill in the form of reduced health insurance costs for their employees, they were intimidated by Gingrich, DeLay, and company into opposing the bill, ultimately leading to its defeat.[21]

The truth, however, is a little simpler. Business came to oppose Clinton's healthcare bill because they perceived it as contrary to their interests. While the Republican Party might have wished for a more vociferous attack on the bill from business, there is little evidence that business groups needed to be intimidated into opposing the bill.

Healthcare reform was one of the Clinton administration's top priorities in its first term. The issue polled well, and Clinton's campaign team had won a long-shot Senate campaign in Pennsylvania when their candidate began talking about a right to healthcare. During the campaign, Clinton had talked vaguely about universal coverage but didn't advance anything resembling a concrete plan. Once in office, the administration turned to the Jackson Hole group, an informal gathering of healthcare policy figures who had coalesced around the idea of "managed competition." In essence, the vision of managed competition was one in which there was some kind of intermediary organization between health insurance consumers and health insurance sellers. This would allow consumers to aggregate their purchasing power and bargain for better deals from insurers. In managed competition, the Clinton administration thought it had found a plan which could contain healthcare costs (which had risen even more quickly than campaign expenditures over the previous two decades) and provide universal coverage without eliminating markets or private insurers.[22]

As a broad vision, managed competition won wide support among American employers. Manufacturers, in particular, suffered from the rising costs of their employees' healthcare plans. Large insurers also looked forward to the additional customers that universal coverage would bring. Small businesses, which typically did not provide health insurance plans to employees, and small insurance companies, who thought they would be squeezed out by increased consumer bargaining power, opposed the plan from the beginning. But this was unquestionably a minority sector of American business. Given the buy-in of big business, the administration was optimistic about its chances as it began rolling out its plan in early 1993.

It was because of this initial support for the plan that a number of authors have concluded that business's volte-face in early 1994 must be explained by the interference of the Republican Party. The key piece of evidence cited in this story is the turnabout by Chamber of Commerce representative Robert Patricelli. On February 2, Patricelli had submitted prepared testimony to the House Ways and Means Committee, which affirmed that, with a few tweaks of the plan, the Chamber of Commerce could go along with the administration. However, when Patricelli came to testify in person the very next day, he told the committee that the chamber "cannot support any of the mandate proposals that have been advanced in legislation by President Clinton or members of Congress." Moreover, in the months before this, the GOP had leaned heavily on the Chamber, with John Boehner telling Chamber leaders in one meeting that it was "the Chamber's duty to categorically oppose everything that Clinton was in favor of." This sequence of events has convinced many "that a number of companies were cowed by into opposition by Republican members of Congress."[23]

Yet a broader look at the episode reveals that this was hardly the case. By early 1994, the vehemence of Republican opposition to Clinton's plan was itself reflective of business sentiment. The key transformation was prompted by the arcana of congressional procedure. In the 1970s, Congress had mandated Congressional Budget Office reporting on the costs of legislation. By the deficit-conscious 1990s, these reports had become politically relevant, and Clinton's healthcare team was desperate to make sure their plan didn't add to the deficit. But the only way to ensure this was to not just rely on the aggregation of consumer purchasing power to hold down costs but to impose caps on insurance premium prices. This shifted the Clinton plan from a market-friendly attempt to expand coverage and contain costs to an initiative that would impose permanent price controls on a sector comprising more than 10 percent of GDP. One Jackson Hole éminence grise denounced the plan as "Single Payer in Jackson Hole Clothing."[24]

The alteration also changed the corporate calculus on health-care reform. Now, even corporations that had previously been supportive of managed competition needed to weigh potential benefits against the cost of legitimizing a large expansion of government control over the economy. For many corporate leaders, with the battles of the 1970s still in mind, the game was no longer worth the candle. Moreover, healthcare costs had unexpectedly plateaued in 1993 and 1994, lessening the urgency of reform even for those companies most exposed to rising costs.[25]

The precise timing of corporate opposition to Clinton's plan supports the idea that this opposition was not initiated by congressional Republicans. Patricelli came out in opposition to the plan on February 3. The day before, however, the Business Roundtable had made public its own opposition to Clinton's plan. While the Chamber had suffered GOP browbeating for its lack of opposition over the previous month, congressional Republicans stepped more lightly around the members of the Roundtable, composed as it was exclusively of the CEOs of the largest firms in the country. There's nothing to suggest that GOP intimidation changed the Roundtable's mind. Moreover, the National Association of Manufacturers, whose members stood to gain the most from Clinton's plan, also came out in opposition soon after the Roundtable did. As with the Roundtable, there is little to suggest that the NAM received the kind of pressure campaign from the GOP that the Chamber did. Instead, the timing indicates that a corporate consensus in opposition to Clinton's plan formed as the plan itself took more concrete shape.[26]

The Roundtable's opposition to the plan proved decisive in Congress as well. John Dingell, a reform advocate who chaired the Energy and Commerce Committee, told reporters that "when the president failed to get the Business Roundtable, there was a big shift in sentiment inside the committee ... That was a defining event." By the summer of 1994, healthcare reform was dead.[27]

The fight against Clinton's healthcare reform certainly show-cased a newly truculent Republican Party. But the evidence suggests that they were encouraged by corporate leaders who also opposed the plan. Business felt that, as one Roundtable member told another at the meeting where they voted to oppose the plan, "the only things these guys in the White House understand is a sharp stick to the nose."[28]

Balanced Budget Conservatism and the Government Shutdowns

Unlike healthcare reform, the budget battles between the Clinton administration and Gingrich's Republicans have attracted relatively little scholarly attention. This is unfortunate, because this episode is every bit as revealing about the relationship between the Republican Party and American capitalists in the early 1990s. Indeed, there's a prima facie case that the government shutdowns that resulted from this conflict (which resulted in some government agencies shutting down for more than twenty days) were, as has been alleged of the healthcare battle, a case of the Republicans going outside the bounds of what business actually wanted. Given the real macroeconomic consequences of shutdowns, the argument that corporate leaders would oppose a strategy that risked a shutdown is certainly plausible.[29]

Yet this was not the case. The push for a balanced budget was enthusiastically supported by a wide corporate coalition. And little evidence exists of any disagreement with Gingrich's hard-ball tactics, even when they resulted in what was, at that point, the longest government shutdown in American history. Like the healthcare battle, this was a case of a Republican Party whose combativity reflected the preferences of its historic patrons in the capitalist class.

The salience of the federal budget deficit had climbed steadily throughout the 1980s, as it grew ever larger under Reagan's peculiar political economy. Walter Mondale had attempted to run on the issue against Reagan in 1984 but had attracted little enthusiasm from either employers or voters. By Reagan's second term, however, concern was growing. In 1988, the chair of the Business Roundtable had declared that "chronic budget deficits pose a grave danger to our economy, to our standard of living, to our leadership role in the world and to the perceived community of interests which unites American society—old and young, rich and poor." During the George H. W. Bush administration, a number of corporate leaders supported tax increases to reduce the deficit. When Clinton proposed a budget with substantial tax increases on the top brackets in order to close the deficit, however, the Roundtable, the Chamber, and the NAM all opposed his plan, arguing that it did not include enough cuts to social spending.[30]

By the mid-1990s, business was engaged in large-scale mobilization against the deficit. On Wall Street, right-wing financiers had banded together to form the Political Club for Growth, a group to coordinate donations to conservative lawmakers who could be counted on to cut government spending. The Business Roundtable formed a group called The Coalition for Change, which conducted a $10 million media campaign for a balanced budget. At the same time, an informal discussion group between Republican leaders like Boehner, DeLay, and Gingrich; conservative policy entrepreneurs like Grover Norquist; and business leaders, dubbed the Thursday Group, spun off to form an organization called the Coalition to Balance the Budget (chaired by a senior vice president of the Chamber of Commerce) to coordinate activity among different business groups.[31]

This wide corporate coalition for a balanced budget served as the backdrop to Gingrich's decision to fight Clinton's budget proposal in 1995 all the way to a government shutdown. Indeed, the connections between this coalition and Gingrich himself were intimate. Members of the Political Club for Growth had donated hundreds of thousands of dollars to GOPAC in the 1980s and 1990s, and the group's treasurer and chief organizer also served as the executive director of GOPAC. Similarly, the Thursday Group conducted its meetings out of Gingrich's conference room in the House.[32]

With the enthusiastic backing of the corporate community, Gingrich embarked on a recklessly confrontational strategy of budget negotiation. Clinton had already by this point moved to the right on budgeting and by 1995 was proposing to balance the federal budget in ten years. For Gingrich and company, however, this was insufficient, and they refused to support any budget that took more than seven years to eliminate the deficit. Gesturing back to his frustrations with Reagan and Bush, Gingrich declared "This is where [Reagan budget director David] Stockman and [Bush budget director Richard] Darman blinked. I will not blink." On November 1, 1995, Clinton and a number of Democratic leaders met with Gingrich and Senate Majority Leader Bob Dole to try and obtain a compromise. As Clinton laid out the programs he wanted to see protected (Medicare, Medicaid, education, and environmental programs), Gingrich rejected any compromise, insisting that his majority would pass the cuts he demanded. Clinton replied, "If you want somebody to sign your budget … you're going to have to get yourself another president."[33] A government shutdown of six days began in November and ended with a short-term spending bill. In December, however, Clinton vetoed the Republican budget, triggering a twenty-one day shut down.

Though the actual differences in spending levels between the Republican bill and what Clinton wanted were small, the White House succeeded in portraying the Republicans as callous extremists eager to cut popular programs. As polls revealed that the public was increasingly blaming the GOP for the shutdown, Gingrich and Dole began softening their opposition and looking to compromise. They were hindered in this endeavor, however, by the rest of the House GOP leadership, which in late December voted 12-0 against Gingrich to reject any compromise with Clinton. Yet political realities could only be resisted so long, and in early January, the Republicans capitulated, giving Clinton a short-term funding bill that set a framework for a longer term compromise. Gingrich had gambled and lost.[34]

The Clinton administration and its allies had tried to make the case that the shutdown was a threat to business. Susan Hering, a representative from Salomon Brothers Inc., had testified before the Senate Finance Committee in mid-1995 that a failure to finance debt payments "would cascade throughout the economy." Similarly, Robert Rubin raised the specter of a payment pause and tried to convince Congress of the threat it imposed. Yet, as *Business Week* put it, "Everybody thinks Rubin is crying wolf." Business wasn't buying it.[35]

In the aftermath of the shutdown, there was little to suggest that corporate leaders had changed their minds. In December, the Chamber of Commerce's magazine, *Nation's Business*, published an editorial commending the 104th Congress for a job well done. The Congress had been elected, the Chamber wrote, to ensure "a balanced budget, lower taxes, less regulation, and a transfer of power from Washington to the states." Even after the first government shutdown, the Chamber commended Gingrich's majority for "an excellent start toward fulfilling their commitment to voters." The next month, the editorial attacked Clinton for vetoing the Republican budget, and the following month, after the compromise had been reached, the message was even more explicit:

> This Congress was sent to Washington to carry out commitments that a majority of its members made as candidates, and that process must continue.
>
> Unfortunately, the president has already given indication that he believes his political survival lies in blocking, or at least diluting, actions taken by Congress to further that program.

Whatever the economic consequences of Gingrich's gamble, the Chamber judged them insignificant next to the goals of cutting spending and balancing the budget.[36]

The End of Dependency

Alongside a balanced budget, entitlement reform was one of the most important policy priorities of Gingrich's new majority. For veterans of Congress in the 1980s like Gingrich, slashing cash aid to the poor was one of the key unfinished tasks of the Reagan revolution. Though Reagan had imposed various new rules and spending restrictions on welfare, his policies produced, in political scientist Paul Pierson's words, "some marginal tightening of benefits and eligibility, but no fundamental reforms." Gingrich's 1994 Contract with America, which laid out his agenda, promised a bill that would "cut spending for welfare programs, and enact a tough two-years-and-out provision with work requirements to promote individual responsibility."[37]

As with healthcare reform and the government shutdown, this was a cause in which the Republican Party and American employers were united. In the early 1990s, the Chamber of Commerce began agitating for welfare reform and promoting various forms of welfare to work, regularly publishing surveys of business owners endorsing retrenchment in *Nation's Business*. As the GOP welfare bills made their way through Congress in 1995, the magazine editorialized that it "offers the nation more hope for optimism than it has enjoyed in a very long time." Richard Lesher, the Chamber's president, explained business's interest in the bill:

> There are lots of jobs. Anytime there's high unemployment, there's also the long list of jobs that go a-begging. The fact of the matter is everyone wants to start at the middle or upper middle, and now you're going to be driven to start at the bottom and begin to work your way up. And that's the beginning of the end of dependency.[38]

With strong support from business organizations like the Chamber, the GOP was able forge ahead with welfare reform even after their costly defeat over the government shutdown. The House, led by Gingrich, advanced an extremely conservative bill, while the Senate, led by Bob Dole, produced a bill closer to what Clinton wanted. Through discussions with Dole, Clinton was able to make sure the reconciliation bill was something he could tolerate, and he signed it in August of 1996. The bill was the only major policy proposal of the Contract with America to be signed into law.[39]

The major policy battles of the early 1990s saw the emergence of a congressional GOP that pursued reactionary politics with an intensity that outdid even the Reagan administration. Determined to cripple the Clinton administration, they embraced confrontation and disdained compromise. In some cases, most notably the government shutdown, this led to costly political defeats. In others, such as healthcare reform and welfare reform, the GOP was more successful, blocking a transformative reform in the first case and enacting their own in the second. Though the belligerence of the GOP, particularly after the 1994 election victory, has led some to conclude that the party was no longer following the lead of big business, on all of the above issues, the party's priorities were actually closely aligned with organized business. Business itself was pushing the party to the right.

Impeachment

However, the GOP's determination to take Clinton down did eventually lead it to embrace a strategy that found little support among corporate boardrooms. The impeachment of Bill Clinton in 1998 for lying under oath in the course of the investigation of his relationship with Monica Lewinsky, was the culmination of the right-wing campaign against him that began as soon as he took office. The impeachment was watershed event in several senses. It was only the second presidential impeachment in the nation's history. The first, of Andrew Johnson in 1868, proceeded from the conflict between the president and Congress over the direction of reconstruction policy after the Civil War. While Richard Nixon resigned before he could be impeached, there is little doubt that, given the rampant criminality he oversaw in the White House, he would have been. Bill Clinton's impeachment, by contrast, ultimately came down to whether he accurately described the specific sexual acts he and Monica Lewinsky performed on one another. Clearly, the political calculus involved in initiating impeachment hearings had changed.

Relatedly, the impeachment campaign testified to a new level of partisan vindictiveness among congressional Republicans. From the beginning of Clinton's presidency, Republicans had despised him. This contempt extended well beyond the party's radical wing. James Baker, for example, who was Reagan's chief of staff and secretary of state for George H. W. Bush, "saw Clinton as sleazy ... Baker was offended at the very notion of Clinton as president." For a large part of the Republican Party, Clinton was, by virtue of his person and his politics, an illegitimate president.[40]

During Clinton's first administration, this implacable opposition kept the GOP closely in line with what corporate boardrooms wanted. As described above, American employers also wanted

Clinton's healthcare plan to fail, and they wanted his budget cut down to size. But Clinton's second term witnessed a dramatic transformation in the relationship between party and class. As Clinton moved right and aggressively courted corporate favor, the Republican Party's determination to see him fail came to be more removed from the preferences of leading business organizations. Similarly, congressional Republicans were showing themselves to be less reliable stewards of corporate interests than those who had opened their pocketbooks for the Republican Revolution had hoped.

The push for impeachment, then, was the moment when the Republican Party began to stray from the path preferred by leading business organizations. Instead, it chose a narrower path, hewing to the dictates of the tobacco industry and the Christian right. As a result, business priorities in the late 1990s, such as tax cuts and social security prioritization, withered under the heat of partisan acrimony. The mainstream business organizations showed themselves unable to discipline the party, while particularistic interests like tobacco set that latter's course. Impeachment was the moment when money-driven politics and a more fractured corporate elite collided, yielding a Republican Party whose rightwards radicalization would not be restrained by the traditional power elite.

How Clinton Got His Groove Back

After the Republican Revolution, Clinton began tacking right. This manifested in policies like the balanced budget proposal of 1995, which went most of the way towards meeting Republican demands and completely abandoned the stimulus spending he had hoped to pass in his first term. Similarly, as described above, Clinton's embrace of welfare reform helped convince corporate leaders that the president was serious about governing as a new kind of Democrat.

Clinton also performed acts of service for some very specific industries, who responded with appropriate gratitude. He courted the media industry, for example, through modifications to the Telecommunications Act of 1996. Largely a Republican initiative aimed at allowing further consolidation of regional telephone landline companies created by the breakup of Ma Bell in the early 1980s, the act enabled a wave of media conglomeration that created the legal framework for our current era of consolidated, hyperpartisan media. The Clinton administration, however, was able to rewrite some of the bill's language to be much friendlier to television networks, newspapers, and movie studios. Moreover, while Gingrich and congressional Republicans brashly declared their intentions to "abolish the FCC," the administration was far more solicitous to the established firms that benefited from the current regulatory regime.[41]

Even more important in the long term than telecom, however, was tech. The 1990s witnessed the political coming of age of Silicon Valley. The immediate catalyst to tech-industry organization was California's Proposition 211, which would have made it easier for shareholders to sue companies whose management was failing to act with appropriate discipline. Tech companies reacted furiously to this threat to managerial prerogative, and Silicon Valley's first PAC was formed in 1996 to combat Proposition 211.[42]

Proposition 211 seemed like the kind of policy that Democrats would love. Trial lawyers, who were, after all, an important Democratic Party constituency by this time, would benefit massively from enabling more shareholder lawsuits. Moreover, the man responsible for pushing the measure, Bill Lerach, was himself the second largest donor to federal political candidates in the country and donated almost exclusively to Democrats. In fact, he had met personally with Clinton and convinced the president to veto federal legislation limiting shareholder lawsuits.[43]

Yet as Silicon Valley organized, it began exerting tremendous pressure on the Democrats to oppose Proposition 211. Executives began showing up at Clinton fundraisers, and, with the requisite donations, finding themselves in private conversations with the president. By August, they had succeeded. Clinton made a public statement, declaring that Proposition 211 would be "highly disruptive to investment in new companies throughout the country. I don't think it's good for the economy." This support from the Clinton administration launched a relationship between Silicon Valley and the Democratic Party that has continued to the present day.[44]

But the most important way Clinton won back corporate support was his stewardship of US international economic policy. Clinton was, at heart, a free trader, and over the course of his presidency, he enacted various policies that numbered among the very highest priorities of American corporate leadership. Clinton was instrumental in securing implementation of NAFTA in 1993 and in passing permanent normal trade relations (which made free trade the default between countries) with China in 2000—basically making China's entry into the World Trade Organization inevitable. In between, Clinton led an ultimately unsuccessful fight for fast-track negotiation powers, which would allow the president to present trade agreements to Congress for an up or down vote, without giving the body the opportunity to add amendments. The fight for fast track in particular was crucial, as it took place concurrently with impeachment.[45]

Clinton's support for free trade was pragmatic as well as ideological. By the 1990s, free trade had become the single most important issue to the corporate elite, resulting in largest corporate political mobilization of the decade. The push for free trade by American corporations in this era (there had been previous such crusades, of course) began with the negotiation of NAFTA. These negotiations began shortly after the election of Carlos Salinas as president of Mexico in 1988. Salinas, a Harvard economics PhD, saw potential in free trade for accelerating Mexican development. He reached out to the CEOs of American Express and Eastman Kodak, both of whom did extensive business in Mexico, and who happened to co-lead the Business Roundtable's task force on trade expansion. By 1990, formal negotiations between the US, Canada, and Mexico had begun, and President Bush announced that he would seek fast-track authority from Congress. This catalyzed opposition in Congress, transforming the negotiations into a political fight.[46]

It was a battle American corporations were only too happy to enter. In March of 1991 business groups, led by the Business Roundtable, the Chamber of Commerce, and the National Association of Manufacturers, formed the Committee for Trade Expansion to support fast track. Their lobbying succeeded in winning fast-track authority for Bush, and in 1992 the initial negotiations were complete. In December, the presidents of the US, Canada, and Mexico signed the agreement creating NAFTA. The next step was ratification of the agreement by Congress.[47]

To ensure Congress made the right decision, corporate leaders significantly expanded their organizing. The Committee for Trade Expansion was converted into USA★NAFTA, and it expanded to more than two thousand corporate members and forty-three trade associations. USA★NAFTA appointed state captains in all fifty states who would coordinate the lobbying of each state's congressional delegation. The Business Roundtable remained at the center of this organizing, mobilizing its firms as leaders in the push for NAFTA. Over the course of 1993, USA★NAFTA conducted an intense pressure campaign, involving everything from corporate leaders personally calling representatives to specially brokered meetings with the president to ensure his continued fealty to free trade. The head of USA★NAFTA proclaimed, "I think we've done more on NAFTA than on any legislative issue in history." In November, the campaign was successful, as Congress approved the treaty by a large margin.[48]

By Clinton's second administration, the focus of foreign economic policy had shifted from the Americas to Asia. Two issues dominated: the fight for fast-track authority for new trade negotiations in Asia and the East Asian financial crisis of 1997. In both of these, Clinton showed himself a loyal steward of corporate interests. The president's fast-track authority had expired in 1994, and Clinton sought renewal for the negotiation of new trade agreements in Latin American and increasingly in Asia as well. In seeking this authority, Clinton was increasingly out of step with the congressional Democratic Party. With the party's conservative wing decimated by the Republican Revolution (itself partly the result of the party's support for NAFTA), trade-skeptical Democrats had become more prominent. To support Clinton, the Roundtable, the Chamber, and the NAM formed American Leads on Trade, a broad corporate coalition comparable to USA★NAFTA.[49]

As Clinton sought fast-track authority from Congress, he and his administration also worked to manage the East Asian financial crisis. Centered in South Korea and Thailand, the financial crisis spread and ultimately threatened catastrophic bank and currency runs across much of Southeast Asia. Preventing a global financial crisis required bailouts by the International Monetary Fund, which the US played a key role in funding and managing. In 1998, the crisis hit the United States as Long-Term Capital Management, a massive hedge fund, found itself carrying $2 billion in capital against $100 billion in debt. The insolvency of LTCM threatened financial markets more broadly, causing Goldman Sachs to lose half its value in a month.[50]

The Clinton administration acted rapidly to contain these threats. Led by Treasury Secretary Robert Rubin and the economist Lawrence Summers, the administration put together bailout packages for a number of East Asian countries as well as LTCM. Rubin and Summers, together with Alan Greenspan at the Federal Reserve, started to be called "The Committee to Save the World," and the three of them won wide praise for their handling of the crisis. The main business organizations supported their efforts. When the IMF needed additional funds to administer the bailouts, the lobbying to get Congress to appropriate the necessary money was led by the Ad Hoc Coalition for IMF Replenishment, whose members included the Chamber, the Roundtable, and the NAM. Shortly before the vote, the Roundtable brought over two dozen CEOs to Capitol Hill to personally lobby for funds.[51]

At the same time that business was finding in Bill Clinton a reliable ally when it came to international economic policy, it was finding that the Republican Party was rather less constant than it had hoped. The GOP had always had a protectionist wing (anchored, in the modern era, in the textile states of North and South Carolina), and this wing had received a fillip by the primary campaign of Patrick Buchanan in 1992. Articulating a fiercely anti–free trade message (and funded by textile magnate Roger Milliken), Buchanan had received a substantial portion of the vote. Many of the freshmen of the class of 1994 were drawn to Buchanan's approach. At the same time, the growing influence of the Christian right among congressional Republicans led them to look askance at efforts to normalize trade relations with China, whom the Christian right viewed as a persecutor of believers.[52]

Both of these influences led the Republicans to attack Clinton's international economic policy in his second administration, much to the displeasure of big business. Already in 1995, signs of divide among Republicans on trade were in evidence, leading some free trader congressmembers to attempt to clarify the party's stance on the issue. By 1996, Republican representatives were making appearances alongside Buchanan denouncing the US government's bailout of the Mexican peso. In early 1998, Republicans, led by Gingrich, blocked a Democratic effort to secure additional funding for the IMF in the midst of the East Asian financial crisis. That same year, a large number of Republicans (though not the leadership) opposed fast track, because it would prevent them from inserting amendments dealing with human rights abuses in China. While the Republican right had been a faithful steward of business interests during Clinton's first term, it now appeared to be turning on its patron.[53]

Business leaders were not hesitant to voice their displeasure with this turnabout. PAC leaders began speaking out. In March, the Business-Industry Political Action Committee wrote a memo entitled "Broken Premises" that called attention to "the very mixed message the business community has been receiving from Republican leaders and members of Congress." The senior vice president of the Chamber of Commerce confided to a reporter that "the business community never expected a Republican Congress to advance isolationism." Similarly, a representative of the NAM said, "It's a little bit scary. The younger Republicans tend to have a more protectionist view or to be susceptible to a protectionist argument." Business groups began talking about the need to rebalance campaign contributions back towards the Democrats.[54]

Ultimately, a rebalancing towards the Democratic Party did not occur. The Democratic Party was, by this point, more solidly protectionist than the GOP. Clinton's main ally in trying to pass fast track was Newt Gingrich. Moreover, since many of the most conservative Democrats had lost their seats in 1994, the remaining congressional Democratic Party was more liberal than ever. At the same time, as Clinton grappled with the impeachment scandal, the GOP looked poised to pick up more seats, meaning that any shift away from them could lock lobbyists out in the cold when the new Congress convened. Moreover, in July, the GOP and the corporate lobbies had negotiated an uneasy truce. In what came to be dubbed "The Treaty of K-Street," Gingrich promised business greater fidelity.[55]

Fidelity, however, was never Gingrich's strong suit. Ultimately, he failed to deliver the GOP votes necessary to pass fast track. The congressional GOP had shown itself to be deeply unreliable when it came to stewarding corporate interests. If this never translated into a windfall for corporate Democrats, that only underscores how crucial Bill Clinton's support for the free trade agenda was. While both parties in Congress moved in a protectionist direction, Clinton was steadfast in his support for free trade and American financial leadership. All of this took place as the Republicans were prosecuting the Lewinksy investigation and subsequently the impeachment. As they did so, they were coming for the one man in Washington corporations knew they could count on.

Risky Business

Most business organizations did not issue statements about impeachment. Business typically stayed out of divisive social issues like abortion, and in 1998 and early 1999, impeachment was, if anything, even more potent. There was simply little to gain from taking a stand either way on Bill Clinton's sex scandals. Despite this, there is good reason to believe that leading business organizations were largely uncomfortable with the Republican push to remove Clinton.

The most basic reason to believe this stems from Clinton's tack to the right discussed in the previous section. During Clinton's second administration, the president had shown himself to be the most reliable steward of business interests in government. While both congressional Democrats and congressional Republicans were deeply divided on the all-important issue of free trade, Clinton consistently pushed for more open trade throughout his presidency. Removing him would only hand a victory to the right wing of the Republican Party, who were following Pat Buchanan and the Christian right on trade.

Moreover, Clinton was promising to deliver on more business priorities in his second term. Most importantly, he was going to advocate the partial privatization of Social Security. The economic boom of the late 1990s had delivered a budget surplus ahead of schedule, making the 1997 budget negotiations between Clinton and Gingrich simplicity itself, as Republicans were able to get some tax cuts and Democrats health insurance for low-income children. With the budget surplus that would accumulate over the next decade, Clinton wanted to transform Social Security both by using the budget surplus to guarantee the fund's solvency and by allowing individuals to invest part of their contributions into the stock market. This was a major initiative, as Social Security had traditionally been considered an untouchable third rail of American politics. Clinton's chief of staff, the conservative Southern Democrat Erskine Bowles, had planned on returning to the private sector after the 1997 budget was negotiated but agreed to stay on when Clinton said he would be backing Social Security privatization.[56]

Business organizations had been pushing Social Security privatization for a few years by that point. The main impetus for this came from banks and financial firms, who stood to reap a massive benefit from individual accounts entering the market. As the head of one bank put it, "With 130 million people in the labor force, you could be staring at 130 million new accounts." These firms poured money into the CATO Institute, a libertarian think tank that launched a Social Security privatization project in 1995. The institute was able to raise over two million dollars for this project. At the same time, nonfinancial firms also mounted a strong push for privatization. The NAM had set up a Social Security task force in 1994, and the following year, the NAM, the Chamber, and the Roundtable formed the Alliance for Worker Retirement Security in order to advance the privatization agenda. In 1997, a survey of chief financial officers of large companies revealed that 78 percent supported individual accounts.[57]

Clinton's agenda had business salivating. Moreover, the president was more than happy to work with the GOP on all of this. Clinton and Gingrich had always deeply enjoyed one another's company on a personal level. As one White House advisor remembered, "When the two of them would start engaging each other on issues of mutual fascination, both of their advisors would feel a panic that each was forgetting they were in a room with political opponents who might use any word they said against them." Now that Clinton was governing from the center and Gingrich was more concerned with passing conservative policy than seeing Clinton fail, they were more than happy to work with one another on privatizing Social Security.[58]

Yet it was precisely at this moment that the impeachment campaign made such cooperation impossible. While, as noted above, business leaders were reticent to speak out on the topic, available evidence strongly suggests that impeachment was rather unpopular in the corporate boardrooms. One CEO of a money management firm told *Business Week* that he was "offended by the partisan nature of [impeachment] in the House" and was worried about Congress's ability to get to issues like financial industry modernization. Other business leaders were even more direct. Barry Rogstad, head of the American Business Conference, which represents mid-sized companies, lamented, "I'm afraid it is going to be a lost year." Even Thomas J. Donohue, the newly appointed president of the Chamber of Commerce, who came into office promising new pugnacity on behalf of business, saw impeachment as disadvantageous, explaining, "We're concerned about the time available for business issues." The Chamber's magazine echoed this disquiet, identifying impeachment as one of the chief "hurdles for business in the new congress." The article quoted Norm Ornstein, a fellow at the conservative American Enterprise Institute, arguing "I don't see how they can [deal with an impeachment trial] while conducting other business ... In effect, the legislative process is going to grind to a halt." Ornstein attacked the Republicans for proceeding with impeachment and blamed them for the resulting gridlock. The article also quoted the Chamber's executive vice president for government affairs, who pronounced the outlook for action "bleak."[59]

The misgivings business leaders expressed about impeachment turned out to be well founded. The campaign against Clinton polarized Congress, and some of Clinton's most ardent defenders were the kind of liberal Democrats to whom Social Security privatization was anathema. When Clinton finally unveiled his detailed plan for the program, individual accounts played a negligible part; they were offered at only four hundred dollars a year for recipients earning under a hundred thousand dollars. Instead, about 20 percent of the fund would be invested in the stock market and administered in the manner of a sovereign wealth fund. Conservatives and business both recoiled from the plan. The chair of the House Ways and Means Committee warned that "if you thought a government takeover of health care was bad, just wait until the government becomes an owner of America's private-sector companies." Similarly, the Chamber's chief economist fumed that "All [Clinton's] doing is adding bells and whistles. Social Security is [still] sliding towards the abyss." As Erskine Bowles later put it, Social Security privatization was a case where "Gingrich wanted to do it; Clinton wanted to do it. It was a real missed opportunity ... Monica [Lewinsky] changed everything."[60]

Though the available evidence is not dispositive, it suggests that the GOP's impeachment of Bill Clinton ran contrary to the desires of the country's corporate leadership. Clinton was a steadfast proponent of policies that the corporate leadership wanted; indeed he was more reliable on this front than either party in Congress. His impeachment derailed a structural transformation of the country's most important entitlement program, which business lobbies strongly supported.

Smokey Ayes

If most of big business was at best uneasy about impeachment, the question remains of what might explain the Republicans' single-minded devotion to it. Some insight can be gained by examining more closely what was happening around the person most responsible for pushing the impeachment campaign in Congress: Tom DeLay. As John Boehner would write in his memoir, "In my view, Republicans impeached [Clinton] for one reason and one reason only—because it was strenuously recommended to us by one Tom DeLay."[61]

As described above, DeLay had quickly mastered the new fundraising structure that Gingrich brought to Congress. His contributors formed a diverse portfolio. Enron was one of his biggest donors, and a number of telecom companies also contributed generously. But one industry stands out—tobacco. Of DeLay's twenty largest donors between 2000 and 2002, three were tobacco companies. This association with tobacco went back to the beginning of DeLay's leadership career in the House. In 1994, when he won election to the whip position against Gingrich's candidate, he hired two political operatives to run ARMPAC, both of whom had worked at a tobacco industry-financed "smokers' rights" group. Appreciative executives at R. J. Reynolds and Philip Morris in turn contributed nearly $30,000 to ARMPAC to help it get running.[62]

The tobacco industry, as it happens, was also one of the few industries to have reason to wage all-out war against the Clinton administration. This animosity went back to his healthcare plan, which was to be financed, in part, with a new tax on cigarettes. The industry reacted with a large-scale mobilization, forming new, supposedly grassroots groups to lobby for "smokers' rights." After the defeat of Clinton's healthcare plan, one R. J. Reynolds executive crowed, "We chased 'Clintoncare' I all over the country and the 'beast' is currently hiding in a cave, somewhere inside a beltway."[63]

The truly existential threat to tobacco, however, came from the Food and Drug Administration. George H. W. Bush had appointed David Kessler FDA commissioner in 1990, with bipartisan approval. When Clinton had kept Kessler on, there was little controversy. However, Kessler had come to believe that the FDA's failure to treat nicotine as a regulated substance needed to be remedied. He and his staff began working on the issue. In 1994, drawing on tobacco industry patents and documents released in previous lawsuits that showed the industry consciously making cigarettes as addictive as possible, Kessler publicly declared the FDA's intent to regulate nicotine. In 1995, Kessler met with Clinton, who had been reading some of his evidence. The president told Kessler, "I want to kill them. I just read all those documents and I want to kill them." Shortly thereafter, Clinton publicly endorsed the FDA's attempt to regulate nicotine.[64]

Clinton's actions precipitated a tectonic shift in tobacco industry political contributions. Before 1996, tobacco industry

Tobacco Industry PAC Spending by Party, 1990–2000

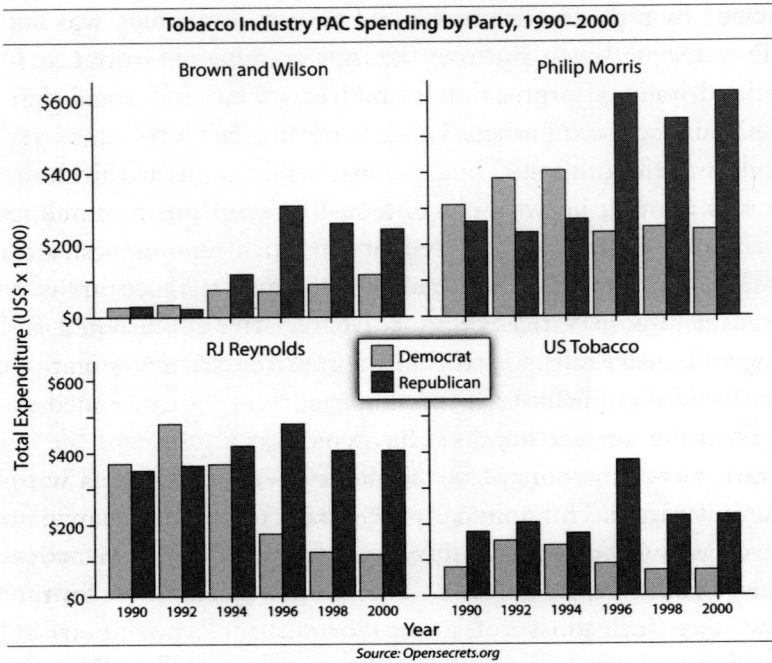

Source: Opensecrets.org

PACs had followed a typical pattern, donating slightly more to Democrats, who had the privilege of a nearly half-century-long congressional majority. However, by 1996, the pattern had flipped, and the industry was giving nearly three times as much to Republicans as Democrats. In 1995, the two leading soft money donors to Republican campaign committees were Philip Morris and R. J. Reynolds, who gave $975,149 and $696,450, respectively. In 1993–1994, when Democrats held the majority, they gave only $199,000 and $126,250.[65]

In addition to playing a critical role in Republican Party financing at the time of the impeachment campaign, there is also some evidence that tobacco interests were involved in the bureaucratic side of the impeachment effort. Bill Clinton's impeachment grew out of the Whitewater investigation, a minor real estate scandal from Clinton's time as governor of Arkansas. As the scandal broke, Attorney General Janet Reno appointed Robert Fiske, a widely respected Republican lawyer, to the position of special prosecutor to investigate. By the time Fiske had concluded his investigation in June of 1994, the special prosecutor had been replaced by the position of independent counsel, which was overseen by a panel of three federal judges. That panel was led by David Sentelle, a jurist from the tobacco state of North Carolina, and political protégé of Jesse Helms. Reno requested that the panel reappoint Fiske as special counsel. On June 14, 1994, Helms and the other North Carolina Senator, Lauch Faircloth, met with Sentelle in Washington, DC. A few days later, Sentelle's panel took the extraordinary step of denying Reno's request, and instead appointing Ken Starr as independent counsel. Starr was a prominent corporate attorney in DC who had represented the tobacco industry in the past. While conducting the investigation that would end in Bill Clinton's impeachment, he continued to represent the tobacco company Brown & Williamson.[66]

Starr wasn't the only player in the impeachment drama with close links to the tobacco industry. For example, the lawyers George Conway and Richard Porter, who worked during 1990s to keep Clinton's earlier sex scandal with Paula Jones in the news, were both tobacco lawyers. Porter worked with Starr at Kirkland & Ellis, and Conway reportedly made $1 million a year defending tobacco companies. Similar links structured the pro-impeachment media. Both the fledgling Fox News and the magazine the *Weekly Standard* were owned by Rupert Murdoch, the reactionary media billionaire who, at the time of the impeachment campaign, also sat on the board of Philip Morris.[67]

All of this suggests the Republican crusade to impeach Bill Clinton was supported by the particularistic interests of the tobacco industry rather than the interests of American employers more generally. Unlike most of corporate America, by the late 1990s the tobacco industry had every reason to seek all-out war against the Clinton administration. Simultaneously, the industry had come to play an important role in the Republican Party; it was closely tied to the single politician most responsible for the impeachment; and the particular bureaucratic appointments that put Ken Starr in position to wage his vendetta appear to have been linked to tobacco interests.

The relationship between the top managers of American corporations and the Republican Party changed significantly over the course of the 1990s. For the first half of the decade, the more confrontational GOP established by Newt Gingrich and his allies moved in sync with employers' organizations. The fight against Clinton's healthcare bill, the government shutdowns, and welfare reform, as ugly as each could be, all reflected the agenda of American corporate boardrooms. However, the transformations wrought by the Republican Revolution also made it possible for the new majority to defy the corporate consensus. The orgy of fundraising and redistribution made it easy for alternative centers of power to emerge in Congress, challenging Gingrich's attempts to forge a united front. These same dynamics meant that, with the tobacco industry pouring money into GOP coffers in the late 1990s, the party could afford to embark on an ill-advised impeachment crusade in defiance of the wishes of most corporate leaders. By the end of the twentieth century, the relationship between the Republican Party and its traditional patrons among American business leaders was more uncertain than it had ever been.

4

The Bush II Years: Coming Together and Falling Apart

By the 2000 election, the GOP right was in bad shape. The Clinton impeachment, in which Tom DeLay and the rest of the congressional conservatives had invested so much, had not only failed to remove Clinton from office; it left him more popular than he had been for most of his first term and made the GOP look like priggish partisan zealots. Indeed, the campaign did more collateral damage to GOP elected officials than it did to the president, most notably when Bob Livingston, who was set to succeed Gingrich as Speaker of the House, resigned after *Hustler* magazine, piqued by the sexual puritanism of the impeachers, offered a bounty for proof of marital infidelity by members of Congress. Livingston preemptively resigned rather than be exposed. While DeLay, Dennis Hastert (who stepped in as Speaker after Livingston's disgrace), and Dick Armey retained firm control of the congressional party, they were largely demoralized and without direction. As the 2000 presidential election loomed, the congressional right was also without a clear standard-bearer for president.[1]

Into this gap stepped George W. Bush. While often derided as a shallow playboy hoisted into his office by his family name and the machinations of party operatives like Karl Rove, Bush actually accomplished a reshaping of the Republican Party that built on and extended what Gingrich had begun. Most centrally, Bush managed, in his first term, to unite the party establishment and the party right around his program of "an ownership society" at home and imperial reassertion abroad. During the Bush II years, a veteran of the George H. W. Bush administration like

Dick Cheney would close ranks with a Gingrich disciple like Lindsey Graham, whose politics were formed in opposition to that administration's moderation. Corporate boardrooms were thrilled with this newfound party unity, which catered to their interests with an attentiveness that had been lacking in the late 1990s. The result was that the party's center of gravity moved decisively to the right, as the establishment learned to love the politics of partisan warfare.

In the aftermath of Bush's reelection victory in 2004, it looked as if this consolidated Republican Party was constructing a new era of party hegemony. But Bush's second term would witness the unraveling of the consensus he had forged, with intraparty battles over immigration policy and, most crucially, how to respond to the 2008 financial crisis. In both of these cases, the GOP right showed itself to be stubbornly independent of the main corporate leadership. At the same time, the bloody failure of Bush's policy in Iraq (which the party right always supported) discredited the GOP as a whole, leading the Democrats to take back the House in 2006 in a victory as dramatic as Gingrich's in 1994. By the end of Bush's second term, the GOP was more intensely divided than any time since the aftermath of Watergate.

A Uniter, Not a Divider

George W. Bush practiced politics with an adroitness that belied his public image as an intellectual lightweight. His campaign for the presidency was based on navigating two dynamics that pulled in different directions: the power of the GOP's right, including the primary electorate, and the American public's skepticism about the politics conducted by that party faction. Bush thus sought to sell himself as at least friendly with the party right, while simultaneously softening his image as much as possible in the general election. At the same time that he attempted to build an electoral coalition, he sought to build a corporate coalition behind first his candidacy and then his administration, which would ensure that he had sufficient funds to accomplish his goals. He succeeded in both of these goals, resulting in one of the most politically successful first terms of any president since Roosevelt.

A Family Affair

Bush's career in politics began when he joined his father's election campaign in 1988. He worked as a media and campaign surrogate, traveling around Texas especially, giving speeches. Four years later, George W. would play a more central role, working as one of his father's top campaign advisors. In this role, Bush showed himself to be a perceptive political strategist, writing memos on campaign strategy and helping to execute several changes in administration personnel assignments.[2]

From this early political work, Bush expressed a healthy skepticism of the new right that was taking shape in Congress. He urged his father to dump Dan Quayle, whose presence on the ticket was meant to reassure the party right, in favor of Dick Cheney, a less polarizing figure. When H. W. lost in 1992, Bush blamed the Republican right for sabotaging his father's ability to win over moderate voters. He singled out Patrick Buchanan's infamous RNC speech, in which the former candidate declared there was "a religious war going on in this country" and fulminated against feminism, homosexuality, and pornography. When George W. became governor of Texas, he eschewed culture war Republicanism, cooperating with the Democratic state legislature and managing to win large portions of the state's black and Hispanic vote in his 1998 reelection. When he began moving towards a presidential run, Bush's team came up with the slogan "compassionate conservatism" as an attempt to fix "the Republican brand at the end of the '96 campaign, all about slashing spending and all that." Bush's road to the presidency began with an off-ramp from Gingrichism.[3]

Yet Bush could hardly expect to win the Republican nomination in 2000 by running a retread of his father's campaign in 1992. He needed the support of the Republican right, even if he kept them at arm's length. Religion provided the means for accomplishing this. Though Bush was a born-again Christian (unlike his father, whose family were mainline Protestants going back to the eighteenth century), he had always maintained his distance from the Christian right, referring to their leaders in private as "wackos." Yet the slogan of compassionate conservatism, along with Bush's fervently sincere personal religiosity, allowed him to convince the Christian right that he would be an adequate vehicle for their agenda. Indeed, Bush's fluency in the vernacular of Evangelicalism allowed him to effectively establish a rapport with Christian right leaders even as he rejected their policy positions, such as when he told a pastor asking him to promise not to hire homosexuals, "I'm not going to kick gays, because I'm a sinner. How can I differentiate sin?" After John McCain's unexpectedly strong showing in the New Hampshire primary, the Bush campaign began leaning more heavily on Christian right leaders like Ralph Reed to ensure he triumphed in other contests.[4]

At the same time, Bush forged various links with the party right. He campaigned as a successor to Reagan, rather than to his father, leading the *New York Post* to christen him "George W. Reagan." His selection of Dick Cheney as his running mate similarly allowed him to appeal to the right. When Bush asked Cheney to serve, Cheney told him, "Look, I'm conservative." When Bush replied, "We know that," Cheney reiterated, "No, I'm *really* conservative." Cheney's ties to the party right went back to his time in Congress in the 1980s, when he had served as a liaison between the House Republican leadership and Gingrich's barn burners in the COS. As Cheney described his role, "I was the grease between the grinding gears ... [Gingrich would] see me when he wanted access lots of times to the leadership, and Bob [Michel] would use me as a buffer to try to make sure those eager young beavers didn't tip and exceed their responsibilities." Even as Bush appealed to the general public with his compassionate conservatism rebrand, he worked to assure the conservative base that his administration would not be a repeat of his father's.[5]

As a result of Bush's outreach to the party right, conservatives were elated when the Supreme Court made him president. The new administration staffed up from conservative think tanks, leading Edwin Feulner, president of the Heritage Foundation, to declare Bush's team "more Reaganite than the Reagan administration." Grover Norquist, head of the influential conservative group Americans for Tax Reform, gloated that "there isn't an us and them with this administration. They is us. We is them." William Kristol, editor of the *Weekly Standard*, agreed, noting that "for conservatives, the good news is you don't need to be a rebel anymore." From the beginning of the administration, conservatives were convinced that Bush was one of them.[6]

The manner of Bush's elevation to the presidency helped to solidify his reliance on the party right and institutionalize Gingrich-style partisan warfare as the administration's default mode of politics. Immediate postelection polling showed a decline in turnout by evangelical voters, with four million fewer showing up to the polls in 2000 compared to 1996. In an internal memo, Karl Rove, who had previously counseled moderation in the campaign, argued that they had "failed to marshal support of the base as well as we should have." The administration would thus have to "spend a lot of time and energy" resurrecting the Christian right's political enthusiasm. Other internal polling pointed in the same direction. Pollster Matthew Dowd found that "independent" voters were a disappearing slice of the electorate. Focusing on winning this shrinking pool of voters had cost Bush the ability to successfully mobilize evangelicals and conservatives. Karl Rove began carrying around a laminated card in his pocket with a graph of the shrinking proportion of true independents among voters. The Bush administration quickly pivoted towards the kind of partisan attacks that Newt Gingrich had perfected, shedding the reputation for bipartisanship he had cultivated in Texas.[7]

George W. Bush never embraced Gingrichism wholeheartedly. He never displayed Gingrich's delight with any maneuver that promised to discomfit Democrats. Similarly, as will be discussed in the next section, his administration advanced new federal programs and responsibilities that Gingrich would have denounced (had they come from a Democratic administration, at least). Yet by the time his term actually began, the president, who had launched his campaign by distinguishing it from the Republican congressional right, had traveled a considerable distance back towards those politics. In so doing, he achieved real unity between the party's warring wings. The establishment of his father was now firmly wedded to the conservatives who had taken over Congress. Over Bush's first term, this unity would be sustained by the concern both wings of the party showed for delivering on corporate priorities in order to sustain their dreams of a permanent Republican majority.

Taking Care of Business

George W. Bush's links with the American corporate leadership class were deep. His father had served for many years as the paradigmatic business Republican, evoking the Republicanism of the 1920s more than that of the post-Goldwater party.[8] Bush himself had moved in these circles socially while at Yale, and later, after organizing a group purchase of the Texas Rangers, as an owner/manager himself. As governor of Texas, Bush built a business-friendly administration that won him overwhelming support from CEOs polled during the 2000 Republican primaries.[9]

In the general election, Bush consolidated an intimidating corporate coalition. While congressional Republicans appeared ever more unreliable to corporate leaders in everything from their lack of enthusiasm for free trade to their quixotic impeachment quest, Bush promised corporate leaders everything Clinton offered, and more. Already by May of 2000, months before Bush was even officially nominated by the GOP, corporate lobbyists were telling journalists that they were now seeking simply to stonewall the Clinton administration on various issues and wait for a friendlier face across the negotiating table once Bush was in office. The tobacco industry was particularly enthusiastic in its support for Bush, with one analyst describing firms as "giddy" over the prospect of a Bush victory. As the election approached, some securities firms began offering stock indices based around companies that would profit from either Bush or Gore winning. *Business Week* described the contents of one company's offerings, noting that the Bush index contained everything from tobacco to defense to the pharmaceutical industry. The Gore index, meanwhile, had a far narrower base, consisting of Microsoft's competitors (who would benefit from Gore continuing the Clinton administration's antitrust stance) and environmental consultants. The set of industries who favored Gore was so narrow that his index was instead filled out with short positions on the companies that would benefit from a Bush victory. The journalist Thomas Edsall described Bush's coalition as a fusion of "the wealthy southern and western renegade backers of the conservative movement ... with a universe of entrepreneurs on Wall Street and in the wider technology-intensive financial services industries." When Bush was finally declared the victor in 2000, Fortune 500 firms were tripping over one another to finance his inauguration to the tune of $100,000 each.[10]

In Congress, Republicans were also consolidating corporate support. Shortly after the Republican Revolution, Tom DeLay began organizing an initiative to require firms and trade associations that wanted access to the new majority of Republican lawmakers to commit to hiring only Republican lobbyists. Such a move not only served to tilt firms away from Democrats but also acted as a powerful source of patronage for Republicans, increasing the resources at the party's disposal. In the 1990s, this plan bore little fruit, and indeed was a source of conflict between the GOP and firms, who were more accustomed to seeing the party as servant rather than master. However, when Bush came to power, DeLay's plans fell into place. Corporate leaders, already enthused about the Republican victory, shifted their campaign contributions radically. By the close of Bush's first term, one study of political giving by nineteen industries found the GOP maintaining a two to one advantage. In this environment, firms were now much more willing to listen to GOP demands about staffing decisions. In both the House (where meetings were chaired by Roy Blunt, Tom DeLay's hand-picked successor as majority whip) and the Senate (where they were led by Rick Santorum), party leaders began holding weekly meetings with lobbying firms and trade associations in order to hammer out which positions would go to which GOP operatives. Business was, it seemed, quick to forgive the imbroglios of the late 1990s and was now marching in lockstep with Bush's Republican Party.[11]

This kind of coordination was something of a return to form for the GOP, after the anomalous rupture between corporate boardrooms and the party in the late 1990s. Yet as DeLay's scheme for K Street revealed, the unity between the party and the corporate elite had been reconstituted on new terms. The party was giving orders to corporations, rather than, as for most of the GOP's history, the other way around. Bush's first major policy initiative, his tax cuts, reveals this same dynamic.

A significant tax cut had been Bush's central domestic policy during the campaign. As the deficits of the 1980s and early 1990s turned into a surplus, the GOP began arguing that the surplus reflected that the tax code was taking more out of the economy than the state required and that taxpayers deserved a refund. Bush made this policy the centerpiece of his campaign, pushing for a much larger tax cut than John McCain proposed in the primary and than Al Gore did in the general election. Though his numbers varied, Bush most commonly cited $1.6 trillion as the right number to be cut. Cognizant of the discord with the party right that resulted when his father had raised taxes, Bush was determined to brand himself as a tax-cutter, leading the *New York Times* editorial board to find "something almost Oedipal in Mr. Bush's revitalization of Republican stereotypes, as if by invoking them he can avoid the conservative revolt on taxes that upended his father's presidency."[12]

Corporate leaders, who had done so much to put Bush in the White House, viewed the promised $1.6 trillion in cuts with concupiscence. As one Washington insider put it, with that kind of number on the table, "companies [would] come out of the woodwork" to try and get a piece of it. At a meeting of corporate leaders from the tech industry alone, lobbyists emerged with a tax wish list costing over $850 billion. Businesses wanted everything from communications infrastructure tax credits to reduced excise taxes on trucks to an across-the-board corporate tax cut. Overall, business organizations put their target at about a third of the total bill (the other two thirds would cut personal income taxes, rather than corporate taxes). The sheer scale of business demands, meanwhile, generated considerable anxiety that there would be a "feeding frenzy" like the one that consumed Reagan's first tax bill two decades earlier. There, the scale of business demands contributed to an unprecedented peacetime budget deficit, leading to further conflict between business and the Reagan administration over how to remedy it. One lobbyist warned that negotiations would be "rough ... It is going to be divisive between industries, within industries, and within trade groups." To forestall conflict, business leaders began organizing a network of different firms to present a united front for business's slice of the pie. As W. Henson Moore, head of a paper manufacturing trade association and a leader of this effort, explained, "we think the only way to get results is to have a coalition of heavy manufacturing, retail, banking, high-tech, and other corporate interests ... [Otherwise] you'll have a cacophony of ideas being deluged on the Ways and Means Committee." If their attempts at unity failed, business leaders worried that their respective attempts to claim the specific tax cuts they desired individually would lessen their leverage, leading to business getting a much smaller portion of the bill's largess. Deeply conscious of the dangers of fragmentation, business entered into negotiations with the Bush administration with caution, moving slowly to avoid disrupting their fragile unity.[13]

They were met, however, with a wall of intransigence from the Bush administration. On February 7, 2001, Bush held a meeting with an assortment of corporate leaders, including Jack Welch of General Electric, Ken Lay of Enron (one of Bush's and Tom DeLay's biggest funders), Jerry Jasinowski of the National Association of Manufacturers, and Charls Walker, who had played a key role in founding both the Business Roundtable and the American Council for Capital Formation in the 1970s. At the luncheon, Bush laid down a hard line: business would get no more than 10 percent of the bill, in the form of research and development tax credits. The rest would go to tax cuts affecting personal income (biased overwhelmingly, of course, towards relieving the tax burdens of the rich), including lowering personal income tax rates, phasing out the estate tax, and expanding the recently created child tax credit. Bush made the case that helping him pass the tax bill would build the political capital to achieve other parts of his agenda that were of more direct service to business. For Walker, the meeting was "Saul on the Road to Damascus. It was an epiphany. After that, I told my coalition that we would hold back."[14]

Following this meeting, the administration deployed a sophisticated strategy to help its business supporters agree to delayed gratification. Treasury Secretary Paul O'Neill, a former CEO himself and widely trusted figure in the business community, was deployed to sell the legislation. Karl Rove and his assistant, Kirk Blalock (formerly a marketing executive at Philip Morris), recruited Dirk Van Dongen, a business lobbyist with deep connections to Bush to form a new group in support of the bill, the Tax Relief Coalition (TRC). About two weeks after Bush's meeting with Walker and company, the TRC was officially announced at a White House event, where the group was endorsed by Van Dongen's National Association of Wholesale Distributors, the Chamber of Commerce, the National Association of Manufacturers, and the National Federation of Independent Businesses. A few days later, the Business Roundtable joined the TRC as well. The group would coordinate an energetic lobbying campaign by its members in favor of Bush's tax cuts.[15]

Business had, it seemed, managed to unite behind a single vision for the tax bill. But the outcome was rather different from what corporate leaders had been clamoring for only a few weeks earlier. Business would not get a third of the tax cuts Bush was seeking. It would get around a tenth. And its unity had not come from within but from without. The administration had told CEOs what it wanted from them and had organized to make sure they stayed in line. Van Dongen made the plan clear, admitting that "the Tax Relief Coalition is an administration coalition. It was brought into existence for the express purpose of supporting the president's package." As with DeLay's K Street Project, the arrangement worked out between the GOP and the corporate leadership was that the party would set the agenda, and in return, the boardrooms could count on their interests being looked after.[16]

Bush kept his word. In 2003, in the midst of the War on Terror and the drive to war with Iraq, he signed another tax bill accelerating some of the phased-in cuts of the 2001 bill and bestowing new cuts on taxes on capital gains and dividends, two causes close to the heart of any C-suite occupant. Then, in 2004, he passed the corporate tax cuts business leaders had been asking for, cutting $137 billion over ten years in the "biggest corporate tax overhaul since 1986." Altogether, the Bush tax cuts dramatically reshaped the fiscal architecture of the American state, reducing federal revenues as a share of GDP to their lowest point since 1950 and income tax revenues as a share of GDP to their lowest point since 1914. Government spending, meanwhile, had hardly decreased at all, leading to a dramatic increase in deficit-financed spending. Unlike the 1980s and 1990s, however, business was no longer clamoring for deficit reduction, apparently agreeing with Dick Cheney that "the Reagan years proved deficits don't matter."[17]

One of the first victories Bush delivered for the business lobby came in his repeal of recent regulations on ergonomic standards by the Occupational Safety and Health Administration (OSHA). Under Clinton's administration, the agency had adopted new regulations governing workplace safety in white collar employment. Business had fought doggedly against these standards, and had lost. When Bush came into office, business lobbyists were confident that he would heed their call. As John R. Block, a business lobbyist and major Republican donor who also served on Bush's transition team put it, the administration would "use every means possible to void regulations." In March, to the glee of employers, Bush signed legislation overturning Clinton's ergonomics rules. He also packed OSHA and the Department of Labor more generally with conservatives and former business lobbyists who were fundamentally hostile to government oversight of employers. As head of OSHA, Bush appointed Edwin G. Foulke, a former union avoidance consultant. One of Foulke's first actions in his new position was giving a speech called "Adults Do the Darndest Things," blaming workplace injuries on the stupidity of workers. Under Foulke, the culture at OSHA shifted to one of voluntary compliance. Ultimately, OSHA under Bush issued the fewest significant safety standards in its history. The only health standard it issued during Bush's tenure was forced on the administration by a federal court ruling. Business could now breathe a little easier, though the same could not be said of employees at polluted worksites.[18]

Another key item on business leaders' wish list was class action lawsuit reform. Class action suits, in which plaintiffs who individually could not pursue litigation are grouped together into one case, had expanded since the mid-twentieth century, and rules had grown more favorable to plaintiffs. In the 1980s, shareholders had begun using these new rules to file class action suits against corporate management, particularly in the tech industry, and against accounting firms for failing to inform them what management was doing with their investments. The growth of these kinds of shareholder class action suits led to a ferocious backlash by corporate managers, who began pouring money into efforts to choke off the growth of litigation. When Thomas Donohue became the head of the Chamber of Commerce in 1997, he committed the organization to a dedicated attack on class action suits, proclaiming that "trial lawyers are sapping the vitality out of American enterprise." The Chamber began pouring money into judicial elections, PR campaigns to sour the public on litigation, and efforts to change the law. As governor of Texas, George W. Bush had enacted some state-level tort reform measures, making him a darling of corporate defense lawyers. When Bush became president, the coalition for class action reform knew it was their time and began a massive push to secure new legislation. In 2005, Bush rewarded the considerable donations the industry had made with the Class Action Fairness Act, making it easier to get class action suits moved from state courts to federal courts, which were far less solicitous of plaintiffs.[19]

Bush was so attentive to the corporate agenda that he was willing to pursue it even when doing so brought him into conflict with his party's right wing. This was most notable with education reform. Since Jimmy Carter had created the federal Department of Education, Republicans had campaigned for its elimination. Bob Dole's platform in 1996 had supported its abolition. However, since the 1980s, a consensus had been developing among leading business organizations that supported an expanded federal role in education in order to raise student performance standards. By the late 1990s, a coordinated lobbying effort by leading business groups was pushing for federal action on schools. By the late 1990s, meetings between the Business Roundtable, the Chamber of Commerce, the National Association of Manufacturers, and others had produced a business agenda for education policy that called for an expanded federal role in schooling. While congressional Republicans had little interest in this agenda, George W. Bush embraced it. In Texas, Bush had pursued education reform by working closely with the Texas Business and Education coalition. As president, he supported the business education agenda wholeheartedly. However, doing so brought him into conflict with the Republican right. Business wanted the federal government to mandate proficiency standards for schools and hold them accountable for reaching them. Congressional Republicans, hostile to anything that resembled federal control over curricula, spurned this agenda in favor of vouchers and school choice, which business, in turn, saw as hopelessly polarizing. As Bush began pushing his education agenda in Congress, opposition from Republican congressmembers mounted. Complaining about Bush's solicitude towards liberal Democrats, who were also signing on to the business education agenda, Jim DeMint quipped that Bush's approach was changing from "leave no child behind" to "leave no Democrat behind." Similarly, a number of Christian right interest groups met with Speaker of the House Dennis Hastert to complain that the bill left them "very upset, discouraged, disappointed and dismayed." Though the bill passed the House fairly easily, conservatives pronounced it more a defeat than a victory.[20]

Bush's Medicare bill, which expanded the program to cover prescription drugs, was another case of pursuing the corporate agenda closely, even at the cost of conflict with the party right. Companies began pushing for an expansion of Medicare to prescription drug coverage as retiree health plan spending ballooned in the 1990s. By the turn of the century, it consumed about 40 percent of spending on retiree health benefits and was growing by 15 to 20 percent a year. Faced with these kinds of costs, a number of companies, particularly those with unionized workforces whose contracts covered health insurance in retirement, began pushing for the federal government to pick up the bill. They were joined by the pharmaceutical industry, who wanted the government to pay for their products but not to negotiate on the price. George W. Bush was happy to deliver on both counts. However, conservative Republicans viewed the plan as another expansion of the welfare state. Dick Armey, who had retired from Congress to head the libertarian group Citizens for a Sound Economy, published an op-ed in the *Wall Street Journal* warning that this expansion of Medicare would only be the beginning, and various interest groups would "be back, year after year, petitioning Congress to massively expand this already oversized new entitlement. Hillary Clinton's wish for ever-increasing government control over the American health care system will come true." In Congress, there was considerable grumbling among Republicans. To win over conservative support, Bush added a Health Savings Account policy to the bill, which would allow people to establish savings accounts for healthcare spending that would be completely untaxed. This measure, essentially a tax cut for those who could afford to save, won wide support on the right and was crucial to its passage. Paul Ryan estimated that as many as forty Republicans voted yes because of the HSAs, far more than the bill's margin of passage. While sufficient to ensure the bill's passage, it did little to endear it to conservatives. The *Weekly Standard* summed up its disillusionment with Bush with a joke—"Want to curb federal spending? Replace President Bush with a Democrat."[21]

Though Medicare expansion and No Child Left Behind produced complaints from the right, they confirmed for corporate boardrooms that Bush was their man. When the 2004 elections came around, business circles began opening their wallets accordingly. The fundraising operation the Bush team put together was awe-inspiring in its scope. The operation was built around bundling donations. Since the Federal Election Commission's individual campaign donation limit was, at the time, $1,000, the campaign encouraged people to bundle donations through their social networks. They would solicit donations from their network, and the resulting cash haul would all get credited to the bundler. The campaign created several different levels of bundlers, who were rewarded with different levels of access to the campaign. At the top were the "Super Rangers," who bundled at least $500,000 for Bush. Below that were "Pioneers," who brought in $200,000, and then "Rangers," who hit $100,000. Leaders of business associations and lobbying firms were prominent among these bundlers. As one lobbyist among the Pioneers explained, "if my clients raise dollars for Bush, it's good for me to be associated with it." And the ranks of businesses raising dollars for Bush were legion. As an official at the Chamber of Commerce explained, on "the major areas of concern, I don't think there is much separation at all" between business and the administration. While John Kerry could count on strong support from trial lawyers worried about Bush's plans for tort reform, Bush was able to put together a massive cross-industry coalition that allowed him to crush Kerry in spending in 2004.[22]

At the time of his reelection, George W. Bush appeared to be a transformative Republican president. He had consolidated the legacy of Reaganism, so that by the end of his term, it was the only political current of any force in the party. Where the late nineties witnessed a rebellion by GOP representatives against the party leadership on issues like trade, conservative opposition to Bush's policies remained politically ineffectual. At the same time, Bush had rebuilt the alliance between corporate America and the GOP on new terms. In this new partnership, the administration was firmly in the driver's seat, setting the agenda and tasking business with building support to make sure the agenda passed. In return, business could rest assured that its interests would be well represented.

Bush's strategist Karl Rove liked to imagine himself as a latter-day Mark Hanna, the political operative who built William McKinley's fundraising machine. When McKinley and Hanna defeated William Jennings Bryan in 1896, it kicked off a three decade period of Republican dominance, broken only by the Great Depression. After the 2004 election, both liberals and conservatives thought similar long-term dominance might be possible. One *Weekly Standard* writer gloated that "Republican hegemony in America is now expected to last for years, maybe decades." It appeared that the GOP, buttressed by its hegemony over corporate boardrooms and the fundraising prowess this brought with it, would continue to dominate in the way it had since Richard Nixon's election in 1968. Bush's presidency would indeed prove to be as transformational as McKinley's. However, his second term would reveal that this transformation would occur via the destruction of Republican dominance, rather than its extension. This process would begin with Iraq.[23]

Iraq

The invasion and occupation of Iraq defined George W. Bush's presidency. The apparent success of the initial invasion, from the rapid collapse of Saddam Hussein's government to Hussein's capture in late 2003, won him reelection in 2004, in a contest that hinged on foreign policy. Soon after the election, as the anti-occupation insurgency gained strength, and Iraq was consumed by civil war, Bush's presidency was fatally wounded. In 2006, the Democrats retook Congress. Though opposition to the Iraq War never penetrated very far into the Republican Party (aside from Ron Paul's idiosyncratic primary campaign in 2008), the destruction of Bush's credibility via the Iraq debacle nonetheless accelerated the fracturing of the party. The hegemony his administration had exercised over all Republican factions collapsed, leading to a level of intraparty conflict that far surpassed the spats in the late 1990s over trade.

Yet if Iraq defined Bush's presidency, it is nonetheless important not to overstate his administration's role in the march to war. The foreign policy establishment of the United States had already settled on regime change as its preferred policy in the late 1990s, during Bill Clinton's administration. While much has been made of the Bush administration's links to oil companies, there is precious little evidence that the decision to invade was made at the oil industry's behest. Instead, the relationship between the administration and the oil companies followed the pattern set during the tax policy debate. The administration set the course and assured the corporations that their interests would be taken care of if they would support it.

Saddam Hussein's regime had been a problem for the United States ever since it invaded Kuwait in 1990. George H. W. Bush's invasion of Iraq put a quick end to the Kuwait campaign and left Hussein's government penned in by sanctions and no fly zones. The hope was that the sanctions, plus low-cost interventions like support for opposition groups, such as Ahmed Chalabi's Iraqi National Congress, would be sufficient to oust Hussein. By the late 1990s, however, it was clear that these tactics would not work. Hussein was too clever and cautious to be assassinated, and the opposition groups were mainly collections of exiles with little following inside Iraq. More importantly, however, the oil market had also changed. While the early 1990s were a period of plentiful oil supplies, by the end of the decade supplies had begun to tighten. In this environment, other states became more interested in cutting a deal with Hussein to gain access to Iraq's bountiful oil. Such a course of action was unthinkable for the United States, however. As Vivek Chibber explains,

> The reason that sanctions could not simply be dismantled was that this would entail a direct, and prohibitive, political cost—a steady decline in power and leverage for the US in the region. It would mean that Hussein had managed to survive a decade-long campaign of strangulation, of attempts at regime change, air-strikes, bombing, vilification—all by the most powerful nation in the world, which had openly called for his overthrow. In any other region, this might have been a tolerable dénouement to the conflict, one that the US could have lived with. But in the Middle East, its ramifications were too serious to ignore.

The very tightening of oil supplies that led other countries to seek an end to the sanctions regime led the US to resist such a move all the more fiercely, since it would mean a humiliating diminution of credibility in precisely the region that the oil market was making ever more geostrategically crucial.[24]

This was what led the Clinton administration to commit the United States to regime change in Iraq. In 1998, Clinton signed the Iraqi Liberation Act, which declared, "It should be the policy of the United States to support efforts to remove the regime headed by Saddam Hussein from power in Iraq." In 1999, he asked Secretary of State Madeleine Albright to begin drawing up plans for overthrowing Hussein.[25]

Before 9/11, George W. Bush's administration did little to change course from what Clinton had set. Before his inauguration, incoming National Security Advisor Condoleeza Rice wrote a memo arguing that a "more aggressive policy toward Saddam Hussein" was warranted but also cautioning that an invasion "would cause serious problems in our relations with NATO

Allies and the moderate Arab world." As late as August 2001, a meeting between key administration figures including Dick Cheney, Secretary of Defense Donald Rumsfeld, and Secretary of State Colin Powell, ended in indecision, with no clear change in policy towards Iraq endorsed. The administration was united in wanting Hussein gone. But the price incurred by any plan to achieve this was too high.[26]

The administration's indecision on the eve of the September 11 attacks casts considerable doubt on the popular narrative that the administration went to war at the behest of the oil industry, which wanted Iraq's oil. Many of these accounts have focused attention on the meetings between the National Energy Policy Development Group (NEPDG), convened by Dick Cheney, and executives from various energy companies. This panel was convened by Bush a mere nine days after he took office, and its task was to formulate a new national energy policy. This rather anodyne endeavor was imbued with political drama when Dick Cheney refused to release the names of corporate leaders who met with the committee, eventually resulting in lawsuits regarding public access to government meetings. As reporters worked on the story, they uncovered that a large number of energy executives, particularly those who had donated to the Bush campaign, were given access to the committee.[27]

The secrecy of the panel fueled speculation as to its purpose, and this only intensified after the invasion of Iraq in 2003. Much of this has focused on the report eventually issued in May 2001, entitled simply *National Energy Policy*. The report's final chapter, on the place of imported oil in the US energy economy, began by declaring that "U.S. national energy security depends on sufficient energy supplies to support U.S. and global economic growth." The chapter went on to note that "by any estimation, Middle East oil producers will remain central to world oil security." Yet any attempt to pin this stance on the oil companies' input during NEPDG meetings runs into the problem that this position, like the general orientation on overthrowing Hussein, was widespread across the foreign policy establishment. A mere month before *National Energy Policy* was released, the Council on Foreign Relations (CFR), together with the James Baker III

Institute for Public Policy, released a report entitled *Strategic Energy Policy: Challenges for the 21st Century* that echoed many of the same conclusions as Cheney's report. It also called for increasing oil production in the Middle East for US consumption. And indeed, it went further than *National Energy Policy* in identifying Saddam Hussein as an obstacle to this. While repeating the consensus that the sanctions regime was not accomplishing its goals, it also called attention to the costs of any policy that left Hussein in power, cautioning that such a policy could be "quite costly as this trade-off will encourage Saddam Hussein to boast of his 'victory' against the United States, fuel his ambitions, and potentially strengthen his regime. Once so encouraged and if his access to oil revenues were to be increased by adjustments in oil sanctions, Saddam Hussein could be a greater security threat to U.S. allies in the region." While it is at least plausible that the Cheney report reflects the undue influence of the oil industry, no similar complaint could be lodged against the CFR's report. The CFR is, quite literally, the primary institution of the American foreign policy establishment, and for decades now, has been densely interlinked with the entirety of the corporate elite.[28] Its recommendations reflected the mainstream of foreign policy thinking by American elites. If there was little difference, when it came to Middle East oil, between the two reports' recommendations, it can hardly be the case that the Bush administration's course was set mainly in oil company boardrooms.[29]

The administration's meetings with energy executives in the spring of 2001 must thus be seen in a different light. Rather than setting US foreign policy on a new course, the meetings were an opportunity for firms to present their needs in the context of a policy that was already in place. Just as Bush's tax cut was calculated to give him the political capital to minister to the needs of actual capital, policy towards Iraq was set by the administration, and corporate elites were then given the opportunity to assert their needs within that framework.

If in August of 2001, the price to be paid for ousting Saddam was too high, 9/11 changed the calculus. In the context of a global war on terror, it would be far easier to enlist allies' support in the invasion and far easier to sell the invasion to the American public. Immediately after the attacks, Bush directed his team to focus on connecting Saddam Hussein to al-Qaeda. When this failed, the justification switched seamlessly to the threat posed by Hussein's weapons of mass destruction. Though substantial opposition to the invasion was mobilized in the run-up to the war, once the war actually began, Bush's conduct of it won super-majority support. This level of support faded quickly, replaced by a clearly partisan stratification of the electorate, with Republicans supporting the war overwhelmingly, independents somewhat less so, and Democrats mostly opposing. Though support for Bush's stewardship of the war was sufficient to win him reelection, it began collapsing in his second term. Hurricane Katrina's devastation of New Orleans, and the administration's unhurried response, posed the question of national priorities sharply. At the same time, as the administration's utterly fantastical postwar plans were revealed to be just that, support for the war dipped sharply. By the 2006 midterm elections, Bush's approval rating was in the low thirties.[30]

Those elections delivered a crushing Democratic victory. Congressional Republicans faced their worst losses since the Watergate midterms of 1974. Democrats won control of both the House and the Senate a mere two years after John Kerry's defeat led Democrats to contemplate permanent minority status. Republicans were all but wiped out in the Northeast, with the New Hampshire state legislature going Democratic for the first time since the Civil War. Iraq was, as Mike Davis argued, "the Archimedean lever" that moved the electorate drastically. Shortly after the election, Bush conceded as much, dismissing Donald Rumsfeld, the cabinet secretary most closely identified with the Iraq War and replacing him with a less polarizing alternative.[31]

The invasion and occupation of Iraq in and of itself did little to fracture the Republican Party. The party's conservative wing was steadfast in its support for the war for the entirety of Bush's presidency. However, when public opinion turned against the war, and by extension, the Bush administration, Bush's capacity to hold together his formerly fractious coalition disintegrated. With Bush a lame duck, conservative insurgents had little to lose by striking out on their own and defying the administration, which they did increasingly over the course of his second term.

From Hubris to Nemesis

By the end of George W. Bush's second term, the dynamics that would dominate the Republican Party up to the present were clearly established. The party was deeply split between its leadership and ranks of insurgents challenging that leadership from the right. Moreover, these fights brought the insurgent factions of the party into conflict with leading business organizations. These conflicts would climax in the financial crisis of 2008, when the congressional GOP stood opposed to the bailout program that virtually the entirety of business held was necessary to avert Depression-era levels of economic dislocation.

At the beginning of Bush's second term, such a fracture in the party was nowhere in sight. Coming out of the 2004 election, the party appeared united. However, the administration made a fatal miscalculation when it imagined that the tactics that had brought such success in the first term could be easily extended to the kinds of projects it attempted to undertake in the second. The administration's ability to pull business behind its policy proposals proved more limited than Bush, DeLay, and company believed. Indeed, evidence that business itself was more divided than its campaign contributions suggested began to mount. The first episode in which these dynamics revealed themselves was Bush's failed effort at Social Security privatization.

Social Security and the Soft Underbelly of the Welfare State

The campaign to privatize Social Security by allowing workers to invest some or all of their savings into the stock market went back to the 1980s. It had previously reached its peak, as discussed in the preceding chapter, in Bill Clinton's second administration, before the Republican impeachment crusade made it impossible. When Bush came to office, Social Security privatization was a major priority, but September 11 pushed foreign policy to the fore, and the effort took a backseat. Though he did not campaign on reforming Social Security in 2004, late in the campaign, he told a group of his biggest donors, "I'm going to come out strong after my swearing in, with fundamental tax reform, tort reform, privatizing of Social Security." After the election, he moved quickly to assemble a team to lead the push for privatization. Rather than policy experts, the team was headed by Karl Rove and Ken Mehlman, who had led the RNC's Bush-Cheney operation. This elevation of political advisors, which one policy advisor in Bush's first term had decried as "the reign of the Mayberry Machiavellis," would prove fatal, as Rove and Mehlman would persistently neglect the importance of answering key policy design questions. As with the tax cut campaign, the launch of the Social Security reform push was accompanied by a new business coalition to support the president's initiative. In 2002, the Roundtable, the NAM, and the Financial Services Forum had formed the Coalition for the Modernization and Protection of Social Security (COMPASS), which promised to spend tens of millions of dollars in support of the policy. It was joined by the Alliance for Worker Retirement Security, run out of the NAM's offices. In January, before Bush publicly announced his plan, the administration had summoned leading business officials to a meeting and told them that active support for Social Security privatization was to be the sine qua non of White House access in the second term. The campaign was shaping up to be a repeat of the push for the tax cut, which similarly began with a meeting where business received its marching orders.[32]

Yet some major differences with the tax cut bill soon emerged. Most centrally, the Bush administration never produced an actual bill, only a framework for a bill. The framework at first focused on the introduction of individual investment accounts, which would partially privatize the program. However, the administration's pitch for this reform involved some sleight of hand. Bush's argument for why his reform was necessary centered on Social Security's funding shortfalls, which projections estimated would start to be felt by about 2040. This funding shortfall, he argued, proved the necessity of reforming the program. However, diverting some funds to private accounts would do nothing to address the funding problem and would in fact worsen it by introducing trillions of dollars of transaction costs over subsequent decades. To address this, Bush eventually conjoined the privatization plan with a plan to reduce Social Security benefits for the upper two thirds of the income distribution, while raising them slightly for the lowest third, which would produce some savings.[33]

This reticence to offer specific legislation stemmed from a fundamental difference between tax cuts and Social Security reform—the structure of public opinion and its effects on interest group mobilization. There is a strong argument that Bush's tax cuts were opposed by the public. The majority of Americans would lose out due to pressures to defund social services and to the generally more unequal society that the cuts would produce, but opposition was inchoate and unorganized. The losses to each individual were generally small, and large numbers of people who each stand to lose a little are difficult to organize. Social Security privatization, on the other hand, threatened fairly large losses for a smaller but well-organized group: retirees. The American Association of Retired Persons (AARP) counted its members in the tens of millions and was ready for the fight before the attempt to reform Social Security. Together with labor unions, it anchored the attempt to defeat Bush's policy. In public opinion as a whole, the arguments against privatization carried the day. Most Americans viewed Bush's plan as a giveaway to Wall Street. The administration's efforts to convince them otherwise were not helped by erstwhile allies like Stephen Moore, former president of the Club for Growth, who told a journalist that "Social Security is the soft underbelly of the welfare state. If you can jab your spear through that, you can undermine the whole welfare state."[34]

This well-organized public opposition dissuaded many corporate leaders from getting involved in the campaign. Early in the campaign, business leaders expressed worries that an endeavor as massive as privatizing Social Security would tie up the legislative agenda for the entire year, crowding out other policies on business's wish list. By May, the *National Journal* reported that COMPASS had only about 300 member companies, less than a third of the number who signed on to the tax cut coalition. One lobbyist explicitly identified the plan's unpopularity as a reason for companies' wariness. Though the leading business organizations, like the Roundtable, the NAM, the Chamber, and the National Retail Federation were all members of COMPASS, their member firms were rather more reluctant to throw themselves into the campaign. It is possible that the leadership of the business organizations, having forged such a close working relationship with the Bush administration during the first term, was out of touch with what their members wanted. However, it is also possible that members wanted the organizations to lead the charge, allowing them to support the privatization plan without having to associate their individual businesses with the controversial plan. What is clear is that business organizations proved much less capable of mobilizing their members to champion Social Security privatization than they had policies such as the tax cuts and tort reform.[35]

With business mobilization sluggish, it was difficult for the administration to win support in Congress. The main obstacle was the Senate. While the Republicans had a sufficient majority in the House to pass whatever legislation ended up being written, in the Senate they would need Democratic votes to overcome a filibuster. This is precisely the kind of problem a sustained business mobilization would have helped with. In its absence, momentum for the entire plan stalled. Republicans in the House were quite conscious of how unpopular the plan was and willing to vote for it anyway. However, if the bill could not pass the Senate, there was no point in taking an unpopular vote in the House. As one representative said, "People are prepared to bleed, but they're not prepared to bleed for no reason." By June, this stance was a consensus across the House leadership, who indefinitely tabled discussion of privatizing Social Security.[36]

The defeat of Social Security reform was the Bush administration's first major legislative failure. It heralded a new period in the relations between the presidency, the Republican Party, and the corporate elite. While some important legislative victories were still in the future, most notably tort reform and a new energy bill, the Social Security experience revealed that the playbook of the first Bush administration would not be as successful in the second.

The Rise, Fall, and Resurrection of Republican Nativism

The defeat of Bush's immigration reform proposals in his second term was in many ways even more surprising than the defeat of Social Security privatization, not least because it came at the hands of his own party. It also marked a sharp turn in the GOP's stance on immigration, which has marked the party's position up to the present. Before the 1990s, however, immigration was an issue that displayed little partisan polarization. When Ronald Reagan legalized the status of several million undocumented immigrants in the 1980s, there was little backlash from his own party. In the 1990s, GOP politicians, led by Governor Pete Wilson in California, articulated a new nativism that scapegoated immigrants as a drain on the welfare state. Newt Gingrich included various measures to disqualify immigrants, both legal and illegal, from federal aid programs in his welfare reform proposals. In the 1996 Republican primaries, in which Bob Dole was challenged by Patrick Buchanan from the right, the Buchanan forces managed to write a plank for repealing the Fourteenth Amendment's guarantee of birthright citizenship into the party platform. All of this, however, was electorally disastrous for the party. Where Reagan had won 37 percent of the Latino vote in 1984, Dole won only 22 percent. In California, where Wilson had first alerted the party to the potentials of nativist appeals, the 1998 gubernatorial election marked the beginning of the end of Republican viability in California politics, as the Republicans' share of the states' growing Latino vote collapsed.[37]

George W. Bush had taken a different path in Texas. From his first election in 1994, he had strongly rejected nativism and had won over a significant share of Latino voters in his reelection in 1998. As he mounted his presidential campaign, with its slogan of compassionate conservatism, he aimed to chip away at the advantage Democrats had accumulated with Latino voters. Ultimately, he spent far more money appealing to Spanish-speaking voters than Gore did, and while Gore still won the demographic overall, Bush nearly matched Reagan's 1984 mark. Newt Gingrich followed this same path in the late 1990s, urging other Republicans to tone down their opposition to bilingual education and starting to issue his press releases with Spanish translations.[38]

Though immigration reform was not a major priority during Bush's first term, he was clear that he had two main policy objectives on this front: some sort of legalization of status for some part of the current undocumented population and a significant expansion of the number of workers who could be let in on work visas of various kinds. In both of these, Bush was deeply in sync with what many large corporations desired. In the late 1990s, the Chamber of Commerce and other business groups had formed the Essential Worker Immigration Coalition (EWIC) to push for more guest workers. They were joined by Compete America, formed by the Business Roundtable and the NAM. At the same time, many companies also took a growing interest in undocumented immigrants as consumers. The financial services industry, in particular, was eager to bring in the savings of undocumented immigrants, which was often held in cash. For these reasons, the corporate coalition behind liberalizing immigration reform was considerable.[39]

Immigration politics, however, had changed markedly from Bush's election to the end of his first term, when policies began to receive serious attention. The attacks of September 11 had breathed new life into nativism, which was now a legitimate subset of security-state policy. Before 9/11, the main anti-immigrant caucus in the House, founded by Colorado's Tom Tancredo in 1999, had just sixteen members. Already by March 2002, it had grown to sixty-two. By 2005, it had ninety. This caucus provided the base for Republican opposition to Bush's immigration reform. The attacks on Bush from these quarters could be quite ugly, as when one representative accused the president of "Hispandering" for votes. Nonetheless, the administration made a calculation that these groups could be ignored. Tom DeLay, still the real power in the House, was willing to go along with the administration, though he himself felt it was doing too little to prioritize enforcement, as opposed to various forms of status regularization. Others in Bush's coalition, from Grover Norquist to the *Wall Street Journal*, assured Bush that immigration reform would ruffle few feathers in his coalition and could even help him win reelection. He followed their advice, and was rewarded with fully 40 percent of the Latino vote in 2004, breaking Reagan's record.[40]

Yet when the administration began pushing for immigration reform in earnest in 2005, it quickly found itself stymied by congressional conservatives. Opposition to immigration reform was fanned by conservative talk radio, which had become a major agenda-setter in the Republican Party. After the 2004 election, with the GOP in unified control of the federal government, talk radio hosts found themselves unable to squeeze much juice out of their usual fulminations against liberals. Now, they had to find the enemy within, and the Bush administration's immigration reform agenda proved the perfect target. Republicans supporting immigration reform faced a barrage of criticism. One senator took to offering bonus pay to staffers tasked with processing the abuse he was receiving. Tom DeLay turned against reform shortly after his indictment for corruption in October of 2005, urging Republicans in Congress to pursue an enforcement-only policy, with none of the expansion of guest-worker programs that business wanted. Representative James Sensenbrenner, who had previously been open to compromise on immigration, followed DeLay's advice, offering a bill that would enact a harsher crackdown on immigrants than had been seen in the US in many decades. The House passed the bill at the end of 2005, but it was so distant from the immigration bills in the Senate, which were more aligned with Bush's vision, that it never became law.[41]

Business's immigration agenda was stalled. To be sure, there were sectors of business supporting the enforcement-only agenda. The US Business and Industry Council (USBIC), which had begun its life as a business organization defending segregation before evolving into an organization for privately owned companies that aligned with the far right in US politics, was strongly supportive of the enforcement-only approach, and opposed to reform.[42] Defense and security corporations also stood to gain from increased enforcement. The bulk of capital was clearly supportive of Bush's agenda, however, and by 2007 they were dispirited even by the bills coming out of the Senate, which were more reflective of their interests than those in the House. These bills still placed the burden for verifying employees' immigration status on business, and business organizations were simply unwilling to accept this burden. By the end of 2007, the Senate immigration reform bill was essentially an orphan, with far too much enforcement for Democrats to support it and still too much expansion of guest worker programs for conservatives to. In the final vote on it, Bush could only get twelve Senate Republicans to support it.[43]

By 2007, relations between the administration and the congressional party had largely broken down. In May, the president attacked opponents of immigration reform in a speech in Georgia, accusing them of "empty political rhetoric" to "rile up people's emotions." The Representatives, he declared, "don't want to do what's right for America." Trent Lott, who continued to support immigration reform, lamented that talk radio was "running America ... We have to deal with that problem." In the aftermath of the 2006 elections, there was no reason for either the president or his critics to the right to hold their fire. Their agendas would not be passing the now-Democratic House and Senate, and opinion on the right was beginning to coalesce around the idea that Bush had never been a real conservative. The unity between the administration, the conservative movement, and corporate America that had defined Bush's first term had been definitively shattered.[44]

"This Sucker Could Go Down"

When the financial crisis of 2008 hit, the Bush presidency was already in ruins. Facing rebellion from his own party and a new congressional majority eager to pay back the partisan warfare that Bush, Rove, and DeLay had waged, Bush was, by 2007, already a lame-duck president simply trying to ride out his term. Yet if the tribulations of his second term brought to mind the sufferings of Job, the arrival of the financial crisis appeared as something from the Book of Revelation. For the broader Republican Party, the crisis was similarly apocalyptic, as it revealed divisions even deeper than those uncovered by the immigration debate.

The crisis's roots extended back into the 1980s. In that decade, the financial system began to be deregulated, as banks, looking for ways to make profits amidst the financial volatility engendered by the Volcker Shock, pushed for the rollback of various parts of the regulatory regime developed in the aftermath of the Great Depression. As more and more regulations were lifted, the financial architecture changed dramatically. Soon, non-bank financial institutions were issuing large amounts of mortgages, while commercial banks were offering more complicated (and riskier) financial products, such as money market funds and mortgage-backed securities. This latter product would prove particularly central. Mortgage-backed securities were derivatives, financial products that derived their value from other financial products. In the case of a mortgage-backed security, the value of the asset was provided by the stream of payments made by the holders of the mortgages that had been bundled to form it. Other derivatives soon proliferated, such as credit default swaps, which allowed holders of an asset to swap particular risks with a counterparty, hedging against specific threats to their assets. These financial instruments grew ever more baroque, and financial firms made huge profits by offering derivatives that were custom made for purchasers. Both the firm offering the product, which could charge huge fees, and the purchaser, who could make big returns by slicing off precise risks to be hedged against, grew richer, but the financial system as a whole grew more and more opaque, as these highly complex financial instruments proved impossible for any outside observer to accurately value.[45]

The risk this represented should have been obvious. Firms were carrying incredibly complex financial products on their balance sheets as assets, but no one could really say if they were worth as much their owners claimed. Calls to regulate these products began to sound, but were met with heroic levels of resistance from Federal Reserve chair Alan Greenspan, along with the Treasury Departments of the Clinton and Bush II administrations. Even as the notional value of derivatives reached $70 trillion in 1998—nearly ten times US GDP—Clinton's Security and Exchange Commission chair, Arthur Levitt, accused regulation advocates of "demoniz[ing] derivatives." At the Fed, Greenspan oscillated between proclaiming the ability of the free market to solve any potential problems and claiming that he did not have the authority to issue the regulations being discussed. By the early 2000s, as home prices rose far ahead of the overall rate of inflation, it was clear that the demand for mortgage backed securities was inflating a housing bubble, as banks could write mortgages to whomever they liked, quickly get the debt off their books by selling it off, and then issue more mortgages. This demand, in turn, pushed mortgage issuers to seek out new customers, leading to the rise of subprime lending and new, more complicated mortgage terms to justify lending to riskier applicants. Complaints of mortgage fraud grew twenty-fold between 1996 and 2005, and doubled again by 2009.[46]

Housing prices peaked in 2006, and in 2007, default rates on nonprime mortgages began to climb rapidly. Default rates on prime-rate mortgages, which went to borrowers who would have qualified even without the new chicanery, followed soon after and eclipsed subprime defaults in both number and the value of equity involved. At this point, Henry Paulson Jr., Bush's secretary of the Treasury, stepped into his role as primary manager of the crisis. His strategy was simple—attempt to bail out the financial system through means that would attract the minimum attention and hope that any more conspicuous intervention could wait until after the election. Three institutions were at the heart of this plan. First were the Federal Home Loan Banks, a system analogous to the system of Federal Reserve Banks but dedicated to mortgage-lending institutions. While the Federal Reserve was an institution of intense media focus, the Federal Home Loan Banks attracted little notice. Through them, Paulson directed billions upon billions of dollars in backstopping loans to failing mortgage firms. Second was the Federal Deposit Insurance Corporation, which, since the Great Depression, had guaranteed small depositors' savings by charging member banks insurance dues. While the risk to deposits was surely climbing in 2007 and 2008, the FDIC would not raise rates on banks. Instead, talk began circulating of the FDIC itself being backstopped by the Treasury, which shifted the burden of financing deposit insurance from the banks themselves to taxpayers. Finally, Paulson turned to Fannie Mae and Freddie Mac, two government sponsored enterprises (GSEs). Fannie Mae had been established as a federal institution during the New Deal to purchase mortgages from banks. In the 1960s, it had been converted to private ownership, and a sister institution, Freddie Mac, was established to provide competition. Though under private ownership, the GSEs remained subject to public governance in key respects. In late 2007 and early 2008, Paulson was able to push through a revision of the GSEs' standards on mortgage purchases, allowing them to start buying some of the subprime mortgages that were choking the financial system. Already by late 2007, the GSEs had become virtually the last institutions buying mortgages. Together, these actions constituted what Thomas Ferguson and Robert Johnson call a "shadow bailout," in which the backstopping of the financial system was attempted through mechanisms that would hopefully evade public attention.[47]

This last maneuver is what ultimately brought the shadow bailout into the light, and in doing so launched a ferocious backlash, driven primarily by the right wing of the GOP. As Fannie and Freddie became loaded down with mortgages that would never be paid, firms that were invested in securities issued by the GSEs began to find their balance sheets deteriorating. The investment bank Bear Stearns was the first institution to buckle. As the prices on GSE securities fell, Bear found itself without collateral, and began to collapse. For Paulson, this failure was doubly catastrophic. First, Bear was a counterparty to a huge number of derivatives across the market, ensuring that its failure would reverberate widely across the market. Second, since Bear was an investment bank, rather than a commercial bank, it was not supposed to be eligible for loans from the Federal Reserve. However, as one of the largest purchasers of government securities like Treasury bonds it could be argued that Bear fell under the Fed's purview as a "primary dealer" of government paper. Paulson and Chairman of the Federal Reserve Ben Bernanke ran with this argument, and the Federal Reserve agreed to take $30 billion in bad debt off Bear's books, which would improve the bank's condition enough that J. P. Morgan would agree to purchase it and prevent its total collapse. Former Fed chair Paul Volcker described the move as stretching the institution "to the very edge of its lawful and implied powers." A move as drastic as this simply could not be hidden, and it thrust bailout politics to the forefront of the nation's attention.[48]

The Democrats were the first to respond, and they used the Bear Stearns bailout to make a case for providing mortgage relief to homeowners. Democrats had begun raising these proposals in 2007 but had faced opposition from both the White House and the congressional GOP. Now they sought to maximize pressure on Bush by accusing him of being willing to bail out the rich while leaving ordinary Americans drowning in debt. This, in turn, led to a response from Republicans arguing that any aid to homeowners was only bailing out irresponsible borrowers.[49]

The opposition was led by Dick Armey, who had retired from Congress in 2002. Armey wore two hats after serving in Congress. First, he worked for DLA Piper, a major law firm, leveraging his political connections on behalf of the firm's clients. Second, Armey went to work for Citizens for a Sound Economy, the libertarian group that oil tycoons Charles and David Koch had set up in the 1980s. However, Armey soon got into trouble with the Kochs, who thought he was using CSE to advocate for policies his clients at DLA Piper desired. A split ensued, and the Kochs formed Americans for Prosperity (AFP) with their loyalists, while Armey formed FreedomWorks with his. Armey proceeded to run FreedomWorks exactly as the Kochs had accused him of running CSE, promoting offshore drilling after he took on oil industry clients and fighting for life insurance deregulation when he took on insurers. In the Spring of 2008, FreedomWorks became the leading voice crusading against aid to homeowners. Freedom-Works' President Matt Kibbe preached the gospel of laissez-faire, arguing that "the market needs to be allowed to reprice mortgage loans and property values, and the government should not exacerbate the situation with policies that create moral hazard, distort prices, and push costs onto taxpayers." They also set up a supposedly grassroots website—the Wall Street Journal described its aesthetic as "a bit like a digital ransom note, with irregular fonts, exclamation points and big red arrows"—complaining that any aid to mortgage holders would be unfair to renters. AFP voiced similar criticisms.[50]

At this point, opposition to mortgage relief united these conservative groups with the mainstream of American finance. When Democrats put forward a plan to allow bankruptcy judges to modify the terms of mortgages, it was strenuously opposed by lending companies. However, as the risk unpaid mortgages posed to the system became more evident, many financial institutions came to support aid to borrowers. In March, just before Bear Stearns went under, Bank of America and Credit Suisse endorsed a plan whereby the government would buy bad mortgages from banks, and then rewrite the terms. This split intensified even further over the summer, when Paulson's plan to use Fannie Mae and Freddie Mac as buyers of last resort finally came crashing down, necessitating the nationalization of both companies. Paulson went to Congress to ask for effectively unlimited funds to back the failing finance houses, famously suggesting that "if you've got a squirt gun in your pocket, you may have to take it out. If you've got a bazooka, and people know you've got it, you may not have to take it out." The White House backed Paulson up, as Bush played an increasingly passive role, doing little beyond endorsing whatever his Treasury Secretary proposed. In Congress, however, opposition was fierce and was growing increasingly histrionic. Senator Jim Bunning of Kentucky snarled that "When I picked up my newspaper yesterday, I thought I woke up in France. But no, it turns out socialism is alive and well in America." While the American Bankers Association backed the bill, FreedomWorks and the Club for Growth opposed it. Ultimately, three quarters of House Republicans voted against Paulson's plan, though the bill had strong enough support from Democrats to pass anyway.[51]

In early September, everything came crashing down. First, on September 7, Paulson's bazooka came out. As Fannie and Freddie's positions fell even lower, they were put into conservatorship, effectively nationalizing them. Then, on September 13, Lehman Brothers, one of the big five investment banks, went bust. Unlike the similar situation with Bear Stearns in the spring, this time Paulson did not step in. Though Paulson and company would later plead impotence, arguing that they could not have helped Lehman if they wanted to, the best evidence suggests that it was a political decision, motivated by "bailout fatigue." The result was cascading market failure, as credit markets across the country seized up, threatening everything from the ability to get mortgages to the ability to make payroll. At this point, truly heroic interventions became necessary to avert financial Armageddon.

Paulson, at Bernanke's urging, proposed a massive fund, over a half a trillion dollars, that the federal government would use to buy distressed assets from financial institutions in order to restore solvency and get credit markets moving again.[52]

As Paulson's plan, formulated initially in a terse three-page memo, reached Congress, the institution began to resemble Bedlam. John Boehner declared, "We don't need more federal involvement in our markets," before reversing and endorsing Paulson's plan. Most of the Republican conference stuck with Boehner's original position, leaving passage of the plan up to Democrats. The Democrats, in turn, saw this for the trap it was —they would supply the votes that would save the economy, and in return, the Republicans would get to accuse them of bailing out Wall Street. Senate Majority Leader Harry Reid insisted that 80 percent of Republicans support the bill before he would pass it. As Representative Louise Slaughter of New York explained, "We're not pulling their chestnuts out of the fire." John McCain, in a desperate attempt to look presidential, declared that he would stop campaigning to attend a meeting at the White House dedicated to solving the crisis. McCain had published an anti-bailout op-ed with his running mate, Sarah Palin, only two weeks earlier in the *Wall Street Journal* but now shamefacedly supported Paulson's plan. At the meeting, he offered nothing but mumbled platitudes, leading an irritated George W. Bush to remind the room, "if money isn't loosened up, this sucker could go down." After the meeting ended and McCain left, Henry Paulson got down on his knees before Nancy Pelosi, the Speaker of the House, and implored her, "Don't blow this thing up, Nancy."[53]

Many of the leading business organizations quickly came out in support of Paulson's plan. Business Roundtable members began calling representatives urging them to vote for it. John Castellani, the group's president, warned, "Every day that [the bill's] delayed, it hurts." Even free market think tanks like the Heritage Foundation and the American Enterprise Institute supported the plan. At the same time, however, Americans for Prosperity and FreedomWorks mobilized against it, as did Grover Norquist's circle of anti-tax groups. They were joined by some sectors of finance, who were exercised by two issues. First, they wanted a revision of recent accounting rules requiring firms to count likely losses on their balance sheets much more quickly. There was, of course, some irony in making such a demand in the midst of a crisis that was brought on precisely by a failure of firm's balance-sheets to reflect their real value, but that did not stop congressional conservatives like Eric Cantor from demanding such a revision before he would vote for the bailout. Second, small banks wanted the FDIC limit on insurable deposits raised from its ceiling of $100,000. The bill's bailout for money market accounts, they argued, effectively disadvantaged small commercial banks, since they could not guarantee their customers' deposits above the FDIC limit.[54]

This opposition, together with that from some Democrats, led Paulson's bailout to fail in the House on September 29, 205 to 228. Republicans had delivered a mere sixty-five votes for the bill. George W. Bush had personally called all nineteen members of the Texas delegation to ask them to vote for it. Four had listened. Subsequent research has revealed that in addition to political ideology, representatives also responded to conditions in their districts and were more likely to vote for the bill if they had a significant number of constituents working in finance or going through foreclosures.[55]

The reaction from markets was immediate and intense, with the Dow Jones Industrial Average logging its largest-ever one-day drop in points. Major business organizations responded with a dedicated push to pass the bill. On September 30, over fifty major business associations, including the Roundtable, the Chamber of Commerce, the NAM, and the Financial Services Forum, put out a letter that warned: "If Congress fails to act and credit markets tighten further, our associations' members will find it more difficult—if not impossible—to secure credit to run their companies, and our members' employees will find it harder to get mortgages, secure auto loans, and borrow money to send their children to college." The Chamber of Commerce took a threatening tone, emailing congressmembers who voted against the bailout, "Make no mistake: When the aftermath of congressional inaction becomes clear, Americans will not tolerate those who stood by and let the calamity happen." Even Americans for Prosperity, quietly and behind the scenes, extended its support for the bill.[56]

A scramble to amend and pass the bailout bill commenced. Amendments were added addressing some interest groups' complaints; FDIC deposit insurance coverage was increased from $100,000 to $250,000 and the new accounting standards that angered banks were eliminated. The bill was also stuffed with pork; everything from tax breaks to energy credits were piled on. This, together with the frenzied lobbying from business organizations, was enough to win passage of the legislation in the late hours of October 1, 263 to 171. Only about thirty Republicans switched their votes.[57]

Passing the bailout managed to avoid the complete collapse of financial markets and the American economy as a whole. Yet even as the bailout held the economy together, it fractured the Republican Party. Significant portions of the party were now decisively alienated from their traditional backers in the large business organizations. The fights about immigration and the bailout had shown that the party right was simply not interested in the opinions of the Chamber of Commerce or the Business Roundtable, no matter how much water they carried for right-wing policies in Bush's first term. At the same time, the fights about the bailout had revealed the power of new groups, like FreedomWorks and Americans for Prosperity, who fought for free market policies even when the big business organizations were opposed. As will be discussed further in the next chapter, it would be a mistake to write these groups off as representatives of idiosyncratic billionaires or newly mobilized small business; they counted the heads of some of the country's largest corporations among their backers and raised money on the same scale as the venerable Chamber of Commerce.

Bush's first term had promised something quite different. Its foundation had been a supposedly unshakeable alliance between business and the Republican Party, with the administration calling the plays and business coalitions executing them. While this alliance held throughout Bush's first term, his second term revealed, crisis by crisis, that both the party and the business community had deep divisions. The dynamics that emerged in these four years would continue to dominate Republican politics up to the present day. The intransigent nativism, in opposition to the preferences of big business, would continue to sabotage any possibility of immigration reform and would give Donald Trump the defining issue he needed to launch his presidential campaign. Similarly, the free market fanaticism that erupted in 2008 would soon coalesce into the Tea Party, forcing repeated games of chicken over the federal debt ceiling and a government shutdown in 2013. Perhaps most fundamentally, they entrenched a pattern in Republican politics whereby the party's right was in near-constant vituperative conflict with the party's leadership. Bush and Karl Rove sought to rewrite the rules of American politics with their reign. They succeeded, but very differently than they had hoped to.

5

Politics Outside the Party

The years following George W. Bush's presidency witnessed a transformation of the Republican Party. This transformation occurred on both political and institutional levels. Politically, the party continued moving to the right, though what that meant concretely would change rapidly. Under the Obama presidency, the GOP adopted a far more extreme vision of free market economics than it had under Gingrich. However, with the Donald Trump presidency—and through the first Biden administration—the party lurched towards a kind of hybrid economic nationalism, embracing tariffs and turning away from attacks on Medicare or Social Security, while also continuing the politics of tax cuts and deregulation. On foreign policy the story was similar, with a retreat from the imperial ambition of the Bush years but a continued commitment to American military supremacy and bellicose nationalism. The one area where the party adopted a clear position was immigration, as the GOP forcefully rejected Bush's attempts to build a Republican majority among Latinos and instead became the party of proud xenophobia.

Underlying this transformation were the two structural changes this book has been discussing: the weakening of American political parties as institutions and the fracturing of the corporate elite. Both dynamics acquired new force in this period. First, the Republican Party, badly damaged by the implosion of the Bush presidency, managed to rejuvenate itself through the Tea Party, a social movement with no strong institutional connection to the party itself. Through this largely decentralized movement, conservative activists were able to wage war against the Obama administration, as well as push the Republican Party far to the right. In so doing, the movement further marginalized the party itself as a decision-making institution.

However, the Tea Party proved largely epiphenomenal and had mostly disappeared by 2014. The emergence of super PACs proved a more enduring change. Vivified by the Supreme Court in two 2010 decisions, super PACs were given the ability to solicit and spend unlimited amounts of money on elections, so long as they did not directly coordinate with candidate committees. GOP operatives seized immediately on the opportunity created by this decision, and the field was soon crowded with super PACs. Official GOP fundraising bodies like the RNC or the NRCC, to whom donations were capped by federal law, now competed with super PACs for funds, staff, and power. An increasingly chaotic party resulted: a single donor could fund a presidential primary campaign, as Sheldon Adelson did with Newt Gingrich in 2012. The parties had been displaced even further, not through internal weakening, as in the twentieth century, but through a change in the organizational ecosystem in which they existed.

This proliferation of super PACs (and their associated organizations like foundations, nonprofits, etc.) itself reflected a political divide among conservative elites. While groups like the Chamber of Commerce and the Business Roundtable had been stalwart supporters of the Bush administration, the 2010s saw the emergence of an alternative ecology of elites, centered on the Koch brothers (Charles and David) and the network they built. This network began drawing attention as a result of its links to the Tea Party and played a major role in the 2010 midterms. At that time, the Koch network and more traditional groups worked together to oppose the Obama administration and bring the GOP into the majority in Congress. However, it soon became clear that there were significant cleavages between more traditional business groups and the Koch network, as Koch-linked politicians pursued strategies like showdowns over government spending that led to government shutdowns and uncertainty about the debt ceiling. From 2010 to 2016, the GOP was a battleground for dueling super PACs, with one side led by Karl Rove and the other by the Kochs. The stalemate between them allowed Donald

Trump to seize the moment in 2016, creating a far different party than either side desired.

Opposing Obama

The first task for the GOP after Bush was stopping Barack Obama. The 2008 elections revealed that the party was in no way up to the task. In the wreckage of the Bush administration, neither the party establishment, which had backed immigration reform and the financial bailout, nor the party right, which had opposed both, were able to put forward a credible presidential candidate. John McCain, distant from both camps, was able to win the nomination but inspired few in the Republican coalition and offered no rejoinder to the majority of the population who blamed the GOP for the wreckage on Wall Street and in Iraq. His defeat bequeathed to the GOP a branding problem that could only be solved outside the party.

Presidential Stalemate

The Republican Party went into the 2008 elections in a kind of stalemate. While the leadership—George W. Bush in the presidency and John Boehner and Bill Frist as minority leaders in Congress—were fairly politically unified, in the House, opposition had been mounting since 2004. The rebellion over immigration signaled the reemergence of open factionalism in the party. But if the party right was newly energized and willing to defy the president, they were also not yet strong enough to produce a credible candidate for the presidency. Tom Tancredo, leader of the House anti-immigrant caucus, attempted to run in 2008 but proved unable to attract more than desultory attention or funding and dropped out before the primaries even began. At the same time, the wing of the party that supported Bush was also unable to produce a strong candidate. Dick Cheney had, in the face of truly abysmal polling, declined to run, making him the first vice president in more than a century to not attempt to succeed his president.[1] Notably, no current Republican governors, who tended to be closer to Bush than the congressional party, attempted a run.

Seeing that 2008 would, in all likelihood, not be the Republicans' year, many of the donors who funded Bush's wins in 2000 and 2004 stayed out of the Republican primaries. As of the summer of 2007, two thirds of Bush's biggest donors had not donated to any of the candidates who had declared themselves.[2]

John McCain had been positioning himself to succeed Bush for several years. After an acrimonious primary contest between the two in 2000, he had largely mended fences with Bush and had worked to ingratiate himself with the Christian right, from whom he had generally been quite distant. In 2006, he gave the commencement address at Jerry Falwell's Liberty University, signaling his bid for evangelical support. Though the establishment wing of the party was suspicious that he was not committed enough to free market principles (McCain had actually discussed switching to the Democrats during the Bush administration, and John Kerry had asked him to be his running mate), they warmed to McCain in 2007 as it began to look like he was their best chance of beating Hillary Clinton, then still the presumptive Democratic nominee.[3]

McCain's main opponent was Mitt Romney, who attempted to run as the candidate of the Republican right. That Mitt Romney, a Massachusetts moderate, was the most credible candidate to play this role was itself a sign of how weak the right was, at least in the presidential field. Romney had had his eye on the presidency for some time. He had won the 2002 governor's race in Massachusetts, and almost immediately began making preparations to run for president. Only a year and a half into his term, he launched a new network of PACs to support a presidential run, and he began courting Bush's donors. While Romney had a clear advantage in the money race, he faced skepticism from the Christian right, whom he pursued wantonly throughout the race. Ultimately, he was able to position himself as the candidate most likely to stop McCain, whom the party right truly detested. With endorsements from a wide range of conservatives, including Rush Limbaugh and Paul Weyrich, Romney appeared to pose a formidable challenge to McCain.[4]

But the race that developed was a clear demonstration of the weaknesses of the Republican right. Even after McCain's campaign very nearly imploded following his endorsement of immigration reform, Romney could never gain a decisive advantage in polling. Evangelical Christians' discomfort with his Mormonism and record of social liberalism as governor created space for Arkansas governor Mike Huckabee to enter the race and attempt to push Romney out. This split the evangelical vote, allowing McCain to overcome his own weaknesses with the religious right and position himself as the candidate most committed to winning the war in Iraq. Unable to act as a disciplined voting bloc, the party right found itself losing to someone who Rick Santorum called "not only against us but leading the charge on the other side."[5]

In the general election, McCain ended up facing not Hillary Clinton, but Barack Obama. In a major reversal from the previous two elections, the Democrats built an intimidating fundraising lead over the GOP. Using a fundraising model that leveraged donations made over the internet, Obama ultimately raised more money than Bush and Kerry *combined* in 2004. This success led him to reject public financing for the general election, something no candidate had done since the public financing system was set up in the 1970s. McCain attempted to build his own fundraising apparatus to compete, appointing GOP operative Fred Malek to lead a bundling operation to replicate Bush's success with Rangers and Pioneers. Yet as one of McCain's fundraisers admitted, among the Bush donor class, there was "bad blood" towards McCain for his position on campaign finance and his initial opposition to Bush's tax cut.[6]

Bad blood with party financiers was soon the least of McCain's problems, however. As the financial crisis erupted in the early fall, he made a last-ditch effort to appear presidential by halting his campaign to go to the White House to discuss the crisis with the president, Nancy Pelosi, and Barack Obama. Caught as he was between the party's intransigent wing, who argued for no more bailouts, and the Bush wing, McCain proved utterly incapable of providing direction amid the crisis. By October, it was clear that Obama would win, and the Republican Party would once again be out of power.[7]

"Insurgency May Be Required"

After Obama's election, the GOP sought to regroup. In various conclaves and consistories, operatives met to plan their way back into power. In all of these various meetings, the same path forward was agreed upon: total war against the Obama administration. Just two days after the election, L. Brent Bozell III, son of Barry Goldwater's ghostwriter and nephew of William F. Buckley, convened a meeting of movement conservatives like himself to discuss how to proceed. Other attendees included movement grandees like Grover Norquist and Richard Viguerie. Bereft of confidence in the GOP, these movement conservatives concluded that the key to opposing Obama was more movement conservatism. Sarah Palin, despite her ignominious performance on the campaign trail, was held up as the kind of leader they needed. The conservative movement, not the GOP, they argued, would lead the opposition to Obama.[8]

The night of Obama's inauguration, a similar meeting took place, this time among Republican Party insiders. Organized by Republican pollster Frank Luntz, the meeting included leading GOP representatives like Eric Cantor and Paul Ryan, senators like Jim DeMint, and Newt Gingrich, the éminence grise. While the mood was understandably dour, there was a certain relief about being free of the burdens of governing. One attendee regretted that, during the Bush administration, they had been too concerned with "making sure the trains run on time. Well, what if the train is heading towards the cliff?" Now, they were free to act as the opposition. While Obama was too popular to attack personally, they agreed to adopt the strategy Gingrich had employed against Clinton of opposing every bill. Kevin McCarthy, then beginning his second term in the House, declared, "We've gotta challenge them on every single bill and challenge them on every single campaign." Gingrich wrapped up the meeting by pronouncing it "the day the seeds of 2012 were sown."[9]

Finally, the next week, a third meeting was convened, this time in California. The last weekend of January 2009 was the annual seminar of the Koch brothers. Held since 2003, these conferences attracted a large and growing audience of extremely wealthy conservatives. The seminars had two purposes. First, they were political educational events, featuring lectures and discussions on various questions of libertarian economics. Second, they were fundraising events, at which attendees donated to various Koch organizations. Both purposes worked together, as the seminars built ideological solidarity among their attendees, allowing the Kochs to function as "collective goods providers for the wealthy right." Since 2006, these seminars had grown rapidly, as the looming prospect of a return to Democratic rule spurred conservative elites to action.[10]

In 2009, the Koch seminar featured a debate between two Republican senators—John Cornyn of Texas and Jim DeMint of South Carolina. Both were extremely conservative and sought a strategy for restoring Republican hegemony. Cornyn argued that the GOP needed to build a bigger tent and do a better job appealing to moderate voters. DeMint argued the opposite, declaring he preferred "thirty Republicans who believed in something [to] a majority who believed in nothing." As the debate went on, the financial bailout, which Cornyn had voted for and DeMint had voted against, came up, and the audience began jeering Cornyn. For the wealthy conservative elite gathered at the seminar, collaboration with the Bush administration during the financial crisis was heresy. Any kind of collaboration with the Obama administration would be even worse. As Richard Fink, the Koch brothers' chief political advisor, told them after Obama's inauguration speech, beating the president would take "the fight of their lives."[11]

Both inside the party and among outside activists hoping to influence it, a consensus was building that Republican hegemony could be reestablished through total opposition to the Obama administration. The new head of the NRCC, Pete Session, gave a hint of Republican thinking in an internal meeting in February of 2009: "Insurgency—we understand perhaps a little bit more because of the Taliban ... And we need to understand that insurgency may be required." Newt Gingrich's Vietcong had been replaced by a new generation of congressional insurgents.[12]

The Party's Over

The strategy of total war against the Obama administration would take the GOP in some unexpected directions, leaving the party itself less influential, even as it experienced some stunning political successes. First, in order to rebrand itself, the party turned to an extra-party social movement, the Tea Party, to relegitimize the politics of free market conservatism. While this strategy yielded considerable success, the autonomy of the Tea Party from the GOP meant that Tea Party priorities, such as electing the most conservative candidate possible in a primary, could easily sabotage Republican plans to win elections. Second, the *Citizens United* Supreme Court decision in 2010, which legalized unlimited expenditures by organizations that were independent of candidate committees, drastically altered the organizational ecosystem in which the party existed. Suddenly, the party found itself working uneasily aside groups who commanded fiscal resources at least as great as its own. While both of these developments contributed to Republican success in the 2010s, they also set the stage for severe intraparty conflicts.

The Tea Party

In the spring of 2008, as the Bush administration was entering the event horizon from which it would never return, one GOP representative decided to get out early. Tom Davis, who had come into office as part of Gingrich's class of '94 and had headed the NRCC from 1998 to 2002, announced his retirement with a memorandum laying out his view of the current state of the party. He didn't mince words, declaring that "the Republican brand is in the trash can ... If we were a dog food, they would take us off the shelf." The GOP needed a way to dissociate itself from the Bush administration, universally seen as a failure, and to create a new identity.[13]

An opportunity arose, appropriately enough, in the city where Abraham Lincoln began his campaign to turn the Republican Party into a party of government—Chicago. On February 19, 2009, a CNBC on-screen personality named Rick Santelli, standing on the floor of the Chicago Mercantile Exchange, launched into a diatribe against a program the Democrats were considering to aid mortgage-holders. Santelli called for a demonstration in a few months: "We're thinking of having a Chicago tea party in July. All you capitalists who want to show up to Lake Michigan, I'm going to start organizing."[14]

Though afterwards Santelli and others would mythologize the moment as an unscripted eruption of popular indignation at an out-of-control government, evidence suggests that the ground had been prepared to take advantage of just such a moment as this. As the journalist Lee Fang has shown, anti-tax tea parties were floated as a tactic by the tobacco industry in the 1990s as a way to shield the sector from new regulation and taxation. One internal industry document outlined a potential advertisement where a narrator ominously intoned, "British policies of minority rule, increased government intervention, unfair taxation ... those same issues face us again today. Excise taxes, advertising restrictions, franchise legislation, price supports, and smoking bans make it necessary to act to protect our rights as citizens of the United States." Dick Armey also embraced the imagery in the 1990s in his campaigns for a flat tax. And Citizens for a Sound Economy, the Koch brothers' organization, organized various anti-tax tea party demonstrations in the early 2000s. In August of 2008, a Chicago Republican organizer and talk radio producer registered the domain www.chicagoteaparty. com. In early January, the Libertarian Party of Illinois had discussions on its listserv of launching a tea party protest against taxation.[15]

All of these forces sprang into action immediately after Santelli's segment aired. Chicagoteaparty.com went live a few hours afterwards. That same day, Eric Odom, an activist in Chicago libertarian circles, registered taxdayteaparty.com, and Americans for Prosperity registered taxpayerteaparty.com. The next day, a series of first weekly and then daily conference calls began taking place between about fifty different conservative activists, coordinating a national day of action in February. Armey's FreedomWorks helped facilitate the calls. All of this culminated in a series of protests on February 27, 2009, that took place in eighteen cities and involved around 30,000 participants.[16]

The sociologist Clarence Lo has provided a useful framework for understanding the Tea Party's growth after this moment. Up to April 2009, he argues, the Tea Party was in a "test-marketing" phase, in which conservative elites like Dick Armey were attempting to see if there was an audience for the kind of anti-government conservatism they were hoping to promote. After proof of concept was produced with the late February demonstrations, the movement shifted into a genuinely grassroots phase, in which local groups, with few connections to groups like AFP or Freedom-Works, proliferated rapidly. The most thorough count of local groups found over 3,500 in existence between 2009 and 2014, with between 140,000 and 310,000 dedicated activists. This isn't to say that elite facilitation did not continue to play an important part in the movement. For example, Fox News promoted the protests relentlessly. Some of their on-screen personalities, like Glenn Beck, actually had paid promotion deals with FreedomWorks, which paid him handsomely to read their content on air. Frank Luntz, the GOP strategist, credited Beck with much: "That rant from Santelli woke up the upper middle class and the investor class, and then Glenn Beck woke up everyone else. Glenn Beck's show is what created the Tea Party movement ... It started on Tax Day 2009, and it exploded at town hall meetings in July. You can create a mass movement within three months." A large body of evidence, however, confirms that while figures like Beck may have helped popularize the movement and keep it salient, there was a huge amount of organizing happening in local groups after February 27.[17]

Throughout 2009 and 2010, thousands of local tea party groups were organized. They tended to form in counties that were both suffering from the economic crisis, with more foreclosures and loss of income, and were highly segregated by race. Using internet services provided by national tea party umbrella groups, like Tea Party Patriots and 1776 Tea Party, local groups sprung up across the country. These websites allowed local groups to set up their own pages, post events and blog entries, and link to other organizations. With this structure, the Tea Party developed a model of social movement organization (or dis-organization) that would be widely adopted over the following years by movements like Occupy Wall Street and Black Lives Matter.[18]

These tea party groups then organized thousands of actions that engaged millions of participants from 2009 to 2014. Demonstrations like those held on February 27 and on tax day 2009 were one common tactic. Another was disrupting legislators' town hall meetings. During the summer recess of 2009, many Democratic legislators returned to their states and districts to hold meetings with constituents and try to build support for healthcare reform. Tea Party activists used these meetings as an opportunity to loudly confront and denounce legislators. These actions both helped publicize opposition to healthcare reform and helped create the impression that the Democrats had lost control, driving down support for Obama.[19]

In doing so, the Tea Party helped to rebrand opposition to the Obama administration from a project of the failed GOP to a project of the resurgent conservative movement. Once the movement became established enough to be widely recognized, it received more support in opinion polls than the GOP itself. By loudly proclaiming their distance from both political parties, Tea Party activists managed to portray their opposition to Obama as above partisan politics. The truth, of course, was rather less inspiring. Tea Party activists tended to be older white Americans, many of whom had extensive backgrounds in GOP politics. Theda Skocpol and Vanessa Williamson report that "a surprising number of the people we met [interviewing tea party activists] dated their first political experience to the Goldwater campaign in 1964." Subsequent research has confirmed that Tea Party activists and sympathizers were extremely conservative, and mainly faulted the Republican Party for not doing *enough* to oppose the Obama administration.[20]

The Tea Party failed to stop Obama's healthcare reform from being passed. But it succeeded in rejuvenating conservatism, and in so doing, it played a significant role in preparing the ground for the GOP's 2010 comeback. Yet if the Tea Party was crucial for the GOP's resuscitation, it also signaled the emergence of a force in Republican politics that was totally outside the control of the party itself and whose relationship with other members of the GOP coalition was not always cooperative. Because of its organizational independence from the GOP, Tea Party activity was not concentrated in areas prioritized by the GOP, instead clustering in areas that were hardest hit by the housing crisis. Moreover, as will be discussed in more detail below, Tea Party groups often threw their weight behind primary challengers who weakened the GOP's chances of winning a seat, costing the party a number of victories in 2010 and 2012. Overall, the Tea Party surely aided the GOP, on net. But it was an ominous sign that the party effectively had to outsource its rejuvenation, showcasing the decline in the party's organizational resources and legitimacy.[21]

The historian E. P. Thompson once said that social movements have a lifespan of about six years. The Tea Party didn't quite make it that long. After 2010, the movement went into decline, and by 2014, it had largely ceased to exist. There were no more large, nationally coordinated days of action like the tax day protests. Protests themselves largely faded, as remaining Tea Party groups tended to hold meetings instead. Now that the GOP had a majority in the House, institutional politics held out greater promise. As one Tea Party organizer related, protest became "much less important, because even though those are exciting, they don't change anything." After 2012, as conflict between the Tea Party and more establishment Republicans became more open, its favorability dropped among conservatives. By 2014, as Patrick Rafail and John D. McCarthy conclude in their exhaustive study of the movement, "the roar of the Tea Party rapidly became a whisper, with more than 90% of local chapters ceasing all visible signs of activity."[22]

Koch Habits

Charles and David Koch had been important figures on the American right for decades by the time Obama came to office. However, before the late 2000s, their involvement had always taken place at arm's length from the Republican Party. That began to change towards the end of the Bush administration, and just a few years later, by 2012, they, and the network of organizations they stewarded, would be some of the most powerful players in the Republican ecosystem. Their rise, however, further marginalized the party itself as a decision-maker.

The Koch brothers inherited right-wing politics from their father, a petrochemical entrepreneur and founding member of the John Birch Society. In the 1970s and 1980s, most of the brothers' energy went into the Libertarian Party and the libertarian think tank, the Cato Institute. In 1984, they founded Citizens for a Sound Economy (CSE), an activist group that campaigned for a balanced budget and the abolition of Social Security. During the 1990s, the group pioneered the business model that the US Chamber of Commerce would later adopt under Thomas Donohue, effectively renting its mobilizing capacities out to various corporations. Since the group was incorporated as a nonprofit, these donations were not public record. However, in 2000 a *Washington Post* reporter obtained documents revealing the group's donors. When CSE mobilized against Clinton's cigarette tax proposals, it received a $1 million donation from Philip Morris. When it pushed for telecom deregulation, it received $1 million from a phone company. When it began campaigning against action on climate change, it received money from ExxonMobil. And when it took on antitrust regulations, Microsoft was happy to chip in.[23]

In the early 2000s, Citizens for a Sound Economy split, resulting in Americans for Prosperity, which was still controlled by the Koch brothers, and FreedomWorks, which was led by Dick Armey. Armey had been the head of CSE since leaving Congress in 2003. However, conflict emerged between the Kochs and Armey in late 2003, and in 2004 the group fell apart. Armey continued to run FreedomWorks on the CSE model, lobbying for firms that had hired the law firm at which he worked, DLA Piper. The Koch brothers, however, began developing a different model. Americans for Prosperity quickly established a more robust organizational presence, with state-level directors in fifteen states by 2007, covering states where 47 percent of the US population lived. Around the same time, they launched the Koch seminars, described at the beginning of this chapter. The fundraising from these seminars quickly reached astronomical levels. In 2007–2008, Koch seminars raised under $100 million in pledges. By 2011–2012, it was over $400 million, equaling what the RNC, the NRCC, and the NRSC *combined* raised. By 2015–2016, their fundraising hit nearly $800 billion, *triple* what the three GOP national committees were raising. By this time, the various Koch organizations, powered by this deluge of cash, employed more than 1,200 people, three and a half times more than the three national Republican committees.[24]

The Kochs used this funding stream to get more involved in GOP politics. In 2004, CSE organized volunteers to collect signatures for Ralph Nader's presidential campaign, clearly hoping he would siphon votes from John Kerry. In 2008, the brothers founded a group called Wellspring. Incorporated as a nonprofit, like CSE, it was not required to disclose its donors. They hired a former RNC official, and used the group to channel over $7 million to other Koch network groups like Americans for Prosperity. Using Wellspring, the Kochs quickly found themselves near the power center of the Republican Party. The group's director met regularly with officials from the Chamber of Commerce and took part in coordination meetings held by Freedom's Watch, a group run by Karl Rove allies and funded by Sheldon Adelson. After Obama's victory, Wellspring was cut loose from the network, but proof of concept had been established. Over the next two years, Americans for Prosperity was the main vehicle for Koch network influence. It was involved in supporting Tea Party mobilization and in 2010 spent heavily on advertising and canvassing to attack Democratic candidates. In 2011, the Kochs created the Freedom Partners Chamber of Commerce, which acted like Wellspring in serving as a hub for the distribution of funds of different groups. The Freedom Partners Chamber of Commerce, however, worked on a far higher level, spending over $230 million in 2011 on grants to Americans for Prosperity, super PACs supporting Mitt Romney, and anti-Obamacare groups. In 2015, they founded the Freedom Partners Action Fund, allowing them to buy political ads directly, rather than providing grants to other groups.[25]

With all of these funds and organizational resources, the Kochs quickly became a major force inside GOP politics. They began throwing their weight behind candidates who embraced their agenda of budget cuts, regulation rollback, and union disempowerment. In Wisconsin, the Kochs helped elevate Scott Walker by using AFP to host massive rallies. Never technically endorsing Walker (which would have been a violation of their nonprofit status), the organization nevertheless contributed mightily to raising his profile around the state and mobilizing volunteers. In Massachusetts, Koch money helped Scott Brown defeat Martha Coakley in the special election to fill Ted Kennedy's Senate seat, depriving the Democrats of their filibuster-proof majority. In 2010, they provided funding for much of the GOP freshmen class of 2010, the most conservative in Congress's history. By 2012, a David Koch–hosted fundraiser for Mitt Romney attracted a wide swath of ambitious Republican politicians, from Jon Kyl of Arizona to Bob McDonnell of Virginia. They used this influence to push the party sharply to the right, working alongside Tea Party organizations to enforce a far more conservative line among GOP politicians.[26]

In creating this network, the Kochs have effectively mobilized an important segment of capital to support the Tea Party and extreme free market politics. There has been some resistance to recognizing this point, with some scholars arguing that "there is little evidence that capitalists lead, finance, or direct the growing populist right." Yet a closer examination of Koch network's funders reveals a substantial contingent of leading capitalists. Far from the small employers of right-wing mythology, many Koch funders were owners or managers of massive enterprises. The 2010 seminar, whose list of attendees was leaked to the media, included Steve Bechtel (of the venerable anti-union construction firm Bechtel), Ken Langone (co-founder of Home Depot), Gary Rogers (former chair of Levi Strauss), Rick Sharp (CEO of Circuit City), and Alan Boeckmann (CEO of the engineering firm Fluor). A number of major figures from finance also attended, including Steven A. Cohen, Paul Singer, and Stephen Schwarzman. More systematic research confirms the extensive support for Tea Party politics among the capitalist class; big business was more likely to donate to Tea Party candidates than individual members of the Fortune 400 were. Far from the work of a few rogue billionaires, the Republican Party's sudden lurch to the right under the Obama administration was the result of a substantial group of American capitalists organizing to support a different kind of conservative politics than what had been practiced by the Bush administration.[27]

While Republicans were certainly glad to have the resources the Koch network supplied, the rise of this network of organizations who were unaccountable to the party and its officials created a series of problems. At the most basic level, the Koch network competed with groups like the RNC for funds. Indeed, at a 2013 Koch seminar, a presenter made this argument explicitly, contending that Americans for Prosperity had developed a voter mobilization machine that was more effective than either the RNC or Mitt Romney's campaign committee. As the journalist Steven Vogel, who attended the seminar, recounted, the message was clear : "the Koch operation was a better steward of the donors' cash than ... the official Republican Party." Around the same time, in the GOP's postelection "autopsy" report, the party leadership complained that "The current campaign finance environment has led to a handful of friends and allied groups dominating our side's efforts. This is not healthy." The report even went so far as to "push hard for campaign finance reform that would help the RNC return to its rightful position as the national Party leader." Like the Tea Party, which it supported, the Koch network had helped the GOP recover from 2008, but in doing so, it further marginalized the party itself as a decision-maker.[28]

Karl Rove's Second Act

By 2007, Karl Rove was used to being around money. For four decades, he had been attached to the Bush clan, ever since George H. W. Bush had elevated him from the College Republicans to the RNC. He had married into a wealthy family in the Bushs's social world, and had been George W. Bush's consigliere as his administration sought to accomplish the ultimate fusion between corporate power and the Republican Party. In the last years of Bush's administration, however, Rove found himself, for the first time in a great while, on the outside looking in. Under investigation for a leak that had exposed a CIA analyst's identity, Rove had become more of a liability than an asset for a lame-duck administration. He resigned in August of 2007.

Rove had always imagined himself as the Mark Hanna of the modern GOP, attempting to emulate what William McKinley's chief fundraiser had accomplished in cementing three decades of virtually unbroken Republican rule. After his resignation from the Bush administration, he would continue in this endeavor. But whereas Hanna had raised funds for the Republican Party, Karl Rove would, in the 2010s, help to develop the new ecosystem of political money, in which super PACs, unburdened by contribution limits, would begin to eclipse the party itself.[29]

Rove's first experiment as an outside spender came with the organization Freedom's Watch, a nonprofit set up to support Bush's troop surge in Iraq. Funded by Sheldon Adelson, and managed by Bush administration veterans like former press secretary Ari Fleischer, the group planned to spend tens of millions of dollars on advertising supporting the administration's strategy. Its organizers, however, had plans to go beyond the surge, and hoped to turn the group into a "Johnny Appleseed" of the right, acting as a central funder and providing grants to other groups. Rove himself was never officially involved with the group, though there is considerable evidence that he acted as an advisor. Soon after its founding, Rove's protégé Carl Forti became its head, and it shifted away from pure issue advertising to more direct electoral efforts, preparing to be a major force in the 2008 elections. It also began to host meetings coordinating strategy between outside groups like the Chamber of Commerce, the Club for Growth, and even the Koch brothers' Wellspring Committee.[30]

As impressive as this effort was, however, it could hardly make up for Obama's small-donor advantage and the general collapse of the Republican project in 2008. Freedom's Watch folded shortly after McCain's loss. Nonetheless, the project had proved substantial sums could be raised for projects outside of the party. As one member of its board said, the group "provided a model for [American] Crossroads and everything that came later." Rove and his allies began planning a new project. The opportunity to launch it came in early 2010, when the Supreme Court handed down its decision in *Citizens United v. FEC*. Within a few weeks of the decision, Rove and his allies were in Texas, pitching their new network of organizations to the members of the Dallas

Petroleum Club, which included long-time financiers of the right like T. Boone Pickens and Harlan Crow. The network would consist of American Crossroads, a new super PAC; the American Action Network, which would be a 501(c)(4) like Freedom's Watch; and Resurgent Republic, which would be a polling firm. Rove sold the project as meeting the right's need to organize in response to Obama, observing that "people call us a vast right-wing conspiracy, but we're really a half-assed right-wing conspiracy. Now, it's time to get serious."[31]

Rove's designs were partially a response to the tribulations of the RNC. After Obama's victory, the RNC selected former Maryland lieutenant governor Michael Steele as its new chair. The first African American RNC chair, Steele had plans to broaden the party's appeal. However, he lacked the kinds of connections to donors that the role required and proved a spectacularly maladroit leader. Within a few months of winning the position, he had declared abortion "an individual choice" in an interview and managed to start a feud with Rush Limbaugh. Soon, major donors were forsaking the RNC, and its cash flow withered.[32]

For Rove, Steele's incompetence was an opportunity. American Crossroads brought together a number of major GOP operatives. Carl Forti was given American Crossroads itself. Fred Malek, who had been McCain's chief fundraiser, was put in charge of the American Action Network. Crossroads GPS, a new group organized as a 501(c)(4) and thus free of the requirement to disclose its donors, was headed by Steven Lew, a former aide to Mitch McConnell who had recently headed up the Chamber of Commerce's efforts to defeat labor law reform under Obama. Former RNC heads Mike Duncan and Ed Gillespie were also involved. With this team, Rove began telling Republican donors that they should cut the RNC off and give their money to him instead.[33]

Rove's network threw itself into the 2010 midterms. One of its first moves was to back Sharron Angle, a Senate candidate in Nevada. A Tea Party favorite, Angle had won an unanticipated primary victory; she would now take on Senate Majority Leader Harry Reid. Angle was hardly Rove's sort of Republican. Gormless and impulsive, she called unemployed people "spoiled" in the midst of the recession and advised pregnant rape victims to try and turn what "was really a lemon situation into lemonade." Yet American Crossroads soon came to Angle's aid, spending $120,000 on attacks on Reid. By doing so, Rove helped ingratiate American Compass with the Tea Party, placing it firmly on the side of the anti-Obama wave that was gathering.[34]

Overall, Rove's strategy in 2010 was to target the Senate first and the House second. By June, American Crossroads and Crossroads GPS had targeted eleven Senate races. As the race entered its final month, it became clear that the GOP had a strong chance to retake the House, and so the Crossroads network broadened its spending into a number of House races, forcing Democrats to spend more in response in places they hadn't counted on needing to defend. Overall, Rove's groups spent about $60 million on independent expenditure campaigns during the elections, accounting for about a third of total independent expenditures for the GOP. In total, Rove's groups alone spent nearly 80 percent of the total that the party committees spent on independent expenditures during the midterms.[35]

Within a year of *Citizens United*, Karl Rove's network was close to eclipsing the Republican Party in its ability to provide outside spending on races. This posed, in some ways, less of a threat than the Koch network did, since Rove's network was deeply intertwined with GOP officialdom. Once Reince Priebus beat Michael Steele for RNC chair in 2011, the party and the PAC went out of their way to emphasize their cooperation. Moreover, American Crossroads stayed out of primaries, adopting a position of neutrality in intraparty fights. Nevertheless, Rove's group contributed to the diminishment of the party itself. It competed for funds and staff and served as an example of what money outside the party could do. In seeking to reestablish Republican dominance, Rove could not help but undermine the party itself.[36]

Containment: The Fight Against Obama's Policy Agenda

The GOP carried out their plan of total opposition. Obama's three major legislative priorities for his first term were the economic stimulus plan, healthcare reform, and financial reform.

Across the three bills that resulted, Obama garnered a grand total of three Republican "yea" votes in the House and two in the Senate. Yet the Republican strategy of total opposition also revealed the split in opinion among corporate elites, for even as Republicans fought Obama's agenda ferociously, it won significant support from many business leaders.

Obama's first major legislative push was for an economic stimulus bill. The economy had contracted violently as the financial crisis developed, and by the time Obama took office, the unemployment rate was already nearing 8 percent. Economists estimated that a stimulus bill of at least one trillion dollars was required to get the economy back near capacity, but that was quickly dismissed as politically impossible. Instead, a package that cost a little over three quarters of a trillion dollars was assembled, and of this, about 35 percent were tax cuts, which were rather less efficient at restoring economic growth than funding public services.[37]

Business support for the stimulus bill was strong. Even before Obama was inaugurated, the Business Roundtable put out a statement calling for "bipartisan legislation to support economic growth through a stimulus package designed to boost consumer confidence and increase business investment to help mitigate the potential for a recession." The Chamber of Commerce was also strongly supportive, kvelling after the legislation's passage that "since the elections, we've worked with the president ... to quickly pass a bill that would apply a defibrillator to the economy and shock it back to life." The NAM got in on the action as well. Amidst economic collapse, Obama's stimulus program won wide approval from business.[38]

Support, however, was not universal. Americans for Prosperity and FreedomWorks both mobilized against the bill, buying ads and organizing demonstrations. AFP started running ads against the stimulus within forty-eight hours of Obama's inauguration, and eventually collected over 500,000 signatures against it. The networks around both groups worked closely with the GOP, whose resistance was total. When the Democratic chair of the House Appropriations Committee asked the ranking Republican what GOP members would like to see in the bill, and what they could live with from Democrats, he was summarily rebuffed. There was, quite simply, no version of the bill Republicans could live with. Because of Democratic majorities in the House and Senate, however, the bill passed anyway.[39]

Obama's healthcare reform bill followed a very similar trajectory, though here the Chamber of Commerce would play a different role. Healthcare reform had been a Democratic priority for decades by the time Obama took office, and the new president believed he had both the political capital and the political intelligence to succeed where Bill Clinton had failed. Obama built his healthcare plan around what Mitt Romney had passed in Massachusetts a few years earlier. The centerpiece of the plan was a mandate requiring people to buy health insurance if they didn't already have it. By providing a guaranteed market to insurance companies, the administration could then extract various cost savings from the industry without automatically pushing them into total opposition to the bill. Crucially, corporate support for this kind of policy had been building. The Massachusetts plan had been designed with extensive input from business organizations in the state, and in 2007, the national Business Roundtable announced its support for a national mandate. The health insurance industry was also on board.[40]

The GOP, however, was determined to defeat the bill, and they were joined by the same groups that had opposed the stimulus. The Koch network had begun mobilizing against healthcare reform after Randy Kendrick, a multimillionaire attendee of the 2009 seminar, had delivered a histrionic plea for other attendees to take up the fight against Obama's legislation. She soon set up her own nonprofit, the Center to Protect Patient Rights, which began channeling money to other Koch groups. Americans for Prosperity spun off a group called Patients United Now to organize protests. Dick Armey's FreedomWorks, with funding from Philip Morris, MetLife, and other corporations, was intimately involved in organizing activists to disrupt events by Democratic politicians by railing against a federal takeover of American medicine. These kinds of theatrics succeeded in hardening popular opposition to the legislation.[41]

These groups were soon joined by the Chamber of Commerce.

The Chamber had remained noncommittal on reform until the fall of 2009, when it began a massive advertisement and lobbying campaign against healthcare reform. In the third quarter of 2009, it spent $39 million on lobbying—more than it had spent in the first six months of the year. Much of this money, subsequent reporting revealed, came from the group America's Health Insurance Plans (AHIP), the health insurance business association. Even as AHIP was publicly declaring its support for reform, it was funneling huge amounts of cash to the Chamber to carry out an aggressive campaign aimed at stopping the bill. These funds totaled $86.2 million, over 40 percent of the Chamber's budget for 2009. The insurance industry had come to loggerheads with the Obama administration in negotiations over cost savings. When the administration persisted with the plan, the insurers publicly continued to profess support but began funding the Chamber of Commerce to tank the bill. Because donations to the Chamber are not public record (they were revealed by journalists), the insurers believed they could shield themselves from any blowback caused by opposing the bill. As formidable as the campaign against healthcare reform was, however, it was insufficient to overcome Democratic majorities in the House and Senate.[42]

Rollback: The 2010 Midterms

Though the GOP failed to stop Obama's first-term priorities, the mobilization of activists and funds achieved during 2009 and 2010 prepared the groundwork for the 2010 midterms. By late 2009, Republicans were growing optimistic that they could retake the House in the midterms and at least restore the filibuster in the Senate. Obama's approval ratings were already hovering near the 50-percent mark, the unemployment rate was at 10 percent, and the Tea Party mobilization had restored vigor to conservatism after its near-death experience in 2008. Scott Brown's victory in Massachusetts in late January provided further evidence that a GOP wave was building.

This optimism did not, however, lend itself to an esprit de corps among Republicans. 2010 would see a record number of primary challengers in Republican races. In 2006, in the last midterm elections, there had been about 350 funded challengers in the GOP primaries. In 2010, there were more than 750. The Tea Party was a major force behind the mushrooming of candidates. Districts with more Tea Party events were more likely to have more candidates in the primary. And Tea Party affiliation proved to be a valuable resource. Candidates who were affiliated with the Tea Party did significantly better in the primaries than candidates who were not.[43]

Many of these Tea Party primary candidates weren't simply contesting open seats; they were challenging Republican incumbents. In South Carolina, incumbent Bob Inglis, with over a decade in office, was unseated by Trey Gowdy. While Inglis himself had been supported by the Koch brothers earlier in his career, his increasing liberalism on climate policy made him an enemy. The Kochs supported Gowdy, and Americans for Prosperity mobilized behind him. In Utah, Bob Bennett, who had been in office nearly two decades, lost to Mike Lee, who was funded by FreedomWorks and the Club for Growth. Finally, in Alaska, Joe Miller, with the backing of Sarah Palin and Tea Party Express, beat incumbent Senator Lisa Murkowski (though Murkowski would win the general election as an independent).[44]

In open races without Republican incumbents, the party establishment also fared badly. In particular, a number of NRSC-endorsed primary candidates lost to Tea Party candidates. In Kentucky, Rand Paul, son of Tea Party godfather Ron Paul, beat Mitch McConnell's preferred candidate by 23 points. In Colorado, the establishment backed Jane Norton for Senate; she was also supported by both the NRSC and the Chamber of Commerce, in one of the very few primary races in which the business group intervened. Her challenger, Ken Buck, was backed by the 501(c)(6) Americans for Job Security, which was funded by the Kochs' Center to Protect Patient Rights. Buck won narrowly. In some of these establishment-insurgent contests, the differences between the candidates were only superficial. In Florida, the NRSC tried to intervene early in the state's Senate primary and endorsed former governor Charlie Crist, a prodigious fundraiser. Marco Rubio, then a state legislator with close ties to Jeb Bush and a reputation as a centrist, had also declared a run. The party right took umbrage at the NRSC's intervention on behalf of Crist, and Rubio took advantage of their resentment. He secured the endorsement of Jim DeMint, patron saint of GOP insurgents and ingratiated himself with the Tea Party. Rubio eventually built such a formidable campaign that Crist dropped out of the primary to run in the general election as an independent. In the process, Rubio learned that the rules for campaigning were changing: "People started realizing that in 2010. You didn't *need* the party."[45]

At the same time that establishment candidates were taking a drubbing in the primaries, the extra-party networks were launching their plans for the midterms. As mentioned above, the Koch network intervened aggressively in the GOP primaries, supporting numerous insurgent candidates. Rove's American Crossroads, by contrast, stayed out of the primaries, as for the most part did the Chamber of Commerce. All three groups, however, worked closely together in the general election to deliver majorities to the GOP. The Chamber had begun running ads against a public option for healthcare in July of 2009, and by the fall the group was moving into a stance of pure opposition to the administration. In March, it announced plans to spend $50 million on the midterms. Americans for Prosperity joined them in June with plans for $45 million. At this point, the Chamber, the Koch network, and the Rove network were all coordinating. The Chamber sent representatives to the meetings of Rove's groups and to the Koch summits. The Kochs sent their operative Sean Noble, who ran the Center for the Protection of Patient Rights, to meetings at American Crossroads' office in New York. Rove concentrated on Senate races, while the Koch network focused on the House. Taking full advantage of the latitude *Citizens United* gave independent expenditure groups to coordinate with one another as long as they were technically independent of the candidates' campaign committees, the extra-party networks produced a campaign apparatus that was anything but half-assed. Together, conservative independent expenditures massively outpaced liberal ones. The two biggest Democratic independent expenditure (IE) campaigns were by the unions SEIU and

AFSCME, who together spent about $24 million, only two thirds of what either the Chamber of Commerce or American Crossroads spent.[46]

The combination of a devastated labor market, Tea Party mobilization, and the newly opened floodgates of political money led to a massive GOP victory. The Republicans gained sixty-four seats in the House, giving them a 242 to 193 majority, and took six Senate seats, reducing the Democrats' majority to fifty-three. The Tea Party played a key role in this victory. First, it revitalized the party by facilitating its rebranding. Looking at public opinion data, Gary C. Jacobson concluded that "insofar as Tea Party sentiments influenced voting in the 2010 elections, they helped all Republicans equally, not just those considered Tea Party favorites." However, there is also strong evidence that the Tea Party mattered in a more local sense as well. Districts with more Tea Party organizations showed higher votes for Republicans than comparable districts with fewer organizations. There is also good reason to believe that *Citizens United* provided a significant boon to the GOP by empowering corporations relative to unions when it came to political expenditures.[47]

Powered by the Tea Party and the GOP shadow parties, the congressional class of 2010 was the most conservative in modern history. Of Republican freshmen, 77 percent were more conservative than the median Republican in the preceding Congress. While Newt Gingrich's Republican Revolution had produced a massive lurch to the right in the House, the movement was even bigger in 2010. The Republican Study Committee, a right-wing caucus set up by New Right activists in the 1970s, had only a minority of the House as members for decades. By the 112th Congress, 70 percent of Republicans had joined up. Immediately following the election, FreedomWorks hosted a two-day retreat in Baltimore for newly elected GOP representatives to steel them against the inevitable pressures for compromise to which they would be exposed.[48]

But if the 2010 midterms delivered nearly everything the various conservative plotters had hoped for after Obama's election, they also exposed the problems the new forces around the GOP were creating. Particularly in Senate races, where candidates had to appeal to broader audiences than in more homogeneous House districts, Tea Party candidates who had succeeded in the primaries crashed and burned in winnable general elections. In Colorado, Delaware, and Nevada, candidates manifesting various combinations of political inexperience, ideological radicalism, and sheer incompetence lost their races. Even before November, some Republicans were expressing reservations. Trent Lott, former Senate majority leader and now a lobbyist, complained, "We don't need a lot of Jim DeMint disciples." One Chamber of Commerce official noted cautiously, "Some of the politics of the Tea Party and legislative practicalities just don't match up." Though the Tea Party and the Koch network had helped restore the GOP to power, they were also creating new fissures in the party that would only widen over the next few years.[49]

Remaking the GOP

The Republican majority of the 112th Congress shared a great deal with its predecessors in the 104th Congress, who took power in the Republican Revolution of 1994. Like Newt Gingrich's famous freshmen, they had taken Congress back from the Democrats —though ending four years of Democratic rule in the House was rather less impressive than ending four decades of it. They also tended to view themselves as an ideologically coherent block, defining themselves in opposition their supposedly more timid precursors. But while the class of '94 was often a headache for Gingrich, the 104th Congress marked the beginning of an unprecedented period of intraparty conflict in the GOP. Three Speakers of the House—John Boehner, Paul Ryan, and Kevin McCarthy—would each be brought down by conflicts with the party right.

At the same time, the conservatism that was introduced into the party by the 2010 midterms would spread throughout the party in this period. While the Tea Party was often identified as the dynamo powering this process, in truth the group quickly faded in importance. The policy conflicts engendered during this process would lead, particularly after the 2012 midterms, to counter-organizing by Karl Rove and the Chamber of Commerce, who felt that the intransigent right was both costing the party seats with its primary challenges and preventing the party from acting as an effective opposition. These efforts appeared to be succeeding, though the conflict that developed between the establishment and insurgents in this period ultimately set the stage for Donald Trump's ascent.

Faction Fights

The Tea Party in Congress signaled its intentions from the very beginning of its time in Congress. Shortly after the election, Michele Bachmann went to John Boehner's office and demanded a place on the House Ways and Means Committee, one of the most powerful in Congress. Bachmann, who had only been in Congress since 2007 and had recently attached herself to the Tea Party, would not normally have been considered for such a powerful post, and Boehner initially denied her. However, Bachmann countered by threatening to tell Fox News and talk radio that "John Boehner is suppressing the Tea Partiers who helped Republicans take back the House." Boehner had no choice but to cave. In his words, "She had me by the balls. She had all the leverage in the world, and she knew it." Though Boehner had himself been one of Gingrich's barn-burners and had attempted to ingratiate himself with the Tea Party in various ways, he was viewed as part of the establishment and therefore part of the problem.[50]

In fact, Boehner's efforts to ingratiate himself with the Tea Party set up the most damaging intraparty conflict of the 104th Congress. As part of the House rules package that is approved at the beginning of every new Congress, Boehner had agreed to eliminate the "Gephardt Rule." This rule allowed budget resolutions, which mandated spending, to automatically increase the debt ceiling as necessary, without the need for a second vote allowing an increase in the national debt to pay for the mandated spending. The House Republicans had eliminated the rule under Gingrich, helping precipitate the 1995 government shutdown, and after the Democrats restored it in 2007, were now eliminating it again. As the total debt approached the debt ceiling in the spring of 2011, House Republicans again sought to use the threat of a default, in which the Treasury would stop making payments on Treasury bonds, to force the Obama administration to make spending cuts.[51]

Though Boehner agreed with trying to force some spending cuts in return for raising the debt ceiling, the party's right settled on demands that the Democrats would not accept, including a balanced budget amendment. The Treasury Department had set August 2, 2011, as the date on which it would no longer be able to pay the bills without additional borrowing. Throughout the spring and summer, House Republicans (joined by a few Senate intransigents) held out for their maximalist demands.

They were joined in this campaign by the Koch network. Charles Koch published an op-ed in the *Wall Street Journal* lamenting that the cuts being demanded by House Republicans weren't deep enough. Americans for Prosperity launched a pressure campaign to dissuade lawmakers from accepting any compromise Boehner reached with the Obama administration. At one point, Boehner even traveled to New York to meet with David Koch and begged him to "call off the dogs." The Kochs were joined by the Club for Growth. The Chamber of Commerce, the NAM, and the Business Roundtable, meanwhile, sent a letter in support of Boehner, warning of the economic consequences uncertainty about the reliability of the US national debt would bring. The fractures between different sectors of business in the Republican coalition were widening.[52]

Most significant of all, however, was the dog that didn't bark: Wall Street. Finance had perhaps the most to lose from a debt default. The downgrading of US Treasury Bonds would wreak havoc with portfolios all over the world, which were built on treating T-bonds as the safest asset in existence. Yet financial firms were putting virtually no effort into lobbying Republicans to support a deal to raise the debt ceiling. This certainly wasn't for lack of capacity. After the passage of Dodd-Frank in July 2010, financial firms had gone on a lobbyist hiring spree. Richard Hunt, president of the Consumer Bankers Association, declared, "This will create more jobs than the jobs stimulus bill." Yet at the same time, both executives and lobbyists were telling journalists that they were "steering clear of the debt debate with the exception of trying to gather intelligence to pass along to their clients." At the same time, finance was building close links with Tea Partiers in Congress, who were committed to repealing Dodd-Frank, at one point making it a condition of raising the debt ceiling. Concentrated monomaniacally on rolling back the thin layer of oversight that had been enacted in the aftermath of the financial crisis, Wall Street bet that they could put all their efforts into rolling back Dodd-Frank, and that the pressure to avoid a default would, even without their lobbying, be strong enough to avert financial catastrophe.[53]

It was the right bet. In late July, Boehner agreed to pass a debt ceiling deal that depended on Democratic votes to pass, effectively bypassing the intransigent wing of his party. Doing so put his speakership on life support. Boehner, always partial to priapic imagery, summed up the difficulties of his position: "It's hard to negotiate when you're standing there naked. It's hard to negotiate with no dick." The fight also hurt the party's right. In July, it was revealed that the executive director of the Republican Study Committee, a conservative House caucus led by Tea Party favorite Jim Jordan, had been working with outside groups to target wavering Republican representatives. At a Republican conference meeting, members excoriated Jordan and the RSC and called for the staffer to be fired. More generally, they had failed to cap spending and failed to prevent tax increases from being a part of the debt ceiling deal. Because the bill ultimately relied on Democratic votes to pass, it was more liberal than what a united Republican conference would have produced.[54]

In 2013, Republicans used a similar funding deadline to attempt to repeal the ACA, leading to a government shutdown in October. Initially, Boehner and Cantor outlined a strategy to the Republican Conference in which the House would hold a vote on defunding Obamacare and would then vote on funding the government, with the second vote not contingent on the outcome of the first. The House Republican leadership was promptly booed out of the room by their own caucus. Boehner, in particular, was worried about his speakership. At the beginning of the 113th Congress, nine Republicans had refused to support his candidacy. As some of the main features of the ACA, such as the online healthcare exchanges, were set to begin operating in the fall of 2013, opposition to the law among conservative groups grew massively. The Koch network spent heavily on advertising and events decrying the law. In August, Representative Mark Meadows began circulating a letter promising to hold government funding hostage to defunding the ACA. Heritage Action, the 501(c)(4) of the Heritage Foundation, headed by Jim DeMint, ran ads in the districts of Republicans who hadn't signed the letter, raising the threat of primary challenges.[55]

Boehner and Cantor attempted to hold out against this pressure but ultimately caved. Boehner was frank with his members, telling them, "The president, the vice president, Reid, Pelosi—they're all sitting there with the biggest shit-eating grins on their faces that you've ever seen, because they can't believe we're this fucking stupid." But the new ecosystem of the shadow parties had changed the balance of power in the House. As one Republican operative told the journalist Steven Vogel, "As a congressman, you went against the Speaker or you went against the party structure? Forget it. You wouldn't get funded, and if you got reelected, they'd lock you out of the bathroom. They can't do that anymore. Now everybody is an independent actor. Everybody has their own funding, and you'll get even more if you tweet 'Boehner just lowered the boom on me and I told him to go fuck himself.'" In September, Boehner told the insurgents he would follow their plan, holding government funding hostage to defunding the ACA. On October 21, without a funding resolution, a government shutdown began.[56]

But Boehner's instincts had been correct. There was no chance the shutdown would end by defunding Obamacare. First, Democrats still controlled the Senate. When the House passed a funding resolution that included defunding the ACA, the Senate simply stripped that language out and sent the bill back to the House. Second, the same coalition of business groups that had opposed the debt ceiling standoff in 2011 once again assembled to express its opposition to a government shutdown. The Chamber, the Roundtable, the NAM, and other groups expressed their appreciation for the effort Republicans made to cut the budget but signaled their disapproval of inducing a government shutdown.

Third, as in the government shutdowns of Gingrich's era, the public blamed the GOP. Even the Koch network distanced itself from the shutdown, with Koch Industries releasing a statement clarifying that "Koch has not taken a position on the legislative tactic of tying the continuing resolution to defunding Obamacare nor have we lobbied on legislative provisions defunding Obamacare." Americans for Prosperity supported the shutdown but said it was out of broader concerns about government spending, rather than a specific attempt to defund the ACA. As the impossibility of defending the defund position became clear, Mitch McConnell was able to negotiate a compromise with Joe Biden, ending the shutdown.[57]

The post-2010 congressional right escalated the discord that had broken out in the GOP ranks during George W. Bush's second term. More confident after their success in the mid-terms and bolstered by a rapidly growing ecosystem of extra-party groups, they succeeded in forcing John Boehner to accommodate their impulses. In doing so, however, the party's intransigent right also increasingly polarized the party establishment against them. From 2012 until 2016, the establishment looked for ways to reassert control over the party.

The Establishment's Last Stand

As the party headed into the 2012 elections, a familiar problem for the party's insurgent wing resurfaced. While the Tea Party and associated forces had succeeded in taking over much of the Republican Conference in the House, they were no more successful than their predecessors on the party's right in producing viable presidential candidates. Various figures who hoped that by kissing the ring they might win the Koch network's considerable largesse presented themselves to the brothers. Rick Perry attempted such a supplication, but he botched it when he counted down his four key points by holding up five fingers, "only to be left with one digit still waving in the air, programmatically unaccounted for." Sean Noble, chief Koch apparatchik, was attempting to get Paul Ryan, author of the austerity budget around which the entire party was rallying, to jump into the race, but Ryan demurred, saying he preferred a vice presidential nomination. The Kochs were charmed by New Jersey governor Chris Christie, but after some coquetry, Christie decided against a presidential run. A network of donors to the Koch network decided they liked Mike Pence of Indiana, who combined Tea Party economic policy with Christian right views on social issues, but Pence had already committed to running for governor of Indiana. Michele Bachmann (who had founded the Tea Party Caucus in the House), former Pennsylvania Senator Rick Santorum, and even Newt Gingrich, who exited his political retirement for one last dance, all also attempted to represent the party right but none could generate a wide enough base of enthusiasm to unite the conservative wing of the party behind them.[58]

The party establishment, however, had consolidated early around Mitt Romney. In the fall of 2010, veterans of Romney's 2008 campaign had established a new super PAC, Restore America's Future, to support Romney's ambitions in 2012. One of the figures they recruited to steer the new vehicle was Carl Forti. Forti had been Romney's political director in 2008 and was currently the political director for Rove's American Crossroads network. Though American Crossroads officially stayed neutral in the primary, it was clear which way its operatives were leaning. Romney's super PAC dominated early fundraising. By the beginning of 2012, it had already raised $30 million, twice as much as the super PACs supporting Obama and the rest of the Republican field combined. In the early primaries, Romney dominated with the traditional Bush electoral base of affluent, college-educated suburban voters.[59]

Yet the new GOP ecology prevented Romney from achieving an early lock on the nomination. A number of candidates had managed to attract the backing of individual billionaires, who could single-handedly fund a super PAC that would keep a candidate on the airwaves and in the race, even when losing contest after contest. Rick Santorum, a dour religious zealot, secured the backing of Foster Friess, an investment manager who had long funded the Christian right. Though Santorum polled in the single digits for much of early 2012 and raised negligible funds for his campaign committee, a super PAC funded by Friess embarked on a major advertising buy before the Iowa caucuses, running ads that feted Santorum as a "visionary that saw and understands the threat of radical Islam." These ads helped push Santorum from an also-ran to a second-place finish.[60] Newt Gingrich also secured a patron in Sheldon Adelson, the casino billionaire. Adelson had been a longtime donor to the GOP and pro-Israel groups— George W. Bush once memorably described him as "this crazy Jewish billionaire yelling at me"—and had connections with Gingrich going back to the 1990s. After a few position adjustments on Gingrich's part—for example, announcing that he now favored clemency for a Jewish American who was convicted of spying for Israel and whom Gingrich had earlier described as "one of the most notorious traitors in U.S. history"—Adelson opened his wallet for Gingrich's campaign, ultimately pumping over $20 million into Gingrich's super PAC. These super PACs turned the candidate committees themselves into background players, as independent expenditure groups outspent them two to one in the Iowa contest.[61]

The super PACs injected an extra dose of chaos into the Republican primary. Santorum was able to stay in the race until April, despite failing to win even 25 percent of delegates. Gingrich's role was even more destructive. He attacked Paul Ryan's budget as "right-wing social engineering," prompting a backlash from most of the rest of the party. Gingrich responded with his trademark megalomania: "The Republican establishment is anti-intellectual and anti-change … I'm running because I want to change the old order." Even worse, Gingrich zeroed in on Mitt Romney's days at the private equity firm Bain Capital, describing the business model as "rich people figuring out clever legal ways to loot a company." This line of attack would be quickly picked up by the Obama campaign and used to devastating effect by his super PAC, Priorities USA. Romney could at least count himself lucky that one agent of chaos was sitting out the campaign—Donald Trump. After amassing considerable political capital with the Republican right for his advocacy of the birther conspiracy theory, he had decided not to run in 2012, concluding that the Paul Ryan austerity budget was an albatross around the party's neck. He would go on to trademark "Make America Great Again" the week following Romney's defeat.[62]

By late April, however, Romney's delegate lead was insurmountable, and the general election campaign began. Romney moved to consolidate his support with the party's right. During the primaries he had pledged obeisance to the Tea Party, denying that climate change was caused by human activity and introducing a budget proposal that was very close to Paul Ryan's. In return, the Koch network went all out for Romney, ultimately spending over $400 million on the 2012 elections. Notably, Americans for Prosperity redirected its spending away from congressional races, spending almost exclusively on the presidential contest. American Crossroads and Crossroads GPS came close to the Koch network, spending about $325 million. Romney's campaign was also able to rack up massive donations from the energy industry and the financial industry, both of which were eager to cast off the regulatory yolk the Obama administration was placing on them.[63]

Backed by this kind of money, the Romney camp confidently expected a win throughout most of the campaign. Paul Ryan, nominated for the vice presidency, told his wife and children to prepare to move to Washington. Obama, however, had his own sources of money. The president won big with telecom, software, and pharmaceuticals—all sectors his administration had built relationships with, both overt and covert, during his first term. What's more, the Obama campaign's network of super PACs showed far greater discipline and coordination than the GOP's. They had a rigid division of labor, in which Priorities USA handled negative advertising for the president, while one super PAC each covered the House and Senate. The groups coordinated so closely that they even formed an umbrella fundraising group so that donors could write one check to be split among the different organizations. Analysis of super PAC spending on Senate seats revealed extraordinarily tight coordination on the Democratic side, while groups like FreedomWorks and American Crossroads pursued quite different agendas. Overall, the rise of the super PACs resulted in the first election in which outside groups outspent the parties themselves, $2.5 billion to $1.6 billion.[64]

The Democrats' organizational advantage, combined with Romney's inability to manifest a personality trait other than wealth, led the Democrats to a significant victory in 2012. Romney and Ryan, convinced by their in-house polling that Obama was about to be a one-term president, were shocked by the results. In Ohio, a key state for Romney, he won fewer votes than McCain had in 2008. In the House and the Senate, Democrats picked up seats. In the Senate, the Republicans once again lost seats as a result of the right. In Indiana, a primary campaign driven by FreedomWorks and the Club for Growth had unseated longtime Senator Richard Lugar. His replacement, Richard Mourdock, would go on to lose the general election after he blurted out that "life is that gift from God ... even when life begins in that horrible situation of rape." In Missouri, Todd Akin, who was from the party right but did not have strong links to the Tea Party, lost after making similarly impolitic comments on the subject.[65]

Following the election, the GOP establishment moved aggressively to reassert control over a right wing that it blamed for the defeat. In December 2012, Boehner removed four particularly intransigent representatives from their committee assignments, in a move that was widely interpreted as a shot across the bow to the party's right. Before the election, Steve Scalise had been campaigning to be the next chair of the Republican Study Committee, the base of the party's right in the House for nearly half a century, on the basis of a more constructive relationship with the party leadership. After the committee's current leadership, led by Jim Jordan, unanimously selected another bomb thrower to lead the group, Scalise used an obscure bylaw that allowed him to force a committee-wide vote for leader. Ironically, Tea Party primary challenges had moderated the RSC by forcing less conservative members to join it for conservative credibility. With over 170 members, nearly three quarters of the entire Republican Conference had joined. Scalise won the vote, prompting Jim Jordan and his allies to create the invitation-only Freedom Caucus in 2015. Even Paul Ryan changed tack, walking away from the austerity budget that had defined him politically to push a compromise proposal backed by Boehner. The Tea Party Caucus, meanwhile, had stopped holding events in summer 2012, and its membership was declining. Outside the House, RNC head Reince Priebus commissioned a report on the defeat, which quickly became known as the "autopsy" report.[66]

Outside the party as well, the right was reeling. Two days after the election, the conservative radio host Sean Hannity told his listeners, "We've got to get rid of the immigration issue altogether," and endorsed a path to citizenship for undocumented people already in the country, a policy he and the rest of the right had been stigmatizing as amnesty since 2005. Exit polls revealing that Romney, who had adopted the right's stance on immigration, had won only 27 percent of Latino voters, terrified conservatives. FreedomWorks, the Tea Party's most important organization for electoral interventions, had suffered a split between its two most important leaders, Dick Armey and Matt Kibbe, which culminated in Armey showing up at the headquarters with a pistol and attempting an armed coup. Armey failed and went into exile, leaving the group soon after. Karl Rove, meanwhile, was abandoning his stance of neutrality on Republican primary elections. In early 2013, American Crossroads launched the Conservative Victory Project, which would intervene in primaries following a maxim coined by William F. Buckley, Jr.: "support the most conservative candidate who can win." After the government shutdown, the Chamber of Commerce also announced its intention to begin contesting Republican primaries to protect establishment candidates from challenge. Dirk Van Dongen, formerly the Bush administration's main operative in the business community, told the *New York Times*, "there's a lot of talk around town about the need for Republicans to get into primaries and protect people who are being attacked because they are only 96 percent pure."[67]

Heading into the 2014 midterms, the GOP leadership was confident that it had the party's intransigent wing on the run. Karl Rove and the Chamber of Commerce were playing an unprecedented role in GOP primaries, spending big to defend legislators who would play ball with the leadership. But throughout the first half of 2014, the party establishment was struck again and again by events that made it queasy. First, near the beginning of the year, John Boehner had met with Roger Ailes, the CEO of Fox News, to ask him to stop giving so much airtime to the craziest figures in the GOP, like Steve King and Louie Gohmert.

The meeting ended with Ailes ranting about how Obama was a Muslim who had Ailes under round the clock surveillance. Then, in June, Eric Cantor, the House majority leader, lost his primary to a right-wing challenger, mainly over Cantor's insufficiently fervent advocacy of anti-immigrant politics. Finally, in Mississippi, the establishment had to work overtime to keep Senator Thad Cochran from losing. To fend off the challenge, Haley Barbour's political machine turned to black Democrats in Mississippi, who were able to vote in the state's open primary. The Chamber of Commerce chipped in by recruiting Brett Favre, not yet embroiled in allegations of misappropriating welfare funds, to cut an ad for Cochran. Cochran won, but by a very slim margin.[68]

Overall, however, the establishment had done well. The party's right had targeted six incumbent senators in the primaries, and the challenges had been beaten back in all six. This year, at least, there would be no more Richard Mourdocks. The Chamber of Commerce had intervened heavily in the primaries, spending nearly $20 million. The Chamber's senior political director, Scott Reed, summarized the group's stance succinctly: "We called them 'the Caveman Caucus,' and we needed to crush them."[69]

Ultimately, the elections were a major success for the Republicans. They picked up nine Senate seats, finally granting them control of the chamber for the first time in Obama's presidency. They also improved their standing in the House. Karl Rove was eager to spin the results as vindication of his perspective, writing in the *Wall Street Journal* that "Voters delivered messages Tuesday to both the president and to the GOP. Republicans would be wise to heed their message first and better."[70]

Yet on a systemic level, the election delivered a more ominous message. Once again, outside spending had surpassed party spending. In 2014, however, candidate fundraising and national committee fundraising both declined compared with 2010. In 2012, Obama and Romney each had their own super PACs. In 2014, there were ninety-four single-candidate super PACs operating, according to the FEC. The balance of power between the parties and the shadow parties was growing even more lopsided.[71]

This surge in outside spending, much of it powered by a vanishingly small number of ultra-rich individuals, was accompanied by one of the largest drops in voter participation in American history. The voter turnout was lower than any midterm since 1942, when World War II depressed voter turnout. As Thomas Ferguson and Walter Dean Burnham pointed out, in many states, voter participation reached levels not seen since the early nineteenth century, before the advent of modern political parties. The tectonic plates of American politics were moving, but few could have predicted the earthquake to come.[72]

6

A Hostile Takeover of
the Republican Party

Most books written about the recent history of the Republican Party are, in one way or another, an attempt to explain Donald Trump's presidencies. This one is no exception. Trump's reign begs to be explained. His lack of political experience, his boorishness, his extraordinarily chaotic administrations, his attacks on free and fair elections, and his unprecedented hold on the Republican Party following his 2020 defeat all represent clear breaks with presidential precedent. As more than one interpreter has observed, Trump's presidency has tended to frustrate existing social scientific schemata, appearing as a chimeric combination of different paradigms.[1]

Compounding the problem of interpreting *how* Trump ruled is the highly uneven nature of *what* he accomplished in his first term. On the one hand, Trump's triumph in the Republican primaries and in the general election were some of the most stunning victories in American political history. Similarly, Trump initiated a new, more protectionist phase of American political economy. His domination of the Republican Party, even after his defeat, is also without parallel in American history. At the same time, however, Trump failed in some truly spectacular ways. His promise to repeal Obamacare was never fulfilled. His signature issue of controlling immigration saw no significant new legislation, and his attempts to accomplish it via executive order led' only to court challenges and reversals. Trump's healthcare and immigration initiatives led to a massive defeat in the 2018 midterms, guaranteeing that any dramatic legislative initiatives were off the table in the second half of his term. Worse still, 2019 and 2020 were consumed by investigations and an impeachment that were all entirely self-inflicted. Finally, Trump's attempts to overturn the 2020 election results, culminating in the abortive putsch of January 6, failed utterly, tainting the GOP and plunging Trump into new depths of historical ignominy.

This unusual combination of victory and defeat flowed from the particular position of the Republican Party as it entered the 2016 election season and the way Trump himself was able to take advantage of it. Split since 2010 by two well-organized factions, the party found its relationship to its voters changing. While in 2008 and 2012, GOP primary voters had coalesced around the candidate who seemed best positioned to defeat the Democrats, by 2016 the constant factional warfare had degraded the ability of party elites to deliver cues to voters. Moreover, GOP voters were themselves turning against the orthodoxies of both the establishment and the Koch network. Both factions supported free markets, entitlement cuts, and immigration reform. But GOP voters were souring on all three. Neither side of the Republican civil war saw the terrain changing under its feet. Trump, by contrast, had an almost instinctual understanding of where Republican voters were going. At the same time, the increasingly extreme rhetoric of the GOP, inflamed by the Tea Party, prepared the party's base to embrace the candidate whose declaration of war on liberalism seemed the most emphatic.

Stepping into a party whose warring elites were out of touch with its base, Trump was able to consolidate something quite unusual in American politics—a strong degree of personalist rule over a political party. After Trump won the election, opposition to his rule was consigned to the margins of the party, where it has remained for the better part of a decade. In much of the country, the Republican Party believes what Donald Trump says it believes and supports what Donald Trump supports. Drawing on his ability to command media attention, Trump has forcibly cowed most Republicans who have attempted to challenge him, turning even his bitterest rivals into mewling supplicants.

Trump's success in establishing personalist rule over the GOP, however, led him to attempt to govern the American state in a similar fashion, producing the many dramatic failures of his administration. The American state, trisected by Madisonian design, is deeply ill suited to personalist rule. Passing legislation requires negotiation with congressional parties, over which the president has no direct authority. Executive orders are subject to judicial review. The massive federal bureaucracy requires coordinated direction, which Trump was unable to provide. This is part of why Trump's reign has appeared chimerical—he combined successful personalist rule over a party with a failed attempt to exert personalist rule over a state. Unable to simply steer the ship of state himself, Trump's first term ultimately resulted in a fairly traditional Republican set of policy outputs—a large tax cut, environmental deregulation, and a conservative judiciary.

The Prophet Unarmed

Heading into the 2016 primaries, both the Republican establishment and the party's insurgents had reason to feel confident about the upcoming contest. The party as a whole was in a stronger position than it had been even at height of the Bush administration in 2003–2005. The party's congressional majority was larger than it had been at any point since the 1920s, when the Republicans held Capitol Hill and the presidency for a decade straight. This dominance also extended down to the state level, with nearly half the country living in states with total GOP control of state government. Only about 15 percent lived in states with total Democratic control. Reince Priebus, the head of the RNC, had also modified the primary calendar, shortening the nominating window and reducing the number of debates in order to minimize intraparty conflict and produce a strong nominee as quickly as possible.[2]

On the establishment side, Karl Rove and his comrades were confident they could build on the momentum of the 2014 midterms. They had beaten back nearly every primary challenge that year and had been rewarded with a Senate majority for the first time since 2006. After the election, the insurgents tried to take over the Republican Study Committee, nominating Mick

Mulvaney for its leadership. He was beaten, however, by Bill Flores, a former energy company executive who ran on continuing the cooperative relationship with John Boehner's team that Steve Scalise had established during his time as head of the committee. Among the electorate, support for the Tea Party, even among conservatives, was lower than ever. On the presidential level, Jeb Bush was positioning himself to win the primaries before they even began. His super PAC, Right to Rise, was announced in January 2015, before Bush declared his candidacy. Because Bush was not technically a candidate, he was able to fundraise directly for his super PAC, evading the strictures against coordination that the FEC still upheld. By June of 2015, he had raised over $100 million. The goal was that numbers like that would act as a kind of "shock and awe" campaign against possible rivals, pushing them out of the race well before the primaries began. A Bush victory in the 2016 general election, the establishment hoped, would crush the insurgency and reunify the party.[3]

Yet the insurgents also had reasons to be hopeful. At the beginning of 2015, House members launched another challenge to Boehner's speakership, this time winning twenty-four votes, the most votes against a candidate for Speaker of any majority party since the Civil War. Afterwards, insurgents like Jim Jordan and Mark Meadows began putting a new caucus together. This one would be by invitation only in order to protect it both from the kind of dilution that, in the insurgents' view, had rendered the RSC useless and from ridiculous figures like Louie Gohmert and Steve King, who would only taint its efforts. They called it the House Freedom Caucus. With more than thirty members, the Freedom Caucus had the power to split the GOP's majority, forcing Boehner to come to the table with them. After several months of the Freedom Caucus sabotaging various leadership initiatives, John Boehner resigned his speakership in October, rather than be deposed by the insurgents. He was replaced by a reluctant Paul Ryan, who only stepped in after it was clear that Kevin McCarthy didn't have the votes.[4]

Outside the party, insurgents were also gathering strength. The Koch network was recentralized after 2012. No longer would huge amounts of money flow to consultants, like Sean Noble, running outside groups. Instead, the Kochs planned to run every-thing in-house. The Freedom Partners Chamber of Commerce would be the main funding vehicle for the network. IT and HR services would become the Center for Shared Services. i360, a for-profit voter-data analysis firm the network ran, would handle number crunching and voter targeting. Its operation had grown so successful by 2015 that many Republican candidates were turning to it rather than the RNC for their data analysis. Alto-gether, the network employed more than 1,200 full-time workers, more than triple what the RNC, NRSC, and NRCC had. The Kochs' ambitions for 2016 were massive. At the beginning of 2015, they announced plans to spend nearly $900 million on the 2016 elections. This would eclipse what the RNC would spend on the race and bring the Koch network close to parity with what the individual candidate campaign committees would spend in the general election.[5]

Both sides of the GOP civil war were preparing for battle on a scale never seen before. Another combatant, however, was about to enter the field.

The Greatest Infomercial in the History of Politics

Donald Trump had flirted with running for president for some time. Going back to the 1980s, he had told interviewers what a great president he would make. In 2000, he had launched a short-lived candidacy for the Reform Party nomination. As the Reform Party gambit might suggest, Trump displayed little in the way of a settled political ideology and donated frequently to politicians in both parties. This began to change during the Obama presidency, as Trump drew closer to the GOP. In 2010, he donated $50,000 to Rove's American Crossroads. In 2011, he gave a speech at the Conservative Political Action Conference (CPAC) in which he attacked OPEC and China for manipulating trade, fueling rumors that he was planning a 2012 run. Shortly thereafter, Trump began promoting the birther conspiracy theory, insinuating that Obama had not been born in the United States. Very quickly, Trump became one of the most prominent proponents of birtherism, which elevated his credibility with GOP voters. Eventually, after observing that Paul Ryan's austerity budget proposals were a significant political liability to the party, Trump decided not to run. His influence in the party was nevertheless such that Romney's campaign manager traveled to Trump Tower to meet Michael Cohen, Trump's fixer and lawyer, to secure an endorsement.[6]

After Romney's defeat, Trump began positioning himself to run in 2016. He started donating primarily to Republicans and made a quarter-million-dollar donation to the Republican Governors Association. In January 2015, he showed up at the Iowa Freedom Summit, an event hosted by Iowa Republican Steve King that was widely viewed as a warm-up for the Iowa caucuses. In Iowa, he had breakfast with Newt Gingrich, whom he peppered with questions about running. In June of 2015, he announced his candidacy. At this point, however, he was still not considering the presidency to be the end goal. Rather, it was primarily an exercise in self-promotion. As he reasoned, "What's the worst thing that happens? We lose? So what? This can be the greatest infomercial in the history of politics." One of his early campaign aides recalled that "he would say this will be the greatest branding exercise of all time."[7]

The 2016 GOP primary field was crowded, but there were really only three candidates besides Trump who had a serious chance at winning. As described above, Jeb Bush sought to raise so much money from the corporate coalition that had backed his brother that he would simply run over any competitors. Marco Rubio, Jeb's old protégé, was also running. Rubio had long sold himself as a kind of bridge between factions in the GOP, popular with Tea Party types but also willing to work with the establishment. As such, he ran an everything to everyone campaign, never consolidating enough support to lead the polls but maintaining a high enough level of support to have hopes of leapfrogging to the front when someone else dropped out. Finally, Ted Cruz ran as the candidate of the party insurgents, appealing to both the Tea Party and the Christian right. He launched his campaign at Jerry Falwell's Liberty University (the same place John McCain had signaled his supplication to the Christian right a decade earlier) and very quickly put together a formidable data and fundraising operation, with a network of super PACs whose war chest was second only to Bush's.[8]

From the time of the first GOP debate, in August of 2015, Trump had been a clear favorite in polls. The question of how to respond to this fact shaped the actions of all other actors in the party going forward. Reince Priebus, as head of the RNC, was actually more worried about Trump losing than him winning. His nightmare scenario was Trump dropping out of the GOP race, running as an independent in the general, and handing the election to Hillary Clinton. To prevent this from happening, Priebus wanted to make Trump sign a loyalty pledge to the Republican Party, guaranteeing he would not run as an independent. In point of fact, Trump had no intention whatsoever of running as an independent, a formidable enterprise in a country with ballot access laws as restrictive as the United States', but he used the resulting speculation to keep himself at the center of the conversation and to make Priebus squirm. Eventually, Trump agreed to sign a piece of paper, but by making Priebus come to Trump Tower for the signing, he left little doubt over whose victory it was.[9]

Both Jeb Bush and Ted Cruz, meanwhile, held off on attacking Trump. Bush's campaign, seeing Cruz and Trump as competitors for the most right-wing GOP voters (a misunderstanding of Trump's base in the party, as we will see), thought it best they fight it out between themselves. Mike Murphy, the chief strategist for Bush super PAC Right to Rise, explained that "Cruz has the grievance issue ray gun ... and we know he's going to use it on Trump, who's very vulnerable." The Bush team did not want to get bogged down criticizing Trump. Cruz, meanwhile, thought Trump was a flash in the pan, stirring up the kind of resentment politics that Cruz's sophisticated campaign operation would have no trouble harnessing. And so, Cruz went out of his way to praise Trump, telling crowds, "I like Donald Trump. I'm glad he's in the race. I think he is having many beneficial effects on the race." Trump, he argued, was only "renting" his supporters. Yet as Cruz would soon learn, with Trump, possession is nine tenths of the law.[10]

The truce between Trump and Cruz broke down, as it inevitably would, in the midst of the Iowa caucuses. The day of the caucuses, CNN mistakenly reported that Ben Carson, a neurosurgeon running as a minor candidate in the primary, had dropped out. Cruz's sophisticated media monitoring and messaging apparatus immediately blasted communications around the state encouraging Carson supporters to caucus for him instead. Cruz ended up winning, and Trump came in second. While there is little evidence that the Carson mishap affected the results, Carson cried foul, and Trump immediately joined him, calling on the Iowa GOP chairman to disavow Cruz's victory. Bush, meanwhile, had taken eighth place, with 2.8 percent of the vote. The next week, in New Hampshire, Trump won by a twenty-point margin, cementing his place as the front-runner and putting Bush's campaign on life support.[11]

At this point, the question of how to stop Trump became the animating issue in GOP politics. In January, a new super PAC, called Our Principles, launched with the aim of stopping Trump. Funded by longtime GOP donors like financiers Paul Singer and Thomas Stuart Ricketts, it aimed to crush Trump under an avalanche of negative advertising. On the other side of the party split, Marc Short, the president of the Freedom Partners Chamber of Commerce, held a meeting with Charles Koch to mobilize the network against Trump. However, other senior managers at various Koch enterprises vetoed the move, arguing that the firm's reputation was becoming increasingly politicized. Short promptly resigned from Freedom Partners and went to work for Rubio's campaign. In the Koch network more broadly, disquiet at Trump's victories mounted, but support was divided between Cruz and Rubio and never coalesced around an alternative.[12]

Without these coordination problems and poor strategic decisions by other campaigns, it is unlikely that Trump would have won. Ultimately, he won only about 40 percent of votes cast in the Republican primaries. With Priebus (against the advice of other RNC officials) going out of his way to accommodate Trump, and Cruz and Bush both holding off from attacking him, Trump was essentially given a free ride in the second half of 2015. Bush and Cruz's failure to coordinate was itself an artifact of the intense factionalism that had developed in the GOP. Cruz in particular was widely despised across the party for his self-promoting pyrotechnics against the party leadership. In this sense, Trump's victory in the GOP primaries was a product of a weak party, whose divisions themselves reflected divisions among the wealthy capitalists who financed the shadow parties.[13]

Trump had other advantages as well. His media footprint was nothing less than titanic. Analysts estimate that Trump's domination of media coverage netted him nearly $5 billion worth of time on the airwaves. After the first GOP debate, the Chamber of Commerce's political strategy shop found that 82 percent of online discussion was about Trump. Trump was also the beneficiary of more direct aid from media figures. In March of 2016, Ted Cruz was his last rival standing, and two Fox News contributors called the Cruz campaign to tell them, "We're not allowed to say anything positive about you on air." Cruz would later muse, "I think it was Roger [Ailes's] dying wish to elect Donald Trump president."[14]

The message was as important as the media. Trump presented a combination of political stances that simply did not exist in the GOP before his candidacy. The autopsy report on the 2012 election had argued that the economic policy of the Mitt Romney campaign—itself based on Paul Ryan's slash and burn budget—was basically fine and that the problem was that anti-immigrant politics were costing the party votes. Tea Partiers and their political scions, meanwhile, argued for even more aggressive action against the welfare state. But, as Theda Skocpol has pointed out, both of these agendas were growing increasingly remote from the hearts of GOP voters, who were becoming more skeptical of entitlement cuts and more hostile to immigrants and multiculturalism. In 2015, shortly before Trump entered the race, a poll revealed that three fifths of Republicans had "very little" faith in party leaders. Trump fit this niche perfectly. He promised to "save Medicare, Medicaid, and Social Security without cuts," denounced trade deals like NAFTA, and attacked immigrants with unprecedented vitriol. Crucially, this distinguished Trump from candidates linked to the Tea Party, like Ted Cruz. Counties that had had lots of Tea Party activism or were represented by a Tea Party congressmember were actually less likely to vote for Trump. One study found that, among the major GOP candidates, Trump was the only one more likely to win voters whose perceptions of the national economy and their own finances was negative. In the GOP primaries, Trump was offering a policy agenda that sharply distinguished him from the rest of the field; it turned out that a substantial plurality of the GOP electorate was supportive of it.[15]

Finally, Trump triumphed over his rivals because he was simply the most anti-liberal figure in the primary. Before 2016, American politics had been increasingly characterized by what political scientists call negative partisanship—feelings of hostility towards the other party. In public opinion, while people's evaluation of their own party remained largely stable, their assessment of the opposing party grew increasingly negative.[16] In the Republican Party, negative partisanship was inflamed by the Tea Party, whose vituperative attacks on Barack Obama portrayed him as a kind of apocalyptic figure come to bury the America they once knew. Throughout the early 2010s, deeply negative rhetoric became standard in the Republican Party, paving the way for a candidate whose attacks on Democratic politicians eclipsed previous standard-bearers in their abusiveness. As Thomas Massie, a GOP representative who was himself excluded from the Freedom Caucus for being too volatile, put it, "All this time, I thought they were voting for libertarian Republicans. But after some soul searching, I realized when they voted for Rand and Ron and me in these primaries, they weren't voting for libertarian ideas—they were voting for the craziest son of a bitch in the race. And Donald Trump won best in class."[17]

Trump's victory in the 2016 GOP primary was an unlikely outcome, and one that few predicted. But it was deeply rooted in the political dynamics that had taken root in the party since 2008. The deep split between the establishment and the insurgents made coordination to stop Trump difficult, if not impossible. The rise of the shadow parties masked the growing discontent with free market economics among the party's voters. And the incendiary rhetoric pioneered by the Tea Party and largely financed by the Koch network created a ready audience for Trump's particular style of politics.

A Pointillist Election

Donald Trump's victory in the 2016 election came as an even bigger shock than his victory in the primaries. The recipient of numerous lectures from RNC chair Reince Priebus informing him that he was headed for a historic defeat, Trump did not even have a victory speech written on election night. Such an unanticipated result has led to some exaggerated claims receiving more currency than is justified. Claims that Trump's election represented a turning point in voting behavior are not at all uncommon. Two such claims that have achieved prominence are that Trump's election 1) represented a turning point for the Republican Party, which had acquired a new, more working-class voting base; and 2) was the result of a massive surge in racism. Neither of these holds up to scrutiny. In fact, in the broadest outlines, Trump's election was extraordinarily ordinary. After two terms of Democratic rule, a Republican was elected after he narrowly managed to flip a few swing states. In this sense, Trump's election was like a pointillist painting, presenting a clear image from afar, but dissolving into chaos when examined closely.[18]

To see the chaos clearly, it is worth first addressing the predominant narratives. The argument that Trump had a unique appeal to the working class has been widely repeated both inside and outside the GOP. And while it is true that Trump improved his margins with working class voters in 2016, the GOP had been gaining ground with these voters for some time. Indeed, all the way back in 2005, conservative writers Ross Douthat and Reihan Salam had launched the "reformicon" movement with the declaration that the Republican Party was "an increasingly working-class party, dependent for its power on supermajorities of the white working-class vote." Trump's higher level of support from working-class voters continued a trend that began long before Trump's pursuit of the GOP nomination.[19]

Second, Trump did not ride a massive wave of white racial resentment into office. In fact, Donald Kinder, the political scientist who developed the most commonly used survey instrument for studying racial resentment, wrote in 2015 that "racial resentment is essentially stationary over the last quarter century ... We detect no sign here that White Americans' racial resentments

hardened during the Obama Presidency." Indeed, the most sophisticated versions of this argument acknowledge as much, arguing
that Trump did not catch a new wave of American prejudice so
much as activate existing "reservoirs" in a few key states. But
even this argument misses the key dynamics. It is true that voters
who expressed more racially conservative opinions in 2016 were
more likely to vote for Trump than voters expressing similar
opinions were to vote for Romney in 2012. However, Trump's
victory can hardly be explained in these terms, since the number
of voters expressing such views declined from 2012 to 2016. As
Justin Grimmer, William Marble, and Cole Tanigawa-Lau have
demonstrated, voters expressing high levels of racial resentment
were a smaller portion of Trump's voters than they were of Romney's. They conclude that "Trump's greatest increase in net votes
among Whites, compared to Romney, comes from those with
moderate racial resentment scores." While Trump certainly pulled
racist voters towards him more sharply than any candidate since
George Wallace, the declining number of such voters renders this
magnetism insufficient to explain his victory.[20]

Instead, to understand how Trump managed to win, it is
necessary to attend to the highly unusual specifics of Trump's
campaign. Of course, mistakes by the Clinton campaign also
played a role. In particular, Clinton's political advertising focused,
to an unprecedented degree, on her personal qualifications and
character, to the exclusion of policy. One study found that more
than 60 percent of her advertising focused on personal characteristics, while in no other campaign since 2000 has such
advertising constituted more than 20 percent of the total. For
a candidate as well defined in the public mind and as personally disliked as Hillary Clinton, this was a disastrous mistake.
But while Clinton's campaign certainly contributed to Trump's
victory, what is more salient is how Trump managed to bring
various parts of the Republican Party into his campaign and how
his message resonated.[21]

When Ted Cruz dropped out of the race on May 3, Donald
Trump became the presumptive Republican nominee. Most of the
party's officials were, at best, ambivalent about Trump. Senator
Jeff Sessions of Alabama had endorsed Trump in February, and

Trump had managed to secure an endorsement from only a single member of the Freedom Caucus: Scott DesJarlais, a former physician who was revealed to have slept with multiple patients and subsequently pressured them to have abortions. By April, more endorsements started to trickle in, but the party was clearly horrified at the choice its voters had made. Nevertheless, bridges began to be laid. In May, Karl Rove received a call from Steve Wynn, a casino magnate and sometime-friend-sometime-enemy of Trump's. Wynn had also been American Crossroads' biggest donor in its early years. Wynn told Rove: "Karl, kiddo, I talked to Donald and he wants you to write something nice about him." A week later, the two met in Wynn's Manhattan apartment, and Rove began to teach Trump the rudiments of electoral strategy (Trump had been under the impression that he was on track to win California). Rove also told Trump he should pick Mike Pence for Vice President.[22]

Choosing Pence was crucial for Trump. Mike Pence had carved out a successful career on the right flank of the Republican Party. He served in the House from 2001 to 2013, rising to chair of the Republican Conference during the first Obama administration. In 2011, when a group of GOP mega-donors from the Koch network asked Republican operative David McIntosh to find a candidate who could beat Romney in the primaries, he came up with Mike Pence. As we saw, however, Pence had already committed to running for governor of Indiana. Pence had been close to Koch network groups like Americans for Prosperity for years. He was also a deeply religious evangelical Christian, with close ties to the Christian right. Evangelicals had been lukewarm on Trump for much of the primary season. Choosing Pence was a way of bringing the Christian right on board. He was also an olive branch to other factions of the party. As a former member of the House leadership team, he had credibility with the establishment. As a fanatical free marketeer, he provided an entrée to the insurgents as well. For example, the Club for Growth, who had acted as the insurgents' battering ram in primaries in the early 2010s, had spent heavily against Trump in the primaries. But when Pence called McIntosh, now head of the Club, for advice on Trump's offer, McIntosh told him that accepting it was "a no-brainer."[23]

Despite this, however, Trump proved unable to achieve any real party unity. He spent much of the summer embroiled in disorder of his own making. His attacks on a Mexican-American judge who was presiding over the Trump University fraud case drew all but universal condemnation from Republican politicians, with Paul Ryan describing the comments as "the textbook definition of racism." Additionally, Trump was lagging far behind Clinton in the money race. With small donors, he was uniquely success-ful, for a Republican. Drawing on the RNC infrastructure that Reince Priebus had spent years developing, Trump amassed an unprecedented number of donors. By the end of August 2016, he had 2.1 million donors to Clinton's 2.3. But with the big donors in the post–*Citizens United* world, Trump was lagging badly behind where Romney had been four years earlier. Major GOP donors like the Kochs, Paul Singer, and Sheldon Adelson were not donating. Adelson, the largest donor in the 2012 election, had promised to spend $100 million on the race in May. But by the end of August, despite endorsing Trump, he still had not put up the money. The campaign's finances were so dire following the RNC that a number of employees responsible for policy brief-ings quit after not being paid. For a moment, it looked like the campaign was not going to make it to October.[24]

Trump needed an angel investor. He found several in the Mercer family. Robert Mercer had made hundreds of millions in finance beginning in the 1990s and had been a partisan of the far right in American politics since at least the Clinton adminis-tration. In the 2000s, his daughter Rebekah began steering the family foundation, which had previously supported charity and research, towards political causes. By the time of *Citizens United*, the Mercers had emerged as power players in the shadow parties, donating to American Crossroads and joining the Koch network. In 2012, at a conference put on by the Club for Growth, Robert Mercer met Andrew Breitbart, an entrepreneur in online political news. Mercer became a major investor in Breitbart's eponymous website. Shortly thereafter, Breitbart died of a heart attack, and the site's management fell to co-founder Steve Bannon, with whom Mercer soon established a close relationship. In 2016, the Mercers started by backing Ted Cruz. Robert Mercer donated millions to Cruz's super PACs, and Rebekah ran one of them, though she was increasingly critical of Cruz's campaign. When Cruz bowed out, they switched their support to Trump.[25]

The Mercer's role in the Trump campaign became absolutely crucial in mid-August. As the campaign was floundering, Trump met Rebekah Mercer at a Hamptons fundraiser hosted by the owner of the New York Jets. Mercer pressured him to fire his campaign manager, Paul Manafort, and bring in a set of operatives closely linked with her family. Kellyanne Conway, a former Pence advisor who had helmed one of the Cruz super PACs, became campaign manager. Steve Bannon was brought on as chief strategist. Finally, David Bossie, head of the conservative group Citizens United, which had won the 2010 Supreme Court case and was itself the beneficiary of the Mercers' largesse, became deputy campaign manager. The new leadership decided to focus on "Florida, North Carolina, Virginia, Ohio and Pennsylvania," reasoning that those states were where "Trump's appeal to working-class and economically frustrated voters has the best chance to resonate."[26]

This shake-up proved to be a turning point. First, it marked an end to Trump's attempts to reconcile with the GOP establishment. Bannon had been a fire-eater in the GOP's internal fights over the previous few years and was seen by party leaders as the kind of irresponsible element that cost them winnable Senate seats. Bannon would "position [Trump] as anti-establishment, the candidate of change, and the candidate who's anti-Washington." Second, Trump's campaign found a new source of cash, particularly from industries that would benefit from his protectionist promises, such as steel, rubber, and machinery.[27]

At the same time, for reasons that are not entirely clear, GOP mega-donors finally began opening their wallets to Trump in September. Thomas Stuart Ricketts, who had funded Our Principles, the anti-Trump super PAC, started donating to pro-Trump super PACs. Sheldon Adelson, after months of refusing to donate, finally kicked in $5 million to a pro-Trump super PAC.[28]

All of this was sufficient to keep the campaign afloat, but by the end of September, there were few who thought he could actually win. GOP donors increasingly looked to hold onto Capitol

Hill, writing the top of the ticket off as a lost cause. Even Adelson was directing $40 million to Republican House and Senate campaigns, far more than he was giving to Trump. Particularly after the *Access Hollywood* tape came out, in which Trump bragged about using his celebrity to sexually assault women, the Republican Party basically gave up on Trump. Reince Priebus, who had become a key campaign advisor, told Trump bluntly, "Either you'll lose in the biggest landslide in history, or you can get out of the race and let somebody else run who can win." Paul Ryan thought about withdrawing his endorsement of Trump and was only convinced not to by Kevin McCarthy's argument that it would hurt the GOP in House races. Senate Majority Leader Mitch McConnell argued the RNC should stop spending on the presidential campaign and put all its funds into Senate campaigns to stop Clinton from appointing federal judges. Even the Freedom Caucus, looking at this point to depose Ryan, was working on the assumption that Trump would lose. Their plan was to blame the loss on the party's lack of support and use the opportunity to move against Ryan. The mood was so morose that Trump himself had planned to have his private plane gassed up and ready to fly to Monte Carlo for some high-roller gambling after his loss was announced.[29]

Trump ultimately won by an extremely thin margin. Clinton beat him by nearly three million votes in the popular vote, and his electoral college victory rested on fewer than 100,000 votes distributed across Wisconsin, Michigan, and Pennsylvania. Part of this stemmed from the failures of Clinton campaign. In Wisconsin, for example, Trump got fewer votes than Romney had in 2012. Clinton's support, however, particularly among black voters, dropped even more. But the evidence suggests that the chaos of Trump's campaign also, improbably, contributed to his victory. First, the massive flow of money to GOP Senate campaigns, itself partially a consequence Trump's slim chances, had a reverse coattails effect, helping to bolster Trump's own campaign. In October, it had looked like the Democrats might retake the Senate. In response, a group of super PACs closely linked to Mitch McConnell and Karl Rove began pouring money into races. With the NRSC almost out of funds, these shadow-party institutions carried the bulk of the load for the final stretch of the race. At the same time, there was a spike of dark money from 501(c)(4) groups, which unlike super PACs, are not required to disclose their donors, that eclipsed the amounts seen during the extraordinarily well-funded Romney campaign. Evidence from political betting markets suggests that this Senate spending benefited Trump as well. In the final two weeks of the campaign, odds for a Trump victory and for the GOP holding onto the Senate rose together. On election day, for the first time in American history, the Senate map and the presidential map matched exactly.[30]

Second, Trump's nationalist message, symbolized by the elevation of Steve Bannon in August, allowed him to speak to specific concerns in the Midwest that the Clinton campaign was not addressing. Though the move led GOP leaders like Priebus and Ryan to despair of getting Trump's campaign on track, the focus on economics and deindustrialization that Bannon advocated proved resonant in key states. Trump's angry insistence that American workers were getting a raw deal found a receptive audience in precisely the upper Midwest states he needed to win. As Mike Davis pointed out shortly after the election, in a number of counties that flipped from Democrat to Republican from 2012 to 2016, "a high-profile plant closure or impending move had been on the front page of the local newspaper: embittering reminders that the 'Obama boom' was passing them by." Subsequent academic research has tended to confirm Davis's insistence on the importance of economic geography. One research team found that commuting zones exposed to competition from China showed a clear shift to the GOP in presidential elections. Another group found that manufacturing layoffs led white voters in the same county to become more economically pessimistic and to vote more Republican; they concluded: "deindustrialization appears to be central to the white voter backlash that culminated in the surprising election of Donald Trump." The strategy Bannon had formulated in August focusing on Midwestern states and doubling down on economic nationalism had, with an assist from a shadow party terrified of losing the Senate, succeeded.[31]

Though the broad outlines of Trump's victory appeared normal, a closer look reveals a campaign unlike any in recent history. Aided by a Clinton campaign that drastically misread how to best sell its candidate, Trump managed to win, albeit on the thinnest of margins. Though the party had in no sense united around Trump, the determination to hold on to the House and Senate ended up propping up his disintegrating campaign. Moreover, the very message that repulsed much of the party was likely what allowed Trump to eke out his narrow victory. As Trump prepared to enter the White House, he thus faced two challenges: first, the normal work of governing, and second, the task of unifying a party that had spent the previous two years attempting to distance itself from him.

The Prophet Armed

Trump came into office facing skepticism from his own party, and vociferous opposition from the Democrats. The latter would remain constant throughout his presidency. The former, however, would change rapidly. By the 2018 midterms, Trump had consolidated a degree of personalist control over the Republican Party that was unprecedented for any party leader in American history. By personalist, I mean the degree to which a party's direction is under the control of a single person who uses the party to advance their own rather than the broader party's goals.[32] Under Trump, the Republican Party became a Trumpist party; even more extraordinarily, it has remained one after his defeat in 2020. Trump's consolidation of control filled in the vacuum created by the hollowing out of the party over the previous decade; it was also enabled by elites in the party who attempted, often successfully, to advance their own goals by accommodating Trump. Their support allowed Trump to effectively purge the party of anyone opposing his leadership. While the congressional party would frequently defy Trump on individual votes, almost anyone attempting to systematically push the party in a different direction was pushed out.

The president is not just a party leader, however. As recent work in political science has emphasized, the president is also the head of one of the world's largest bureaucracies—the federal government.[33] In this role, Trump attempted to operate in the same way he operated in the Republican Party: forcing supplication from subordinates and ruling by diktat. In essence, he attempted to operate as his own political enforcer, leading longtime Chamber of Commerce operative Scott Reed to comment that "[Trump] is the White House political director." But the federal government is hostile to such rule. Policies the president wishes to pass are subject to judicial oversight, and legislation must pass through Congress. Navigating these institutions requires the successful coordination of a large group of people. Trump, who enjoyed watching subordinates compete for his favor, was utterly uninterested in achieving this kind of coordination among his staff. As a result, Trump was largely unable to achieve the distinctive policy change he sought. Where he was most successful was where he pursued very standard GOP objectives, such as inegalitarian tax cuts and a conservative federal judiciary. Even in areas where he achieved a certain reorientation of policy, such as international trade, he was moving in concert with some very traditional GOP constituencies. This combination of unprecedented control over a party and a weak presidency is part of what made the first Trump administration so unique and difficult to understand.[34]

A New Patrimonialism

Personalism runs deep in Trump's political career. His electoral appeal was suffused with it. He often voiced his rather high opinion of his own capabilities. But more importantly, Trump argued that his position among the hyper-rich made him uniquely qualified to govern. First, in line with traditional Republican arguments comparing the government to a business, he emphasized his experience as a business owner. Second, Trump argued that his wealth allowed him to be politically independent of the monied interests that corrupt politics. As he bragged to voters in Iowa, "You know the nice part about me? I don't need anybody's money. They [lobbyists, donors] have total control over Jeb [Bush] and Hillary [Clinton] and everybody else that takes that money. I will tell you this: Nobody's putting up millions of dollars for me. I'm putting up my own money." Third, Trump argued that as part of the elite, he knew exactly how elites were screwing over ordinary Americans. Speaking in Pennsylvania, a state he would flip in 2016, Trump declared that "globalization has made the financial elite, who donate to politicians, very, very wealthy. I used to be one of them. I hate to say it, but I used to be one. But it has left millions of our workers with nothing but poverty and heartache." Trump argued that he was uniquely positioned to tell truth about what was happening to American workers, because he had been in the rooms where the decisions were made. Trump even tried to turn his campaign into a patrimonial enterprise like the Trump Organization. According to Rick Gates, one of his senior campaign staffers, Trump spent several weeks in mid-June of 2016 arguing that his daughter Ivanka would be the ideal vice presidential candidate.[35]

For most of the campaign, Trump was unable to rule the GOP on personalist grounds. Key figures like Ted Cruz refused to lend Trump their endorsement. Other officials, certain that he was headed for a loss, saw no point in tying themselves to him. A number of officials even rescinded their endorsements after the *Access Hollywood* tape came out. His unexpected win thus led to an awkward situation for party elites. Both the establishment and the insurgents reacted to it by attempting to tame Trump. Reince Priebus accepted the job of White House chief of staff, telling bewildered friends, "We need a sane voice in the Oval Office. There has to be a reasonable person in the room with him." Other supposed oppositionists operated on a similar logic. Marc Short, who had quit the Koch network when they refused to go all out opposing Trump, accepted a job as head of White House legislative affairs, taking responsibility for the administration's agenda in Congress. Trump's cabinet was similarly filled with a mixture of establishment figures, like Gary Cohn, a former Goldman Sachs executive who served as director of National Economic Council, and figures from the intransigent right, like Betsy DeVos, a Koch network donor who served as Secretary of Education. In this way, Trump's administration did not, initially at least, overcome the divide between insurgents and the establishment —it simply imported the divide into the administration. And since Trump was unconcerned with setting a clear line of march for his staff, intrigues and conflicts between different wings of the administration were ubiquitous.[36]

Outside the White House, the party also began to accommodate itself to Trump. With Priebus now in the White House, a new RNC chair was needed, and the post went to Ronna McDaniel, a Michigan RNC official who had been a Trump delegate, and was pushed by Priebus. Paul Ryan thought the best way to control Trump was to present him a ready-made legislative agenda that would leave him no room for deviations. Similarly, Mitch McConnell told Trump that his priority was appointing as many conservative judges as possible. The insurgents also sought alliances with Trump that could advance their agenda. Jim Jordan of the Freedom Caucus quickly figured out that Trump was strongly influenced by what he watched on Fox News every morning (which he often watched for several hours before starting meetings). Jordan told his aides to book him on the shows Trump watched; he explained, "Every time we were on TV, we weren't just talking to people in the television audience; we were talking to POTUS." Even the Koch brothers, who had remained cool to Trump throughout the entire election, began finding ways to work with the administration on deregulation and judicial appointments. This accommodation paid dividends, both political and financial. At the Trump International Hotel, which opened in Washington, DC, before the election, the top four clients in the first year were the Republican National Committee, Trump's campaign committee, the Republican Governor's Association, and a pro-Trump super PAC.[37]

At the same time that Republican officials were learning to accommodate themselves to Trump, they were also learning that opposing him was politically costly. A speaker at CPAC in February 2017 gave voice to the convictions of much of the Republican base when he declared, "In many ways, Donald Trump is the conservative movement right now. And the conservative movement is Donald Trump." Trump's ability to merge so thoroughly with the conservative movement was greatly facilitated by his use of Twitter to communicate directly with his followers. As he described his use of the site, "This is my megaphone. This is the way that I speak directly to the people without any filter." In just the first few months of the administration, Trump established that a Twitter attack from him could bring a great deal of unpleasantness into any Republican politician's life. When Freedom Caucus members were refusing to support Trump's ACA repeal bill, Mike Pence was sent in to straighten them out. After his tongue-lashing was finished, "several of the members, grown men, broke into tears, fearful less of disappointing the vice president than of winding up on the business end of a Trump tweet."[38]

Part of the reason Trump was able to exert such dominance over members of his party was that he pursued a unique approach to party building. As the political scientist Daniel Galvin has explained, since World War II, Republican presidents have been remarkably consistent in using their presidency to invest in building party capabilities and broaden their base of support. Reagan, for example, famously courted "Reagan Democrats," while George W. Bush pursued the Latino vote. Trump, however, displayed no similar interest in expanding his flock. Instead, he has sought "to swell the number of like-minded supporters who are active in electoral and party politics." On the one hand, this has minimized the pressure Democrats feel to cooperate with Trump's agenda. While a number of George W. Bush's priorities, from his tax cuts to Medicare Part D, passed with not inconsiderable Democratic support, Trump's strategy of looking only to his base created no such incentives. On the other hand, by looking only to his base, Trump has won their support more completely than any president in living memory. Because he did not attempt to win groups that did not already support him, Trump had no need for the kind of compromises that can sap enthusiasm from a base.[39]

By the time the 2018 midterms came around, Trump's control over the party was near total. Again, it is worth emphasizing that this does not mean that Trump never faced opposition from the party on individual issues. Rather, it means that virtually any attempt to change the direction of the party, or worse, side with the Democrats against Trump, was quickly quashed. In addition to Trump's use of his Twitter account to direct attacks against his opponents, he also used the RNC to ensure that the party was stacked at all levels with loyalists. Ronna McDaniel proved a loyal enforcer, dutifully denouncing Trump opponents. At the same time, White House officials played an active role in overseeing the leadership of state parties, announcing that "we are monitoring, tracking, and ensuring the president's allies are sitting at the top of state parties." As Galvin points out, this control extends downwards throughout the party, as "through the quiet politics of within-state candidate recruitment, Trump's loyal state party chairs are able to insure that only vocal, committed Trump supporters are recruited to run for office and receive the state party's valuable services and support." The Republican Party, already hollowed out by its competition with the shadow parties, proved unable to resist this takeover. Already by early 2018, scarcely a year into Trump's presidency, nearly 60 percent of registered Republicans said they identify more as supporters of Donald Trump than as supporters of the Republican Party. By the summer of 2020, the Republican National Convention featured seven speakers with the last name Trump.[40]

Yet if Trump was able, in a relatively short period of time, to achieve an unprecedented level of personalist domination over the GOP, his attempts to rule in a similar manner over the state resulted in a far more mixed record. Again and again, Trump would attempt to enact a policy on the basis of his authority, only to be stymied by actors from institutions outside the White House. For example, immediately after coming to office, Trump attempted to fulfill his campaign promise to shut down immigration from Muslim countries by issuing an executive order halting migration from seven largely Muslim countries for ninety days. Unconcerned with legal niceties, Trump rushed the order through, skipping the Justice Department review of executive orders, which examined possible legal weaknesses. He had also failed to coordinate the order with John Kelly, the Secretary of Homeland Security who would be responsible for enforcing it. As a result, there was no procedure in place to deal with people already on planes headed for the United States when the order was signed. The order was promptly challenged in court, and less than a week after it was issued, the court ruled against the administration, suspending most of the order. Similarly, in the summer of 2018, Trump pushed his new Homeland Security secretary, Kirstjen Nielsen, to take a tougher approach to deterring immigration via the southern border. Drawing on a plan developed by Jeff Sessions and Stephen Miller, Trump pushed Nielsen to begin separating children from families apprehended during border crossings. Though Nielsen and other cabinet members warned the administration was not prepared to implement such a policy, since it would require massive mobilization of the social services bureaucracy to care for children separated from parents, Trump insisted on putting it into action. Within a few weeks, the images of children living in hastily constructed camps or held in cages created a massive backlash, leading Trump to issue an executive order rescinding the policy. Though he had campaigned on addressing immigration, Trump's insistence on issuing policy himself, without institutional cooperation, meant that his signature policies were haphazardly enacted and easily reversed.[41]

Trump took an analogous approach to diplomacy. He described his diplomatic method to Japanese president Shinzo Abe: "I go in and I look the other guy in the eye and I make the big play and that's how I built my business empire—and that's why I am the greatest negotiator in the history of the presidency." Trump attempted to put this approach to work in dealing with North Korea. At first, in 2017, Trump reacted to news that North Korea was testing new missile systems with an escalating series to bellicose threats and personal insults against Kim Jong Un. In early 2018, North Korean officials began to signal increasing openness to further diplomatic initiatives, and Trump jumped at the opportunity to be the president who finally ended the Korean War. He seemed to believe that a certain quotient of flattery and charm would be enough to convince Kim Jong Un to abandon his country's nuclear weapons program. Trump's strategy was to schedule a meeting between himself and Kim, which would be the first meeting between North Korean and American leaders since Kim Il Sung came to power in 1946. Virtually the entirety of the diplomatic and defense establishment opposed such a move, since normally such a meeting would be the product of prior negotiations over exactly what kind of deal would be announced.

But Trump was convinced that his negotiating skills alone would be sufficient to resolve the conflict on the Korean peninsula, and he went ahead in the summer of 2018. The talks ended up produced nothing but vague commitments to denuclearization, and in 2019, further talks broke down, as it became clear the North Koreans would not significantly scale down their nuclear program without some real concessions from the United States, which Trump was not willing to give.[42]

Trump's personalist approach to diplomacy ultimately led to his first impeachment. Influenced by his lawyer Rudy Giuliani, Trump had decided that Ukraine's government needed to help him in his reelection campaign by launching an investigation to discredit Joe Biden, who had just declared his candidacy for the 2020 Democratic nomination. Biden's son Hunter had served on the board of a Ukrainian energy company, and Trump was hoping an investigation into the younger Biden's activities could help tar the elder as corrupt. Trump's pressure campaign began with various bureaucratic effronteries, such as refusing to send Mike Pence to Ukraine as part of a delegation to congratulate the new president, Volodymyr Zelensky, after his election, and holding up a White House meeting with the Ukrainians until they agreed to open an investigation. In June of 2019, however, Trump went even farther and paused the transfer over $400 million worth of congressionally-mandated military aid. At the end of July, in a phone call with the Ukrainian president, Trump responded to a request for further military aid with: "I would like you to do us a favor though." He went on to describe how he wanted the government to launch an investigation into Hunter Biden. Trump's insistence on diplomacy as a game of individual quid pro quos between countries' leaders and his refusal to recognize boundaries between electioneering and ruling formed the basis of the first impeachment trial against him. When the Democrats began moving towards impeachment hearings in the fall of 2019, Trump again undermined himself through personalist diktat by releasing the transcript of his call with Zelensky, believing, against the advice of all advisors, that it would exonerate rather than further incriminate him. The resulting impeachment investigation and trial would consume months of Trump's presidency, further weakening his administration's ability to achieve any other objectives.[43]

Finally, Trump was more concerned with receiving personal credit for things than he was in affecting policy. For example, after Hurricane Maria hit Puerto Rico, Trump prioritized a photo op in which he threw paper towels into a crowd. The federal response, meanwhile, was uncoordinated and insufficient for the magnitude of devastation. This same tendency manifested a few years later during another crisis. When COVID started spreading in early 2020, Congress began debating the economic stimulus legislation that would be necessary to counteract the massive disruption the pandemic would bring. Trump, who had stopped speaking to Nancy Pelosi after being impeached, played virtually no role in shaping this legislation. His one policy proposal, a payroll tax cut, never made it into the final legislation.[44] Instead of shaping the legislation, which was one of the most expensive spending bills in American history, Trump was instead focused on making sure his name was on the stimulus checks Americans would receive. By trying to make sure he received personal credit for various initiatives, Trump tended to actually weaken his influence.[45]

In some areas that were institutionally conducive to a personalist mode of operation, the administration achieved important political successes. Judicial appointments were a notable example. Here, Trump and Senate Majority Leader Mitch McConnell formed a close partnership, with Trump agreeing to appoint judges well disposed to McConnell's establishment conservatism and McConnell modifying Senate procedure to allow Trump's nominees to proceed through confirmation more smoothly. Because Trump was effectively preclearing his judicial choices with conservative legal activists, he could simply send his nominees to the Senate and rely on the Senate to confirm most of them without any additional lobbying, horse-trading, or coordinating on the part of the administration. The results of this partnership were impressive. Trump appointed three Supreme Court justices in a single term, swinging the court's balance sharply to the right. He also appointed 174 district court judges and fifty-four circuit court judges. These appointments flipped the balance of power in three of the circuit courts, so that now seven of twelve circuit courts lean conservative. While the results of Trump's judicial appointment strategy were impressive, they reinforced the general weakness of his personalist style in two respects. First, his success here was conditional on cooperation with McConnell and the conservative legal movement. He was not able to nominate whomever he pleased. Second, and as a consequence of the first weakness, Trump's judicial nominees did not represent any kind of break with the Republican Party of the pre-Trump years. While Trump certainly put his stamp on the federal judiciary, he was able to do so only because it so closely resembled that of his partisan predecessors.[46]

Trump's personalist approach to both party and government distinguished him from his predecessors. With the party, he achieved unprecedented success. In two years, he had thoroughly routed his opposition such that challenges to his power were all but impossible. With government, however, Trump's approach mostly failed to deliver policy results and repeatedly led to self-inflicted defeats. Because of this combination, the sociologist Dylan Riley is quite right to label Trump a "patrimonial misfit."[47]

The Revolution Betrayed

In terms of policymaking, Trump's first presidency represented continuity rather than change with the GOP of recent history. A failed attempt to roll back entitlements, a large tax cut targeted at the richest Americans, and an aggressive foreign policy against Iran would have been likely outcomes of a Mitt Romney presidency. In some areas, notably trade, Trump did pursue policies that were markedly out of step with the Republican Party of the past few decades. But even here, closer attention reveals that, rather than fundamentally reorienting the policy direction, he accelerated shifts that were already underway. Though Trump represented himself as a sharp break from previous Republican politicians—as did his Democratic opponents—his mode of operation repeatedly frustrated his ability to execute any such break. As the political scientists Jon Herbert, Trevor McCrisken, and Andrew Wroe put it, "Trump's improvised and instant decision-making damage[d] White House planning so badly that they amount[ed] to a surrender of power to other players in the political system." For the first two years of Trump's presidency, these other players were primarily the Republican majorities in the House and Senate. After the Democrats won a majority in the House in the 2018 midterms, Trump's ability to execute any kind of radical break was even more constrained.[48]

Coming into the White House, Trump's major policy priority was repealing the ACA. This did not represent a shift in GOP politics. Since 2010, the GOP-controlled House had voted more than fifty times to overturn the law. Trump, for his part, sold himself as a master negotiator who could, unlike previous Republicans, turn these votes into signed legislation. Yet from the beginning of his term, efforts to repeal the ACA spurred political infighting and ultimately fell apart. Leadership of the effort was handed over to House Speaker Paul Ryan, though the White House suggested a few vague policies. Ryan produced the American Health Care Act (AHCA), a synthesis of various Republican proposals over the previous few years. The AHCA canceled subsidies for insurance plans bought on the ACA's marketplaces (though the marketplaces themselves would remain) and not only canceled Medicaid expansion but converted Medicaid into a block grant. Near the end of February, Ryan began attempting to push his plan through the House.[49]

The plan encountered opposition from multiple angles. The ACA had facilitated a wave of mergers among hospitals and insurers, and trade associations for both groups waged an energetic fight against repeal. A number of Republican governors also came out against repeal, as repealing Medicaid expansion would eliminate what had become an important stabilizer for state budgets. Though the Chamber of Commerce supported the AHCA, making it a key vote for its voting scorecard, it does not appear to have engaged in the kind of intensive mobilization it did to stop the ACA's passage in the first place. The plan also encountered opposition from the right. The House Freedom Caucus, the Heritage Foundation, and the Koch network all argued that AHCA did not go far enough in repealing Obamacare, demanding an end to various consumer protections and taxes levied by the ACA.[50]

Negotiating this crowded field of interest groups delayed passage of the AHCA in the House until early May. In the Senate, however, the adjustments to the demands of conservatives in the House meant the loss of support from numerous GOP senators. Swayed by the arguments of their governors that the loss of the ACA's Medicaid expansion would be catastrophic, senators from a number of states announced their opposition to the Senate version of the bill. With these defections, McConnell fell short of the 60 votes needed. In response, Rand Paul introduced a simpler bill, which would simply repeal most aspects of the ACA, without the various positive proposals contained in the AHCA. This bill won even fewer votes than its predecessor. By the summer of 2017, the Republican agenda had diminished from "repeal and replace" to "repeal" to "partially repeal." By late July, the Senate bill on offer "proposed only to repeal the ACA's individual and employer mandates for eight years, the medical device tax for three years, eliminate funding for Planned Parenthood for one year, and introduce increased flexibility on innovation waivers and health savings accounts." On account of this reduction in ambition, it was popularly referred to as "skinny repeal." It failed when John McCain, dying of brain cancer, dramatically gave it a thumbs down during voting. Though this moment has generally been identified as the moment when the GOP drive to repeal Obamacare failed, it is important to recognize that even before McCain's vote, the agenda Paul Ryan had proposed at the start of the year had already largely been defeated. Though Trump had intervened personally multiple times with Republican legislators, telling them to "Forget about the little shit" and "focus on the big picture here," his efforts to compel Republicans to vote his way were unsuccessful. McConnell, for his part, identified Trump's personalist mode of operation as a source of the initiative's failure; Trump, he complained, had "excessive expectations about how quickly things happen in the democratic process." Though the GOP would, finally, manage to repeal the ACA's mandate for individuals to buy health insurance in late 2017, the ACA did not collapse as conservatives had hoped it would. It was an anticlimactic end to the crusade.[51]

After the failed effort to repeal the ACA, the Trump administration turned to tax reform. Trump had promised massive tax cuts on the campaign trail, pledging to slash individual and corporate tax rates while closing loopholes like the carried interest provision. However, once in office, he devoted little attention to the problem, issuing a one-page plan summary in April that accomplished little besides embarrassing the tax policy specialists in the White House. As with the attempt to repeal the ACA, all the action would take place on Capitol Hill.[52]

The passage of what would become the Tax Cuts and Jobs Act represents a marked contrast to George W. Bush's tax cuts. As discussed in chapter 5, the Bush administration had corralled the major business organizations, telling them they had to accept a massive cut to the personal income tax first and that they would then be rewarded for their loyalty with the kinds of tax measures they desired. During the Trump presidency, however, the situation was reversed. Rather than a strong administration organizing business to lobby for its priorities, the Trump tax cut was profoundly shaped by business lobbying. The plan the administration put forward had been written by Paul Ryan and Representative Kevin Brady, chair of the Ways and Means Committee. It offered a major corporate tax cut, repealed the estate tax, and reduced the number of brackets for the income tax. With all of this cutting, the bill promised, without some other source of revenue, to massively increase the deficit. To address this, Ryan and Brady advocated a Border Adjustment Tax (BAT). Essentially, the tax would shift the target of corporate taxes from profits earned on things made in the United States to profits on things sold in the United States. As such, it would be a boon to exporters, but a major new tax on importers. Projected to raise nearly a trillion dollars over ten years, it would allow the tax bill to be revenue neutral.[53]

Because of this, the BAT drew significant opposition from firms who imported many of their products. This included retailers like Walmart and Best Buy, as well as leading petrochemical firms. While business groups were strongly supportive of the overall tax plan, divisions over the BAT led the Chamber of Commerce to decline taking a position on it. The Kochs, who imported massive amounts of petroleum, were vehemently against the tax, and set Americans for Prosperity to work mobilizing against it. Tapping their connection with Marc Short, the White House legislative affairs director, the Kochs convinced Trump to eliminate the BAT from the bill. At the end of June, Paul Ryan announced that the BAT, which he had supported to the very end, had been removed from the bill. The Kochs were not the only ones to leave their stamp on the bill like this. In early December, Trump attended a fundraiser hosted by the private equity billionaire Stephen A. Schwarzman. At the fundraiser, his donors were complaining that while the corporate tax cut was all well and good, they wanted something on the personal income end as well. Trump agreed, and the final bill knocked the rate of the top personal income bracket down as well.[54]

In the end, the process of passing Trump's tax bill looked more like Reagan's than George W. Bush's. As David Stockman, Reagan's budget director, recalled of the process leading to Reagan's 1981 tax cut, "The hogs were really feeding. The greed level, the level of opportunism, just got out of control." The result was a bill that gave something to everyone, and consequently blew such a massive hole in the budget that it had to be followed by the largest peacetime tax increase in American history. George W. Bush, on the other hand, had gathered business leaders in a room and told them that they would not be adding their preferred cuts to his tax plan but that if they supported his strategy, they would be richly rewarded. Trump's plan clearly resembled the former. Far from creating an administration able to stand above the fray of special interests, he had built one far less capable of exerting any leadership over them than the last Republican president.[55]

Trade policy is one area where many have claimed that Trump genuinely reoriented American politics. In early 2018, the administration imposed tariffs on a number of Chinese goods, from washing machines to steel. Together, these tariffs increased the average tariff on Chinese imported goods by 600 percent and covered two thirds of trade between the US and China, making them the most sweeping tariffs since the Smoot-Hawley Act during the Great Depression. Yet Trump's agency in these developments has been greatly overstated. In fact, many American elites had been moving in this direction for the better part of a decade by the time Trump was elected. From the mid-2000s onwards, China-bashing had been on the rise among members of Congress, particularly those in areas that were affected by Chinese import competition. After the financial crisis of 2008, this anti-Chinese rhetoric intensified, especially among Republicans. As the political scientist Jack Zhang has explained, "blaming the negative externalities of import competition on China rather than on trade policy has allowed Republican incumbents to continue to support their party's free trade platform." While Democrats, encouraged by the trade unions in their coalition, could more forthrightly advocate for protectionism, congressional Republicans during the Bush and Obama years doubled down on blaming China for deindustrialization, while remaining silent on the American policies that had enabled it. Democrats, however, were also becoming more hostile to China. In 2006, Chuck Schumer co-sponsored the Currency Manipulation Definition Act, which was part of a push in Congress that also involved threatening tariffs quite similar to those Trump would levy a little over a decade later. The Obama administration had negotiated the Trans-Pacific Partnership trade treaty with the express goal of containing China economically, and Hillary Clinton was even more hawkish on China than Obama. By the time Trump came to office, the consensus in favor of engagement with China, which had reigned throughout the H. W. Bush, Clinton, and W. Bush administrations was already falling apart.[56]

Initially, the Trump administration did not break dramatically with the Obama administration's posture. In withdrawing from the TPP, which he did soon after inauguration, he reversed the single most important anti-Chinese trade policy of the Obama administration, though he did not present the withdrawal in those terms. For about the first year of the Trump administration, no dramatic actions towards China were taken. The administration had a number of prominent China doves in important positions, including Treasury Secretary Steve Mnuchin; director of the National Economic Council, Gary Cohn; and Trump's daughter Ivanka, who was attempting to trademark some of her fashion lines in China. There were also influential China doves outside the administration, such as Sheldon Adelson and Steve Wynn, both of whom had extensive investments in casinos in Macao. By the latter half of 2017, however, the China hawks, led by former steel-industry lawyer Robert Lighthizer, were winning out. In August, Trump ordered the US trade representative to investigate China's intellectual property infringements, setting the stage for the tariffs he would impose the following year.[57]

Perhaps the most curious aspect of Trump's tariff policy has been American business's muted response. This is not to say there was no response. Many firms joined various coalitions, which organized against the tariffs, such as Americans for Free Trade and the US Global Value Chain Coalition.[58] Firms also submitted a huge number of public comments on the case Trump brought under Section 301 of the Trade Act of 1974, with the vast majority critical of some aspect of the tariff regime. However, this public mobilization has tended to obscure a growing disillusionment with trade with China among many sectors of American business. Manufacturing, in particular, had soured on trade with China, and many tech companies were increasingly vocal about Chinese intellectual property infringements. By the 2010s, the massive corporate coalition that had assembled in the late 1990s in favor of expanding trade with China had fallen apart. The tariffs themselves further disorganized companies. Since lobbying costs resources, it makes sense for firms to concentrate their lobbying on the issue of most relevance to them. In the context of Trump's tariffs, this meant companies lobbied for exemptions rather than against the tariff regime as a whole. As Zhang concludes from an examination of firm participation in the Section 301 process, "only a small number of the largest and most profitable [multi-national corporations] that operate in China made any sort of public statement against tariffs on the eve of the trade war. Three times as many filed for exclusion requests and many more were lobbying the USTR [United States Trade Representative], likely seeking individual exclusions, behind closed doors." Because of the massive number of firms submitting requests for exemptions, very few achieved their goals.[59]

Trump's China policy was thus built on a foundation of general elite disillusionment with the past quarter century of engagement with China. Both political elites and economic elites were increasingly deciding that the game was not worth the candle. Firms that did oppose the tariffs were thus forced to rely on an individualistic strategy to oppose them, yielding an intractable collective action problem. While Trump undoubtedly pursued his policy in a more truculent manner than other administrations would have, it is incorrect to suggest that he fundamentally changed the direction of American trade policy. Indeed, this is confirmed by the reactions to Trump's China policy from establishment figures as varied as Antony Blinken and Hank Paulson, both of whom endorsed the administration's posture.[60]

Ultimately, Trump failed in his first term to achieve a significant reorientation of Republican policymaking. His main priorities were policies that had been central to Republican politics since before his primary campaign. His presidency was distinguished by Trump's personalist approach to politics and by the administration's general disregard for bureaucratic procedure. However, these features primarily had the effect of weakening Trump's presidency, thrusting the administration into avoidable conflicts with either the judiciary or the legislature, or embroiling it in investigations that consumed tremendous administrative resources. In this regard, Trump's administration was truly distinct from the preceding GOP administration of George W. Bush, who particularly in his first term, built a fusion of corporate, administrative, and party power that was able to decisively steer American politics. Trump accomplished none of this.

The Prophet Outcast

American political history is full of resurrections. Figures from Grover Cleveland to Richard Nixon to Joe Biden have been given up as political corpses, only to rise like Lazarus. Since 2020, Donald Trump has joined their ranks. Losing the 2020 election was only the beginning. Almost immediately afterwards, Trump launched a campaign of conspiracy-mongering, alleging he had been denied the presidency through mass voter fraud. This extraordinary attempt to overturn the election results culminated in the riot at the Capitol on January 6, 2021, during which a pro-Trump mob broke into the Capitol in a failed attempt to disrupt the certification of the electoral college results. In the aftermath of this abortive putsch, many thought Trump had consigned himself to political oblivion. Mike Davis gave voice to widely held sentiments when he argued that "the Republican Party has just undergone an irreparable split" in the aftermath of the riot. Yet what followed confounded all such predictions. Trump retained his hold over the GOP. Throughout the country, state parties became more Trumpian than before, as figures with no discernible principles beyond loyalty to Trump came to power. Though anti-Trump forces made a game attempt to challenge his nomination in 2024, Trump triumphed in the primaries easily, losing only two contests to Nikki Haley. The GOP continues to lack any unifying force beyond a faith in their salvation through the leadership of Donald Trump.[61]

The 2020 election continued some of the same trends visible in 2016. Most notably, the Democrats once more decisively outspent the Republicans. In virtually every category in the presidential race, from candidate committees to super PACs to dark money groups, the Democrats spent between 150 and 200 percent as much as the Republicans. Though GOP megadonors like Sheldon Adelson once again opened their wallets, they were eclipsed by a corporate leadership class that was tired of the instability and incompetence of the first Trump administration. One survey of 100 CEOs in September found that seventy-seven were planning to vote for Biden, with many citing Trump's hopelessly inept pandemic response as a key reason. Though Hillary Clinton had maintained a comparable fundraising advantage in 2016, in 2020 Biden's fundraising edge brought victory over Trump.[62]

Ironically, Trump's failure in 2020 came despite the fact that he had an advantage he lacked in 2016: the Republican Party was almost entirely united in support of his candidacy. While in 2016 figures like Mitch McConnell and Paul Ryan had looked forward to a Trump defeat, which would allow their party to return to the kind of business Republicanism they preferred, this time the party was fully backing its candidate. Their commitment to Trump was so total that the party did not bother drafting a platform in 2020, a vulgar reminder that the GOP was no longer motivated by any policy vision beyond what Trump happened to endorse on any given day.[63]

Another change from 2016 was that Trump expected to win. He spent the months leading up to the election declaring over and over that only massive electoral fraud could get in the way of his victory. Even before the election took place, Trump and his supporters had filed more than forty lawsuits challenging various electoral procedures in various states. When Fox News called Arizona for Biden on election night, a result which all but guaranteed a Biden win, Trump's team began the campaign to overturn the election. Assembling a cadre of grotesqueries from the margins of the legal profession, Trump and his closest advisors began searching for some maneuver that would allow them to set aside the election results. All attempts they made met with failure, and on December 14, the electoral college met to cast its votes. A few days later, Trump announced on Twitter that there would be a protest in Washington, DC, on January 6, the day the Senate would meet to certify the electoral college results.[64]

The January 6 riot, more than any other incident during Trump's presidency, marked his administration as an aberration in American political history. To be sure, the use of violence to overturn election results was not without precedent in American history, from the Wilmington race riot of 1898 to the Brooks Brothers riot in 2000 that helped deliver the presidency to George W. Bush. Nonetheless, in terms of scale and audacity, the January 6 riot, in conjunction with Trump's attempts at litigation to overturn the election, eclipses anything that came before it. Even now, the details of Trump's conduct that day have the capacity to shock. Before the riot, he placed a call to Mike Pence, trying to inveigle him one last time into invalidating the electoral college votes. "You can either go down in history as a patriot, or you can go down in history as a pussy," Trump told him. After telling his supporters to march on the Capitol, Trump attempted to force his Secret Service retinue to take him there as well. And during the riot, even when Trump sycophants from Don Jr. to Fox-host Laura Ingraham frantically attempted to convince the president to condemn it, he refused. Though the riot only lasted a few hours and was largely dispersed by the time the National Guard arrived at the Capitol that evening, it nonetheless marked the greatest crisis for the American constitutional order since Watergate.[65]

Trump's attempt to overturn the election on January 6 led to a massive backlash from corporate America. Already in November, when Trump first began broadcasting his intention to challenge the election results, CEOs of major companies had met to formulate plans on how to use their influence to stop him. After January 6, the response from boardrooms was furious. The National Association of Manufacturers, anchor for the some of the most reactionary politics in twentieth century America, called on Mike Pence and the cabinet to remove Trump from office via the twenty fifth amendment. One hundred and twenty-three firms on the Fortune 500 list, with collective revenues of around a quarter of US GDP, announced a pause in all donations to federal candidates in order to assess their donation criteria. For a moment, it looked as if American corporations were organizing on a class-wide level to challenge the direction of the Republican Party.[66]

Things soon fell apart, however. In March 2021, the Chamber of Commerce announced, "We do not believe it is appropriate to judge members of Congress solely based on their votes on the electoral certification." While members of Congress who objected to certifying the election faced large penalties in the 2022 primaries, losing nearly $100,000 in donations from Fortune 500 PACs on average, that penalty was smaller in the 2022 general election, and smaller again in the 2024 primaries. By the 2024 elections, it was difficult to find a Republican who would publicly dispute Trump's continued claims that the election was stolen.[67]

There are a few reasons the corporate boycott failed to hold. First, Republicans proved able to survive it with funds from other sources. In fact, in January of 2021, Republican fundraising for the House and Senate outpaced Democratic fundraising. The rise of small donors allowed mobilized Republican partisans to easily make up for the collapse in contributions from corporate PACs. At the same time, a handful of far-right multimillionaires poured money into candidates and organizations that have continued to try and challenge the results of the 2020 election. Richard and Elizabeth Uihlein, for example, moved from being relatively modest Republican donors in the 2010s to being the largest donors to Republican federal candidates in the 2021–2022 midterms—their generosity extending to candidates who embraced the most unlikely of conspiracy theories. Between small donors and big ones, Republicans who embraced election denial were able to maintain sufficient funds, even with the hit they took from corporate PACs.[68]

The fact that election deniers were able to maintain their position led companies to begin defecting from the boycott. A great deal of corporate political donation is fundamentally about maintaining access to politicians. It is a pragmatic, rather than an ideological, donation. Faced with the survival of Republicans who denied the election results, companies tended to return to acting on their narrow, individual interests, which required them to maintain access to legislators, rather than organize according to their collective, class-wide interests, which would require them to continue the boycott. By mounting his challenge to the election, Trump had precipitated the largest conflict between the Republican Party and American business in the country's history. However, faced with an intransigent party who had the resources to survive their first strike, business's army gradually abandoned the field.[69]

Throughout this conflict, Donald Trump retained his hold over the Republican Party. Throughout 2021, he aggressively pushed GOP candidates to support his claims of election fraud, threatening to support primaries against anyone who refused. He was aided in this endeavor by the depth of negative partisanship among GOP primary voters. Trump's logic was crude but effective: the Democrats say I'm lying, therefore anyone who agrees with them is on the side of the Democrats. In a party whose base had imbibed ever more rancorous partisan antipathy over the previous decade, this argument resonated. On the state level, Trump's support for candidates pledging loyalty to him led to the dominance of state parties by true believers. Yet as the political scientist Julia Azari has argued, Trump's dominance over the GOP has yielded a curious result. He has not, by and large, drastically changed the policy orientation of the party. Nor has his dominance led to increased electoral success. More often, it has been a detriment to the party's performance. Trump's backing of loyalist candidates has time and again led to primary victories that result in general election losses. In the state parties, the reign of Trump believers has led to parties run by political dilettantes, whose incompetencies have greatly hampered fundraising. In Michigan, for example, party chair Kristina Karamo's total ignorance of campaign finance law led to numerous violations that left the party deeply in debt in a key swing state.[70]

Trump announced his campaign for the 2024 nomination immediately after the 2022 elections. He was challenged by two potential rivals. Ron DeSantis, governor of Florida, attempted to run a campaign that was little more than Trumpism without Trump. Lacking Trump's showmanship and charisma, he flailed as he refused to attack Trump directly, leaving voters with little reason to prefer the imitation to the real thing. A more direct challenge to Trump's dominance came from Nikki Haley, who had served as ambassador to the UN in the Trump administration. Haley ran as a unity candidate bringing together the party establishment and the Koch network, a strategy that would have been unimaginable during the Republican civil wars of the early 2010s. Indeed, Haley herself had run as a Tea Party candidate for governor of South Carolina in 2010 and had drawn the opposition of the state Chamber of Commerce, who confessed "We prefer candidates who are not extreme." Nonetheless, by 2024 Haley had rebranded herself as a the voice of reason and was the preferred candidate for voters and donors who wanted to change the direction of the party. Despite drawing funding from a host of deep-pocketed donors, Haley's campaign against Trump drew little voter enthusiasm; she only won New Hampshire and Washington, DC. By February, the Kochs announced they would stop funding her.[71]

Trump thus entered the 2024 election still the undisputed master of the Republican Party. Though his reign had brought the party electoral defeat and led to ruptures with its historic backers in the business community, there is, as yet, little indication that appetites among the party's voters will change. In this sense, Trump's dominance of the party has displaced the factional conflicts that wracked the party before his presidential run. While George W. Bush subsumed factional conflict with a strategy that enlisted both the insurgents and the establishment in the administration's agenda, Trump only managed this successfully with his tax cut legislation. Elsewhere, his personal dominance over the party has tended to crowd out factional conflict, rather than hegemonize the factions. At the same time, Haley's campaign is evidence of how, during Trump's reign, new alignments have been visible. It is unlikely that the forces in conflict in a post-Trump GOP will resemble the alignments that preceded him. But given the continued fractiousness even under Trump's personalist rule, there is little doubt that intense conflict of some sort will continue to structure the party.

Conclusion

All Tomorrow's Parties

The Republican Party's transformation over the last three decades is one of the most striking developments in world politics. Two decades ago, its leadership, for a moment, imagined they bestrode the narrow world like a colossus; those leaders have now largely abandoned the party. In the fall of 2024, former Representative Liz Cheney campaigned for Kamala Harris and told reporters that her father Dick Cheney would also be voting for Harris. Such an alliance would, of course, have been unthinkable a decade earlier. Yet as this anecdote reveals, it is not only the Republicans who have changed in this period. The Democrats have undergone a transformation of their own as well, as they have somehow become the party of both Dick Cheney and Bernie Sanders. If this book has focused on how the Republican Party has changed, it is only because its changes have been so much more dramatic.[1]

Yet this asymmetry itself demands an explanation. Why has the Democratic Party's evolution not simply mirrored the Republicans'? Regarding all three dimensions of change raised at the beginning of this book—increased conservatism, increased internal conflict, and increased conflict with business—a look at the Democrats' recent history will uncover only pale echoes. This puzzle is only deepened by the fact that the Democrats have also had to contend with a weakened party apparatus and a fractured corporate class. On first glance, it seems as if the same forces that deranged the Republican Party should also be at work on the Democrats.

The conclusion will take up the question of this asymmetry. It will examine the Democratic Party and explain its comparative coherence. It argues that the Democratic Party's long-standing relationship to various interest group organizations who represent women, LGBT voters, unions, African Americans, and so on keep the party from treading a similar path as the GOP. Yet the party has certainly changed, losing part of its working class base and gaining more allegiance from the American elite than in any period in modern history. This realignment of the law partners and the C-suites, however, has not produced the kind of retreat from redistribution that many feared; instead, it coexists uneasily with the kinds of insurgent energies that powered Bernie Sanders's presidential campaigns.

Finally, the chapter returns to the GOP, considering its likely future in the new American party system.

A Different Kind of Hollow

The Democrats have been subject to the same kinds of dynamics that have hollowed out the Republican Party. Their congressional leadership is preoccupied with the money race in the same way the Republican leadership is. Like the GOP, the official party organs exist in a state of simultaneous competition and collaboration with extra-party organs like super PACs and dark money groups. And like the GOP, the party has been deprived of control over its ballot lines through the primary system.

Despite all of this, the Democratic party has manifestly not followed the GOP. Political scientists generally agree that it has not moved off-center with the same speed the Republicans have. Perhaps even more surprisingly, the party has retained much of its internal coherence. This is not for a lack of challenges. Bernie Sanders's presidential campaigns in 2016 and 2020 were proudly anti-establishment in their posture and certainly increased the political salience of dissatisfaction with the party leadership. Yet, as exemplified by the conduct of Sanders himself, these challenges have not led to the kind of internal conflict the Republicans have witnessed. While Joe Crowley, the House Democratic Caucus

Chair unseated by democratic socialist Alexandria Ocasio-Cortez in 2018, loosely presents as a Democratic counterpart to Eric Cantor, there is no Democratic equivalent to John Boehner, Paul Ryan, or Kevin McCarthy. There is similarly no stream of formerly Democratic officials joining the GOP, as has been the case with the Never Trump Republicans. While there are Democrats, like Michigan's Rashida Tlaib, who persistently challenge their party's leadership, it is doubtful that anyone in the Democratic leadership has the same kind of naked contempt for Tlaib Republican leaders regularly voiced towards Florida's Matt Gaetz.[2]

A central reason for this divergence is the place of interest groups in the Democratic Party. As political scientists from very different perspectives have recognized, the Democratic Party is built around interest groups in a way the GOP is not. While the Republicans have, since the 1970s, been a party in which success has often hinged on how convincingly a candidate can claim the mantle of ideological conservatism, the Democrats are a party in which candidates succeed by

> assembl[ing] a policy agenda from the aggregated preferences of the party's numerous constituencies, [and] courting the mass electorate with a large assortment of concrete benefits favoring targeted populations. Although the particular groups inside the Democratic "big tent"—as well as their specific programmatic demands—have evolved over time, the party's foundational partisan character has remained constant across decades of electoral history.[3]

Democrats do not win primaries, for the most part, on the basis of who is the most liberal. They win primaries on the basis of who can most effectively claim to unite the different interest groups that make up the party's base by delivering specific benefits to them.[4]

Candidates, in turn, depend as much on interest groups as the party does to secure victory in an election. Democrats have depended on the labor of unions to win elections going all the way back to the high point of the New Deal coalition. Since then, unions have been joined by women's groups, African American groups, environmental organizations, and others to carry out fundraising and voter mobilization operations. While pro-life groups, and the Christian right more broadly, carry out similar work for the GOP, their contribution is not nearly so pivotal to the party's fortunes as that of Democratic interest groups.[5]

The centrality of interest groups to the Democratic Party has tended to inhibit ideological polarization. Democratic primary voters and the institutions that organize them are not looking for the left-most candidate. In states in which Republicans regularly win elections, they are looking for the candidate who can most effectively protect their group from Republican attacks. In one-party states like New York or California, they are looking for someone who can most effectively deliver for their interest group. From this perspective, the Sanders insurgencies are themselves partially the product of the disorganizing of American society, as large numbers of Democratic voters have found themselves outside of the traditional interest group institutions. Yet as Joe Biden's victory in 2020 revealed, if the interest group structure of the Democratic Party is bending, it has not yet broken.[6]

The dense interest group landscape of the party has left precious little space for polarizers. Ideological consistency means very little if a candidate cannot deliver real benefits to the party's interest groups. While some, like women's groups, may demand ideological rigidity on a question like abortion, the interest groups nevertheless understand two things. First, they know that, sometimes, theirs will be the ox that gets gored (as with Hillary Clinton's nomination of pro-life Virginia Senator Tim Kaine to be her running mate) in the interests of electability. Second, they understand that every other interest group must sometimes lose. Therefore, the groups tend to defend their key interests and attempt to push the burden of compromise onto others; broader politics of principle are thus generally avoided. This contrasts sharply with the Republican Party in the heyday of fusionist conservatism, when conservative groups worked in concert to police any deviations from the famous three-legged stool of libertarian economics, social conservatism, and aggressive militarism. This meant that, from the 1970s onwards, it was nearly impossible for a Republican candidate to go too far in their embrace of all three principles. In fact, candidates who did not position themselves as the most conservative frequently had to worry about primary challenges from their right, particularly after 2010. This dynamic ensured a steady stream of political entrepreneurs trying to take the Republican Party to the right. The interest group foundation of the Democratic Party provides no such wellspring.

Political entrepreneurs trying to take the Republican Party to the right could always count on finding funds, while any entrepreneur attempting something similar in the Democratic Party would find fundraising nearly impossible. This was particularly true before the online fundraising revolution of the 2010s, when large donations were the lifeblood of campaigns and parties. While there have been deep-pocketed donors willing to support the Democratic Party left, of course, their numbers have been far, far fewer than the donors willing to back the Republican right. The rise of online fundraising, which has made it vastly easier to harvest small donations, has gone some way to rectifying this. Bernie Sanders and Alexandria Ocasio-Cortez have shown that it is possible for candidates to be competitive in campaign funding by relying strictly on small, ideologically motivated donors. However, there is nothing on the left of the Democratic Party that resembles the networks of ultra-rich donors who have assembled at different times to push the GOP to the right. From Gingrich's GOPAC network to the Koch seminars to the billionaires who funded Trump's efforts to overturn the 2020 election, the GOP right has the means to create lavishly funded institutions that support their efforts to make the party even more conservative. Nothing comparable exists on the Democratic Party left.

Finally, the different policy goals of conservatizing and liberalizing political entrepreneurs create different relationships to the party leadership. Conservative political entrepreneurs have, since the 1980s, been primarily focused on getting the party to be more aggressive in blocking Democratic legislation. Particularly during periods of divided government, these figures, from Newt Gingrich to Ted Cruz, have wanted the party to reject compromise and hold out for the most stringent possible cuts to Democratic budgets, even at the cost of government shutdowns and debt ceiling showdowns. Because their main objective is to get the party to say "no," they are not as reliant on their party leadership to fulfill their priorities. Even if the leadership refuses, they can still go back to their districts and tell their supporters that they fought the good fight. Liberalizing political entrepreneurs, by contrast, stake their reputations on their ability to get the party to deliver more. Whether it's Medicare for All or a Green New Deal, liberal political entrepreneurs want to pass big, ambitious spending legislation. There is simply no way to accomplish this without working closely with the party leadership. This is why there is no Democratic counterpart to Matt Gaetz or Marjorie Taylor Greene.

If the Democratic Party has not undergone a metamorphosis that mirrors the Republican Party's, it has changed, nonetheless. As a number of commentators have noted, the Democratic Party has been losing its hold on working-class voters for some time. Where working-class voters were once a dependable Democratic constituency, they are now much more evenly split between Democrats and the GOP.[7]

Even more striking than the exit of working class voters, however, has been the influx of affluent voters—a relatively recent development. One study of CEO political contributions covering the years 2000–2017 found that 57 percent of CEOs gave at least two thirds of their donations to Republicans, while only 19 percent donated as much to Democrats. Studies focusing on the last decade, by contrast, have found a clear shift to the left among corporate leaders and a fracturing of support for the old conservative consensus. Writing shortly before the 2024 election, Matthew Karp summarized Wall Street's realignment:

> Since 2020, venture-capital donors have made 75 percent of their contributions to Democrats, while hedge-fund donors have given 68 percent. Big Pharma leans blue, as does Big Law. In the same period, donors at the Big Three management-consulting firms—McKinsey, Bain, and Boston Consulting Group—have given 95 percent of their combined contributions to Democrats.[8]

Affluent Americans more broadly have also moved towards the Democratic Party. As Sam Zacher has demonstrated, a host of evidence from different sources confirms the realignment of the upper strata of society. While the vote of working class Americans is now split between Democrats and Republicans, the vote of affluent Americans has become reliably Democratic.[9]

One might predict from this realignment that the Democrats have retreated from redistribution, following the preferences of their new upper-class voters. Yet this is not what has happened. Indeed, under Joe Biden, the Democrats attempted to pass the most ambitious piece of redistributive policy since the Great Society. The fact that it was blocked by the two most conservative senators in the Democratic caucus hardly diminishes the fact that the rest of the party supported it.[10] More broadly, there is little evidence of Democrats growing more conservative on economic issues over the past two decades. In fact, evidence suggests that on a wide range of economic issues, from taxation to financial regulation, high income Democrats consistently hold a more liberal opinion than low income Democrats.[11]

This suggests that the party is in a state of transition. The interest group structure of the party that has held for the last half-century is weakening, and ideological candidates are becoming more common. This has been driven, in part, by the increasing ideological liberalism of college-educated voters, and it is in districts with more of these kinds of voters that some of the most stridently egalitarian Democrats have been elected. The insurgent energies of the 2016 and 2020 Sanders campaigns, therefore, while at a lull as of 2024, are unlikely to simply dissipate. In this sense, the Democrats seem poised to follow the path of polarization that the Republicans forged, but at a lag.[12]

Yet there are good reasons to think that the evolution of the Democratic Party will be different. The budget constraints on left-wing political entrepreneurs are unlikely to change; they will not be able to mount a frontal challenge to the party establishment nearly as quickly as the right wing of the GOP did. Second, the fact that left-wing political entrepreneurs want to pass policy makes a left-wing equivalent to the Freedom Caucus, all too happy to sabotage their leadership, unlikely. Finally, it is unclear whether the ideological liberalism of the educated upper class will continue to encompass redistributive politics. The kind of social democratic welfare state envisioned by Democratic Party egalitarians will not be funded with taxes on the rich alone but will require more broad-based tax increases. It remains to be seen if moneyed liberals' hearts will still bleed in the face of substantial tax increases.[13]

Republicans and the End of Ideology

The Republican Party is also in a state of transition. Donald Trump has profoundly changed the party. Acknowledging this does not require any sort of romanticization of the Republican Party before his ascension. The party of Ronald Reagan and George W. Bush was a party of racist backlash and imperial thuggery and was perfectly at ease disregarding the law when it suited them. Trump's novelty was not in plumbing new depths of reaction. Rather, his personalist rule over the party and attempt to exercise a similar mode of rule over the American government are what is genuinely new. This personalism has called into question the place of conservatism in the new Republican Party.

Since 2016, loyalty to Trump, and whatever he might claim to believe at the moment, has replaced conservative ideology as the motivating force in GOP politics. To be sure, Trump's victory in the GOP primaries revealed an already attenuating attachment to conservative ideology, particularly on economics and foreign policy, among GOP voters. Trump won precisely because he, unlike virtually every other Republican candidate, was willing to jettison the decades-long GOP consensus on attacking entitlements and supporting aggressive militarism. While his administration governed closer to the party's traditional positions on both these questions, there's no question that his rhetoric in the 2016 election marked a clear break from the conservative ideology that had dominated the party.

Since 2016, ideology has continued to take a back seat to Trump's whims in the GOP. In 2020, the party did not bother to write a party platform. The platform was simply whatever Trump said it was. In 2024, the party released a desultory document it called a platform, but that showed scarcely any more interest in a policy vision than it could muster in 2020. At the same time, Trump has also largely abandoned the pro-life politics that have been so central to the GOP since the 1970s. Where George H. W. Bush was once required to disavow his pro-choice past and bend the knee to the Christian right, Trump has sworn off anything resembling a principled position on abortion, despite the fact that the number of abortions continued to rise even after the overthrow of *Roe v. Wade*. Ideologically oriented groups in the party ecosystem have also withered. In the spring of 2024, FreedomWorks officially shut down, its leaders acknowledging that that there was simply no more appetite in the Republican Party for their stridently ideological libertarianism.[14]

As the FreedomWorks example suggests, one candidate for replacing a fusionist ideology in the GOP is so-called national conservatism, which rejects free market economics but retains strong cultural conservatism. Institutionalized in the think tank American Compass, and strongly associated with politicians like J. D. Vance, national conservatism has acted as a kind of over-eager successor ideology. Yet there are strong reasons to doubt that it is up to replacing the three legged stool. For one thing, the movement's main funders support it only half-heartedly. The tech billionaire Peter Thiel is the movement's biggest backer and a major patron of Vance's. Yet Thiel was until a few years ago a deeply ideological libertarian, investing in "seasteading" ventures to escape the state. Now, he funds the National Conservatism Conference, though his ideology seems limited to anti-liberalism, rather than avowing any positive vision. He is most enthusiastic about using the state to attack tech companies who are rivals to Meta (formerly Facebook), on whose board he sits. Similarly, American Compass is funded by largely liberal foundations hoping to cultivate more support for market regulation on the right. True believers in the movement seem rather rare.[15]

More generally, there's very little evidence that the movement is having much policy influence. It's true Trump has proposed extraordinary new tariffs, which national conservative intellectuals have defended. But this is hardly due to the influence of national conservative ideology; it stems instead from Trump's decades-long mercantilism. In the rest of the party, enthusiasm for tariffs remains low. Other planks of the movement's economic platform, like moving the GOP to at least a neutral position on unions and embracing more progressive taxation, have even less support. This should hardly come as a surprise. The GOP's regional, as opposed to national, backbone consists of what Patrick Wyman has called "the local gentry" of the United States—an assortment of car dealership owners, operators of medium-scale commercial agriculture, fast food franchisees who run a few dozen restaurants, and a congeries of other small capitalists. Rich enough for a luxury lifestyle but resentful of the Fortune 500, this social layer is the base of the GOP in much of the country. They are every bit as hostile to unions and taxes as any Goldwaterite. Trump's proposal for more tax cuts to both the personal and corporate rates holds tremendous appeal to the local gentry. Raising taxes and accommodating unions does not.[16]

National conservatism's appeal has less to do with its economic program, and more with its willingness to embrace anti-liberalism. In this respect, its current prominence reflects the fact that the GOP has become a party not so much of ideas as of opposing Democrats. As Newt Gingrich observed of Trump, he "is not essentially a conservative. Trump is an anti-liberal. They're not the same phenomenon. But he may be the most effective uprooter of liberalism in my lifetime." Political scientists have discussed this dynamic in terms of "negative partisanship"—many people cast their votes less out of enthusiasm for their own party than antipathy to the other party. In the Republican Party, negative partisanship has become all-consuming. Politicians compete with one another to see who can enrage liberals more. The actual content of whatever does the enraging is secondary.[17]

As this dynamic suggests, media attention is a crucial currency in the contemporary GOP. In the era of small-donor fundraising, media attention is an extremely effective means of raising cash. Thus, a figure like Marjorie Taylor Greene who has never exercised any influence as a policymaker is one of the best fundraisers in the House, because her ravings attract considerable media attention. This attention—including liberal condemnation

—allows her to promote herself as the politician who is most effectively opposing liberalism and to harvest donors accordingly. The success of this tactic virtually guarantees its persistence. At the same time, it also guarantees continued conflict *within* the GOP. The politicians competing to be the most anti-liberal inevitably turn on their own caucus leadership for being insufficiently anti-liberal. Once again, Greene exemplifies this dynamic. After Kevin McCarthy's ouster in 2023, Greene began agitating for the overthrow of the new Republican Speaker of the House, Mike Johnson, declaring herself "sick and tired of watching our so-called 'conservative' Speaker bend the knee to the communist Democrats." The de-ideologization of the party only reinforces this dynamic. Without clear ideological guardrails, the scope of potential conflict between insurgents and the party establishment has widened.[18]

None of this is to say the Republican Party will stop claiming conservatism. Party officials and candidates will no doubt continue to cast the party in stridently ideological terms. However, conservatism has now been largely emptied of content. It is not clear if it means aggressive militarism or opposition to US intervention abroad. Mitch McConnell, who has never been anything but deeply conservative, thinks the party should embrace free trade, while more Trumpian voices call for tariffs. Both calls for a clientelist, pro-natal welfare state and more traditional attacks on the social safety net tout court now jostle for which is the truly conservative position. The GOP will continue to be a conservative party, but there is no consensus about what this means.

All of this suggests continued turbulence ahead for the Republican Party. The forces that produced a more coherent right-wing politics for much of the twentieth century have been exhausted. The development of more substantial party structures is unlikely—parties are now considerably weaker institutions than they were in the late 1970s, when a chorus of political scientists first warned that the parties were dying. Any real renewal would need to run through a campaign finance reform agenda that would restrain the power of extra-party vehicles like super PACs. Such an agenda would, after the *Citizens United* and *SpeechNow* decisions, require either a constitutional amendment or a total remaking of the Supreme Court, neither of which is foreseeable. Similarly, it is unlikely that American capitalists will engage in the kind of disciplined collective action seen during the 1970s without a major challenge from the state or unions. These basic structural facts will likely continue to shape American politics for decades to come.

The party's ideological unmooring and the bad incentives that continue to be generated by the media-fundraising nexus compound these structural infirmities. They promise continued conflict within the party, perhaps at levels surpassing the already fractious 2010s. For the Republican Party, there is no end in sight for the turbulence through which it has been passing.

Notes

Introduction

1 Ellen Schrecker, *Many Are the Crimes: McCarthyism in America* (New York: Little, Brown, 1998), 259; Joseph R. McCarthy, *America's Retreat from Victory* (New York: Devin-Adair, 1951), 43, 95–6.

2 Schrecker, *Many Are the Crimes*, 250. On business support for anticommunism and McCarthy, see Peter H. Irons, "American Business and the Origins of McCarthyism: The Cold War Crusade of the Chamber of Commerce," Robert Griffith and Athan Theoharis, eds., *The Specter: Original Essays on the Cold War and the Origins of McCarthyism* (New York: New Viewpoints, 1974), 72–89; Martin Trow, "Small Businessmen, Political Tolerance, and Support for McCarthy," *American Journal of Sociology* 64:3 (1958), 270–81; Larry Tye, *Demagogue: The Life and Long Shadow of Senator Joe McCarthy* (Boston: Houghton Mifflin Harcourt, 2020), 352–4.

3 Tye, *Demagogue*, 218–20; David M. Oshinsky, *A Conspiracy So Immense: The World of Joe McCarthy* (Oxford: Oxford University Press, 2005 [1983]), 218. On Benton's role in the CED, see Robert M. Collins, *The Business Response to Keynes, 1929–1964* (New York: Columbia University Press, 1981), 81–4.

4 Shelby Scates, *Maurice Rosenblatt and the Fall of Joseph McCarthy* (Seattle: University of Washington Press, 2006), 88–90; Richard M. Fried, *Men Against McCarthy* (New York: Columbia University Press, 1976), 266–7, 295.

5 Collins, *The Business Response to Keynes*, 148; Gerald R. Rosen, "The Blue Ribbon Business Council," *Dun's Review* (January 1970), 37–41; Philip H. Burch Jr., *Elites in American History: Volume III: The New Deal to the Carter Administration* (New York: Holmes and Meier, 1980), 126; Tye, *Demagogue*, 341–6; Oshinsky, *A Conspiracy So Immense*, 357–8; Stephen Maher, *Corporate Capitalism and the Integral State: General Electric*

and a Century of American Power (Cham: Palgrave MacMillan, 2022), 44.

6   Tye, *Demagogue*, 384; Fried, *Men Against McCarthy*, 280.

7   Burch, *Elites in American History*, 149; "The Business Council Background," The Business Council, thebusinesscouncil.org; Kim McQuaid, *Big Business and Presidential Power: From FDR to Reagan* (New York: William Morrow, 1982), 180; Rosen, "The Blue Ribbon Business Council," 40.

8   Tye, *Demagogue*, 448; Burch, *Elites in American History*, 149; Fried, *Men Against McCarthy*, 292; Scates, *Maurice Rosenblatt*, 107; Burch, *Elites in American History*, 165, n.88.

9   Thomas Ferguson, Paul Jorgensen, and Jie Chen, "Industrial Structure and Political Outcomes: The Case of the 2016 US Presidential Election," in Ivano Cardinale and Roberto Scazzieri, eds., *The Palgrave Handbook of Political Economy* (London: Palgrave MacMillan, 2018), 333–440. "Club for Growth Steps Up Fight with Donald Trump," *Dow Jones Institutional News*, September 4, 2015; Michelle Conlin, "Powerful Koch Brothers Rebuff Big Donors' Calls to Back Trump for White House," *Reuters*, August 2, 2016; David Gelles, Karl Russell, and Ashwin Seshagiri, "The Business Leaders Who Were on Trump's Advisory Councils," *New York Times*, August 16, 2017; Matt Egan, "Wall Street Is Shunning Trump: Campaign Donations to Biden Are Five Times Larger," *CNN*, September 25, 2020; Katie Arcieri, "Donors Affiliated with Amazon, Big Tech Throw Support Behind Biden Campaign," *S and P Global*, October 7, 2020.

10 Zhao Li and Richard DiSalvo, "Can Stakeholders Mobilize Businesses for the Protection of Democracy? Evidence from the U.S. Capitol Insurrection," *American Political Science Review* 117:3 (2023), 1130–6.

11 Thomas E. Mann and Norman Ornstein, *It's Even Worse Than It Looks: How the American Constitutional System Collided with the New Politics of Extremism* (New York: Basic Books, 2012); Jacob S. Hacker and Paul Pierson, "Confronting Asymmetric Polarization," in Nathaniel Persily, ed., *Solutions to Political Polarization in America* (Cambridge: Cambridge University Press, 2015), 59–70.

12 Matthew N. Green and Jeffrey Crouch, *Newt Gingrich: The Rise and Fall of a Party Entrepreneur* (Lawrence: University Press of Kansas, 2022), 152–6; Paul Heideman, "With Kevin McCarthy's Removal, a Long Government Shutdown Just Got More Likely," *Jacobin*, October 4, 2023.

13 Sam Rosenfeld, *The Polarizers: Postwar Architects of Our Partisan Era* (Chicago: University of Chicago Press, 2017).

14 David D. Kirkpatrick, "How Marjorie Taylor Greene Raises

Money by Attacking Other Republicans," *The New Yorker*, April 27, 2024.

15 William Greider, *The Education of David Stockman and Other Americans* (EP Dutton, 1982), 58.

16 Green and Crouch, *Newt Gingrich*, 91.

17 Jeff Stein, Jacqueline Alemany, and Josh Dawsey, "Some Billionaires, CEOs Hedge Bets as Trump Vows Retribution," *Washington Post*, October 28, 2024; Brian Schwartz, Dana Mattioli, and Rebecca Ballhaus, "The Week CEOs Bent the Knee to Trump," *Wall Street Journal*, December 13, 2024.

1. The Fractured Elite

1 Adam Smith, *An Enquiry into the Nature and Causes of the Wealth of Nations* (London: Methuen, 1904 [1776]), 68–9.

2 Wolfgang Streeck and Philippe Schmitter, "The Organization of Business Interests: Studying the Associative Action of Business in Advanced Industrial Societies," Max Planck Institute for the Study of Societies Paper 99/1 (1999), 14; For a discussion of how this plays out in practice, see Peter Swenson, *Capitalists Against Markets: The Making of Labor Markets and Welfare States in the United States and Sweden* (New York: Oxford University Press, 2002).

3 Claus Offe and Helmut Wiesenthal, "Two Logics of Collective Action," *Political Power and Social Theory* 1 (1980), 74.

4 F. W. Hilbert, "Employers' Associations in the United States," in *Studies in American Trade Unionism*, eds. Jacob H. Hollander and George E. Barnett (New York: Henry Holt, 1906), 185. More recent cross-national comparative research has reached much the same conclusion, finding that employers' organizations are significantly more likely to form when strong unions exist. See Cathie Jo Martin and Duane Swank, *The Political Construction of Business Interests: Coordination, Growth, and Equality* (Cambridge: Cambridge University Press, 2012).

5 To be sure, the degree of coordination even in these countries has decreased since the 1980s. However, their overall level of business organization is still the highest in capitalist societies. See Wolfgang Streeck, *Re-Forming Capitalism: Institutional Change in the German Political Economy* (New York: Oxford University Press, 2010).

6 Colin Gordon, "Why No Corporatism in the United States? Business Disorganization and Its Consequences" *Business and Economic History* 27:1 (Fall 1998); Cathie Jo Martin, "Crossroads Blues: Business Representation, Public Policy, and Economic Growth for the Twenty-First Century," in William J. Crotty, ed.,

The State of Democracy in America (Washington, DC: George-town University Press, 2001), 178.

7   On early unionization figures in the US, see Leo Wolman, *The Growth of American Trade Unions, 1880–1923* (National Bureau of Economic Research, 1924).

8   Cathie Jo Martin, "Sectional Parties, Divided Business," *Studies in American Political Development* 20:1 (2006), 160–184; Robert A. Brady, *Business as a System of Power* (New York: Columbia University Press, 1943), 198–9.

9   Richard W. Gable, "Birth of an Employers' Association," *Business History Review* 33:4 (1959), 535–45.

10   Jennifer Delton, *The Industrialists: How the National Association of Manufacturers Shaped American Capitalism* (Princeton University Press, 2020), 11; Colin Gordon, *New Deals: Business, Labor, and Politics in America, 1920–1935* (Cambridge: Cambridge University Press, 1994), 141–3.

11   Richard Hume Werking, "Bureaucrats, Businessmen, and Foreign Trade: The Origins of the United States Chamber of Commerce," *Business History Review* 52:3 (1978), 321–41.

12   Werking, "Bureaucrats, Businessmen, and Foreign Trade"; Robert M. Collins, *The Business Response to Keynes, 1929–1964* (New York: Columbia University Press, 1981), 23–4.

13   Gordon, *New Deals*, 145–7; Collins, *The Business Response to Keynes*, 50–4.

14   G. William Domhoff, *The Myth of Liberal Ascendancy: Corporate Dominance from the Great Depression to the Great Recession* (New York: Routledge, 2013), chapter 4; Mark S. Mizruchi, *The Fracturing of the American Corporate Elite* (Cambridge: Harvard University Press, 2013), 40–1.

15   Mizruchi, *The Fracturing*, 58; Charlie Whitham, "The Committee for Economic Development, Foreign Trade and the Rise of American Corporate Liberalism, 1942–8," *Journal of Contemporary History* 48:4 (2013), 862; Domhoff, *Myth of Liberal Ascendancy*, chapter 4.

16   Gerald A. Epstein and Juliet Schor, "The Federal Reserve-Treasury Accord and the Construction of the Postwar Monetary Regime in the United States," in *The Political Economy of Central Banking: Contested Control and the Power of Finance, Selected Essays of Gerald Epstein* (London: Edward Elgar, 2019), 116–57; Robert A. Collins, "American Corporatism: The Committee for Economic Development, 1942–1964," *The Historian* 44:2 (1982), 151–73; Collins, *The Business Response to Keynes*, 135–7.

17   Mizruchi, *The Fracturing*, 292 n.5; Howell John Harris, *The Right to Manage: Industrial Relations Policies of American Business in the 1940s* (Madison: University of Wisconsin Press, 1982), 184.

18 See Domhoff, *The Myth of Liberal Ascendancy* for a thorough cataloging of corporate dominance during these years.

19 Charles Noble, *Liberalism at Work: The Rise and Fall of OSHA* (Philadelphia: Temple University Press, 1986), 85–6; David Vogel, *Fluctuating Fortunes: The Political Power of Business in America* (New York: Basic Books, 1989), 68–9.

20 Kim McQuaid, *Uneasy Partners: Big Business in American Politics, 1945–1990* (Baltimore: Johns Hopkins University Press, 1994), 139; Leonard Silk and David Vogel, *Ethics and Profits: The Crisis of Confidence in American Business* (New York: Simon and Schuster, 1976), 52–3.

21 Benjamin C. Waterhouse, *Lobbying America: The Politics of Business from Nixon to NAFTA* (Princeton: Princeton University Press, 2014), chapter 5.

22 Marc Linder, *Wars of Attrition: Vietnam, the Business Roundtable, and the Decline of Construction Unions* (Iowa City: Fǎnpìhuà Press, 2000), 28–32, 109.

23 G. William Domhoff, *The Corporate Rich and the Power Elite in the Twentieth Century: How They Won, Why Liberals and Labor Lost* (New York: Routledge, 2020), 191; Robert Brenner, "The Political Economy of the Rank-and-File Rebellion," in Aaron Brenner, Robert Brenner, and Cal Winslow, eds., *Rebel Rank and File: Labor Militancy and Revolt from Below During the Long 1970s* (London: Verso, 2010), 37–76.

24 Brenner, "The Political Economy," 57–8; James Gross, *Broken Promise: The Subversion of U.S. Labor Relations* (Philadelphia: Temple University Press, 1995), 197.

25 Gross, *Broken Promise*, 200–209.

26 Gross, 201.

27 Domhoff, *Myth of Liberal Ascendancy*, chapter 8.

28 Domhoff, chapter 10.

29 Domhoff, chapter 10; Mizruchi, *The Fracturing*, 174.

30 Linder, *Wars of Attrition*, 182–8; Domhoff, *Myth of Liberal Ascendancy*, chapter 6.

31 Linder, 188–95.

32 Benjamin C. Waterhouse, *Lobbying America*, chapter 3.

33 Kim Phillips-Fein, *Invisible Hands: The Making of the Conservative Movement from the New Deal to Reagan* (New York: W. W. Norton, 2009), 190; John S. Saloma III, *Ominous Politics: The New Conservative Labyrinth* (New York: Hill and Wang, 1984), 67; Michael Useem, *The Inner Circle: Large Corporations and the Rise of Business Political Activity in the US and the UK* (Oxford: Oxford University Press, 1984), 163.

34 Thomas B. Edsall, *The New Politics of Inequality* (New York: W. W. Norton, 1984), 123.

35 Waterhouse, *Lobbying America*, chapter 2.

36 Phillips-Fein, *Invisible Hands*, 200; Waterhouse, *Lobbying America*, chapter 2; Alyssa Katz, *The Influence Machine: The U.S. Chamber of Commerce and the Corporate Capture of American Life* (New York: Spiegel and Grau, 2015), chapter 3.

37 Patrick Akard, "The Return of the Market: Corporate Mobilization and the Transformation of U.S. Economic Policy, 1974–1985" (PhD diss., University of Kansas, 1989), 106.

38 Mark Green and Andrew Buchsbaum, *The Corporate Lobbies: Political Profiles of the Business Roundtable and The Chamber of Commerce* (Public Citizen, 1980), 108–18; Patrick Akard, "Corporate Mobilization and Political Power: The Transformation of U.S. Economic Policy in the 1970s," *American Sociological Review* 57:5 (1992), 597–615; Patrick Akard, "The Political Origins of 'Supply-Side' Economic Policy: The Humphrey-Hawkins Bill and the Revenue Act of 1978," *Political Power and Social Theory* 10 (1996), 95–148.

39 Domhoff, *Myth of Liberal Ascendancy*, chapter 11; Laurence H. Shoup and William Minter, *Imperial Brain Trust: The Council on Foreign Relations and United States Foreign Policy* (New York: Monthly Review Press, 1977), 302; Judith Stein, *Pivotal Decade: How the United States Traded Factories for Finance in the Seventies* (New Haven: Yale University Press, 2010), chapter 10; Tim Barker, "Other People's Blood," *n+1* (Spring 2019); Michael A. McCarthy, "The Monetary Hawks," *Jacobin*, August 3, 2016.

40 Stein, *Pivotal Decade*, 234, 265; Domhoff, *Myth of Liberal Ascendancy*, chapter 11; William Greider, *Secrets of the Temple: How the Federal Reserve Runs the Country* (New York: Simon and Schuster, 1987), 571; see also Thomas Ferguson and Joel Rogers, *Right Turn: The Decline of the Democrats and the Future of American Politics* (New York: Hill and Wang, 1986), 116–17. Judith Stein argues that the Roundtable opposed Volcker's austerity. However, the testimony she cites by Roundtable member Stanton Williams does not support this. In his testimony, he complains extensively about inflation, calls for "fiscal restraint by the government," and offers no criticism of the high interest rates. Compare Stein, *Pivotal Decade*, 237 with "Capital Formation and Inflation," *Hearing Before the Joint Economic Committee*, 96th Congress, 2nd session, June 18, 1980, 43–50.

41 On business support for Reagan in 1980, see Thomas Ferguson and Joel Rogers, "The Reagan Victory," in Thomas Ferguson and Joel Rogers, eds., *The Hidden Election: Politics and Economics in the 1980 Presidential Campaign* (New York: Pantheon, 1981), 3–64; Ferguson and Rogers, *Right Turn*, 119–24.

42 Waterhouse, *Lobbying America*, chapter 7; Ferguson and Rogers, *Right Turn*, 121; Akard, "Corporate Mobilization and Political Power," 608.

43 Ferguson and Rogers, *Right Turn*, 122; Akard, "Corporate Mobilization and Political Power," 610–11.

44 Waterhouse, *Lobbying America*, chapter 7; Akard, "Corporate Mobilization and Political Power"; William J. Lanouette, "Chamber's Ponderous Decision Making Leaves It Sitting on the Sidelines," *National Journal*, July 24, 1982; Akard, "Return of the Market."

45 Katz, *The Influence Machine*, chapter 3; Mizruchi, *The Fracturing*, 198–204.

46 Mizruchi, *The Fracturing*, 200–4; Waterhouse, *Lobbying America*, chapter 7; Jacob Hacker and Paul Pierson, *American Amnesia: How the War on Government Made Us Forget What Made America Prosper* (New York: Simon & Schuster, 2017), chapter 7.

47 Michael C. Dreiling and Derek Y. Darves, *Agents of Neoliberal Globalization: Corporate Networks, State Structures, and Trade Policy* (Cambridge: Cambridge University Press, 2016); James Shoch, *Trading Blows: Party Competition and U.S. Trade Policy in a Globalizing Era* (Chapel Hill: University of North Carolina Press, 2001); Hacker and Pierson, *American Amnesia*; *Fortune*, "The Fallen Giant," December 8, 1997; Peter H. Stone, "Business Strikes Back," *National Journal*, October 25, 1997, 2130.

48 Hacker and Pierson, *American Amnesia*; Bo Becker, Daniel Bergstresser, and Guhan Subramanian, "Does Shareholder Proxy Access Improve Firm Value? Evidence from the Business Roundtable's Challenge," *Journal of Law and Economics* 56:1 (February 2013).

49 Mark A. Smith, *American Business and Political Power: Public Opinion, Elections, and Democracy* (Chicago: University of Chicago Press, 2000), 45.

50 Hacker and Pierson, *American Amnesia*; G. William Domhoff, "Is the Corporate Elite Fractured, or Is There Continuing Corporate Dominance? Two Contrasting Views," *Class, Race, and Corporate Power* 3:1 (2015); McGee Young, *Developing Interests: Organizational Change and the Politics of Advocacy* (Lawrence: University Press of Kansas, 2010); Ronald G. Shaiko and Marc A. Wallace, "From Wall Street to Main Street: The National Federation of Independent Business and the New Republican Majority," in Robert Biersack, Paul S. Hernnson, and Clyde Wilcox, eds., *After the Revolution: PACs, Lobbies, and the Republican Congress*, 18–35.

51 Hacker and Pierson, *American Amnesia*; Katz, *The Influence Machine*, 58–63.

52 John B. Judis, *The Paradox of American Democracy: Elites, Special Interests, and the Betrayal of Public Trust* (New York: Pantheon, 2000), 238–40; Hacker and Pierson, *American Amnesia*; Katz, *The Influence Machine*.

53 Katz, *The Influence Machine*, chapter 4; Jeff Nesbit, *Poison Tea: How Big Oil and Big Tobacco Invented the Tea Party and Captured the GOP* (Thomas Dunne, 2016).

54 Katz, *The Influence Machine*; Hacker and Pierson, *American Amnesia*.

55 Richard Lachmann, *First-Class Passengers on a Sinking Ship: Elite Politics and the Decline of Great Powers* (Verso, 2020).

2. The Enfeebled Parties

1 Liam Stack, "Denounced by His Party as a Nazi, Arthur Jones Wins Illinois G.O.P. Congressional Primary," *New York Times*, March 20, 2018; Elise Hu, "Meet Kesha Rogers," *Texas Tribune*, March 16, 2010.

2 J. A. W. Gunn, *Factions No More: Attitudes to Party in Government and Opposition in Eighteenth-Century England* (London: Frank Cass, 1972); Richard Hofstadter, *The Idea of a Party System: The Rise of Legitimate Opposition in the United States, 1780–1840* (Berkeley: University of California Press, 1969); Martin Shefter, *Political Parties and the State: The American Historical Experience* (Princeton: Princeton University Press, 1994), 66; Ronald P. Formisano, "Federalists and Republicans: Parties Yes–System No," in Paul Kleppner et al., eds., *The Evolution of American Electoral Systems* (Westport, CT: Greenwood Press, 1981), 37–76.

3 Lynn L. Marshall, "The Strange Stillbirth of the Whig Party," *American Historical Review* 72:2 (1967), 445–68; Shefter, *Political Parties and the State*, 70–1.

4 John H. Aldrich, *Why Parties? A Second Look* (Chicago: University of Chicago Press, 2011), 99; Stephen Skowronek, *Building a New American State: The Expansion of National Administrative Capacities, 1877–1920* (Cambridge: Cambridge University Press, 1982), 26.

5 James M. McPherson, *The Battle Cry of Freedom: The Civil War Era* (New York: Oxford University Press, 1988), 52–64; Marc W. Kruman, "The Second American Party System and the Transformation of Revolutionary Republicanism," *Journal of the Early Republic* 12:4 (1992), 509–37; William G. Shade, "Political Pluralism and Party Development: The Creation of a Modern Party System, 1815–1852," in Kleppner et al., *The Evolution of American Electoral Systems*, 104.

6   William E. Gienapp, "The Republican Party and the Slave Power," in Stephen E. Maizlish and Robert H. Abzug, eds., *New Perspectives on Race and Slavery in America: Essays in Honor of Kenneth M. Stampp* (Lexington: University of Kentucky, 1986), 51–78; James Oakes, *Freedom National: The Destruction of Slavery in the United States, 1861–1865* (W. W. Norton, 2014); Eric Foner, *Reconstruction: America's Unfinished Revolution* (New York: HarperCollins, 1988) On the organization of the prewar Republican Party, see Michael D. Pierson, "'Prairies on Fire': The Organization of the 1856 Mass Republican Rally in Beloit, Wisconsin," *Civil War History* 48:2 (2002), 101–22.

7   W. E. B. Du Bois, *Black Reconstruction in America: An Essay Toward a History of the Part Which Black Folk Played in the Attempt to Reconstruct Democracy in America, 1860–1880* (New York: Atheneum, 1977); Edwin Godkin, "Socialism in South Carolina," *The Nation* 18:459 (April 16, 1874), 247–8; Foner, *Reconstruction*, 527. On Godkin's connection with New York business, see Sven Beckert, *The Monied Metropolis: New York City and the Consolidation of the American Bourgeoisie, 1850–1896* (Cambridge: Harvard University Press, 2001), 190–1.

8   R. Hal Williams, "Dry Bones and Dead Language: The Democratic Party," in H. Wayne Morgan, ed., *The Gilded Age: A Reappraisal*, rev. ed (New York: Alfred A. Knopf, 1970), 130; Philip H. Burch Jr., *Elites in American History: The Civil War to the New Deal* (New York: Holmes and Meier, 1981); Thomas Ferguson, *Golden Rule: The Investment Theory of Party Competition and the Logic of Money-Driven Political Systems* (Chicago: University of Chicago Press, 1995).

9   Austin Ranney, *The Doctrine of Responsible Party Government: Its Origin and Present State* (Urbana: University of Illinois Press, 1962 [1954]), 32–4; Max Weber, *Charisma and Disenchantment: The Vocation Lectures*, Paul Reitter and Chad Wellmon, eds. (New York: The New York Review of Books, 2020), 105–6.

10 Ferguson, *Golden Rule*, 71–9; J. Morgan Kousser, *The Shaping of Southern Politics: Suffrage Restrictions and the Creation of the One-Party South, 1880–1910* (New Haven: Yale University Press, 1974).

11 Shefter, *Political Parties and the State*, 75–81; Alexander Keyssar, *The Right to Vote: The Contested History of Democracy in the United States* (New York: Basic Books, 2000), chapter 5.

12 Frank Parsons, *The City for the People: Or, the Municipalization of the City Government and of Local Franchises* (Philadelphia: C. F. Taylor, 1900), 471. See Nancy Rosenblum, *On the Side of the Angels: An Appreciation of Parties and Partisanship* (Princeton: Princeton University Press, 2008), 196–7; Samuel P. Hays, "The

Politics of Reform in Municipal Government in the Progressive Era," *Pacific Northwest Quarterly* 55:4 (1964), 157–69; James Weinstein, "Organized Business and the City Commission and Manager Movements," *The Journal of Southern History* 28:2 (1962), 166–82.

13 Adam Winkler, "Voters' Rights and Parties' Wrongs: Early Political Party Regulation in the State Courts, 1886–1915," *Columbia Law Review* 100:3 (2000), 873–900; Leo Alilunas, "The Rise of the 'White Primary' Movement as a Means of Barring the Negro from the Polls," *Journal of Negro History*, 252 (1940), 161–72; Mark Lawrence Kornbluh, *Why America Stopped Voting: The Decline of Participatory Democracy and the Emergence of Modern American Politics* (New York: New York University Press, 2000), 127; Adrian Ware, *The American Direct Primary: Party Institutionalization and Transformation in the North* (Cambridge: Cambridge University Press, 2000).

14 Frances Fox Piven and Richard A. Cloward, *Why Americans Don't Vote* (New York: Pantheon, 1989), 73; Brian F. Schaffner, Matthew Streb, and Gerald Wright, "Teams Without Uniforms: The Nonpartisan Ballot in State and Local Elections," *Political Research Quarterly* 54:1 (2001), 7–30; Kornbluh, *Why America Stopped Voting*, 126–8; Michael E. McGerr, *The Decline of Popular Politics: The American North, 1865–1928* (New York: Oxford University Press, 1986), chapter 7.

15 V. O. Key Jr., *American State Politics: An Introduction* (New York: Alfred A. Knopf, 1956) 119; Charles R. Adrian, "Some General Characteristics of Nonpartisan Elections," *American Political Science Review* 46:3 (1952), 766–76; Ware, *The American Direct Primary*, 235–41.

16 Kornbluh, *Why America Stopped Voting*, 127; V. O. Key Jr., *Politics, Parties, and Pressure Groups* (New York: Crowell, 1964), 342

17 Ware, *The American Direct Primary*, 244–6.

18 Michael Kazin, "What Did Gompers Start?" *Labor History* 40:2 (1999), 189–92.

19 David Montgomery, *The Fall of the House of Labor: The Workplace, the State, and American Labor Activism, 1865–1925* (Cambridge: Cambridge University Press), 269–75; Daniel Schlozman, *When Movements Anchor Parties: Electoral Alignments in American History* (Princeton: Princeton University Press, 2016), 52–5. On the cracks in voluntarism, see Howell Harris, "The Snares of Liberalism? Politicians, Bureaucrats, and the Shaping of Federal Labour Relations in the United States, ca. 1915–1947," in Steven Tolliday and Jonathan Zeitlin, eds., *Shop Floor Bargaining and the State: Historical and Comparative Perspectives* (Cambridge: Cambridge University Press, 1985), 152–9.

20 Franklin D. Roosevelt, "The 'Forgotten Man' Speech," radio address from Albany, New York, American Presidency Project, presidency.ucsb.edu; Irving Bernstein, *The Turbulent Years: A History of the American Worker, 1933–1941* (Chicago: Haymarket Books, 2010 [1969]), 3; Barry Eidlin, *Labor and the Class Idea in the United States and Canada* (Cambridge: Cambridge University Press, 2018), 171.

21 Arthur M. Schlesinger Jr., *The Coming of the New Deal: 1933–1935* (New York: Houghton Mifflin, 1958), 139; James A. Gross, *The Making of the National Labor Relations Board: A Study in Economics, Politics, and the Law, Volume I (1933–1937)* (Albany: State University of New York Press, 1974), chapter 1.

22 For an overview of the law's contents, see Bernstein, *The Turbulent Years*, chapter 7; Schlozman, *When Movements Anchor Parties*, 58; Gross, *The Making of the National Labor Relations Board*, 145; David Plotke, *Building a Democratic Political Order: Reshaping American Liberalism in the 1930s and 1940s* (Cambridge: Cambridge University Press, 1996), 122; Eidlin, *Labor and the Class Idea*, 180.

23 Harvard Sitkoff, *A New Deal for Blacks: The Emergence of Civil Rights as a National Issue, Volume I: The Depression Decade* (Oxford: Oxford University Press, 1978), 41, 95–6; James L. Sundquist, *Dynamics of the Party System: Alignment and Realignment of Political Parties in the United States* (Washington, DC: The Brookings Institution, 1983), 217–18.

24 Schlozman, *When Movements Anchor Parties*, 60–70.

25 Sundquist, *Dynamics of the Party System*, 226–8, 244–52.

26 Nixon is partial exception to this, having come from the party's conservative wing initially. But his conservative bona fides were insufficient to stop the party right from mounting an attempt at a Goldwater nomination. See Rick Perlstein, *Before the Storm: Barry Goldwater and the Unmaking of the American Consensus* (New York: Hill and Wang, 2001), chapter three.

27 James T. Patterson, "A Conservative Coalition Forms in Congress, 1933–1939," *Journal of American History* 52:4 (1966), 757–72; Ira Katznelson, Kim Geiger, and Daniel Kryder, "Limiting Liberalism: The Southern Veto in Congress, 1933–1950," *Political Science Quarterly* 108:2 (1993), 283–306; Shefter, *Political Parties and the State*, 84.

28 Susan Dunn, *Roosevelt's Purge: How FDR Fought to Change the Democratic Party* (Cambridge: Belknap Press, 2010); Doris Kearns Goodwin, *No Ordinary Time: Franklin and Eleanor Roosevelt: The Home Front in World War II* (New York: Simon and Schuster, 1994), 525–6; Paul Heideman, "It's Their Party," *Jacobin* 20 (Winter 2016), 23–39.

29 Harvard Sitkoff, "Harry Truman and the Election of 1948: The Coming of Age of Civil Rights in American Politics,"' *Journal of Southern History* 27:4 (1971), 597–616; Adam Hilton, *True Blues: The Contentious Transformation of the Democratic Party* (Philadelphia: University of Pennsylvania Press, 2021), 42.

30 Sundquist, *Dynamics of the Party System*, chapter 11; Hilton, *True Blues*, 33–5.

31 Paul F. Boller, *Presidential Campaigns* (Oxford: Oxford University Press, 1984), 295.

32 Doris Kearns Goodwin, *Lyndon Johnson and the American Dream* (New York: Open Road, 1976), 154.

33 Committee on Political Parties, *Toward a More Responsible Two-Party System*, supplement, *American Political Science Review* 44:3 (1950), v–99. On the report, see Ranney, *The Doctrine of Responsible Party Government*; Rosenfeld, *The Polarizers*, chapter 1; Philip A. Klinkner, *The Losing Parties: Out-Party National Committees, 1956–1993* (New Haven: Yale University Press, 1994), 20.

34 Klinkner, *The Losing Parties*, 26–40; On Acheson and Nitze, see Luke Fletcher, "The Collapse of the Western World: Acheson, Nitze, and the NSC 68/Rearmament Decision," *Diplomatic History* 4:4 (2016), 750–77.

35 Julian Zelizer, *On Capitol Hill: The Struggle to Reform Congress and its Consequences, 1948–2000* (Cambridge: Cambridge University Press, 2004), 44.

36 Zelizer, *On Capitol Hill*, 37–8, 49–50, 54–6; Rosenfeld, *The Polarizers*, 41–2.

37 Rosenfeld, *The Polarizers*, 52.

38 Frances Fox Piven and Richard Cloward, *Poor People's Movements: Why They Succeed, How They Fail* (New York: Vintage, 1977), 221–4; Jack Bloom, *Class, Race, and the Civil Rights Movement* (Bloomington: Indiana University Press, 1987), 114–49; Joseph E. Luders, *The Civil Rights Movement and the Logic of Social Change* (Cambridge: Cambridge University Press, 2010), 54–77; Hilton, *True Blues*, 45–6.

39 Dominic Sandbrook, *Eugene McCarthy and the Rise and Fall of Postwar American Liberalism* (New York: Alfred A. Knopf, 2004), 133–41. In response, Johnson began referring to Fulbright as a Soviet agent in private.

40 William H. Chafe, *Never Stop Running: Allard Lowenstein and the Struggle to Save American Liberalism* (New York: Basic Books, 1993), 267–72; Sandbrook, *Eugene McCarthy*, 162–73; Lowenstein would later claim that the MFDP had been his idea, much to the vexation of SNCC activists. Lowenstein's biographer concludes that MFDP organizer Ed King was correct when he

observed that "Al deserves more credit than SNCC gave him and less than he took."

41 Hilton, *True Blues*, 54.

42 Hilton, *True Blues*, 62–4; Melvin Small, "'Hey, Hey, LBJ!' American Domestic Politics and the Vietnam War," in David L. Anderson, ed., *The Columbia History of the Vietnam War* (New York: Columbia University Press, 2011), 345–6; Rosenfeld, *The Polarizers* 123–4.

43 Hilton, *True Blues*, 69.

44 Rosenfeld, *The Polarizers*, 136; Hilton, *True Blues*, 72–87. Importantly, a number of unions broke with Meany and vocally supported reform, including the UAW, AFSCME, and the Communications Workers.

45 Hilton, *True Blues*, 79.

46 Rosenfeld, *The Polarizers*, 151; Hilton, *True Blues*, 125.

47 Hilton, *True Blues*, 110–28; Christopher Lydon, "The Democrats and Reform," *New York Times*, December 1, 1974, 5.

48 Hilton, *True Blues* 197.

49 David Rosenbaum, "5 Mississippians Retain Seniority," *New York Times*, January 20, 1971, 14; Rosenfeld, *Polarizers*, 161.

50 Eric Schickler, Eric McGhee, and John Sides, "Remaking the House and Senate: Personal Power, Ideology, and the 1970s Reforms," *Legislative Studies Quarterly* 28:3 (2003), 301–2. A few years later, House Democrats instituted some more centralizing reforms, giving more committee appointment power directly to the caucus leadership. However, as will be explored later in this chapter, the massive increase in campaign costs over the course of the decade made the leadership contest itself into a function of fundraising prowess, further hollowing out the autonomous institutional decision-making power of the party itself.

51 Patterson, "A Conservative Coalition," 763–4; Robert Mason, *The Republican Party and American Politics from Hoover to Reagan* (Cambridge: Cambridge University Press, 2012), 44–8; Clyde P. Weed, *The Nemesis of Reform: The Republican Party During the New Deal* (New York: Columbia University Press, 1994), 89–90.

52 Mason, *The Republican Party and American Politics*, 61; Elliott A. Rosen, *The Republican Party in the Age of Roosevelt: Sources of Anti-Government Conservatism in the United States* (Charlottesville: University of Virginia Press, 2014), 32–6; George Wolfskill, *The Revolt of the Conservatives: The American Liberty League, 1934–1940* (Westport, CT: Greenwood Press, 1962) 214–5; Eric Schickler and Devin Caughey, "Public Opinion, Organized Labor, and the Limits of New Deal Liberalism, 1936–1945" *Studies in American Political Development* 25 (2011), 162. One Roosevelt surrogate said of the Liberty League. "They have appropriated

the Liberty Bell as their symbol, but they apparently think the Revolution was fought to make Long Island safe for polo players."

53   James T. Patterson, *Congressional Conservatism and the New Deal* (Lexington: University of Kentucky Press, 1967), 149–54; Katznelson, Geider, and Kreiger, "Limiting Liberalism." A backlash among voters against the sit-down strikes of 1937 appears to have been crucial in delivering GOP seats. Schickler and Caughey, "Public Opinion."

54   James T. Patterson, *The New Deal and the States: Federalism in Transition* (Princeton, Princeton University Press, 1969), 140–2; Rosen, *The Republican Party in the Age of Roosevelt*, 85–8; Mason, *The Republican Party and American Politics*, 76–7.

55   Rosen, *The Republican Party in the Age of Roosevelt*, 97–105; Philip H. Burch Jr., *Elites in American History, Volume III: The New Deal to the Carter Administration* (New York: Holmes and Meier, 1980), 45; Donald Bruce Johnson, "Wendell Willkie and the Republican Party" (PhD diss., University of Illinois, 1952), 84–94. Willkie also had the support of the Du Ponts, who viewed him as their best chance after the dismal failure of the Liberty League.

56   Rosen, *The Republican Party in the Age of Roosevelt*, 109–13; Mason, *The Republican Party and American Politics*, 95.

57   Mason, *The Republican Party and American Politics*, 96–101; Rosen, *The Republican Party in the Age of Roosevelt*, 153–6.

58   Rosen, *The Republican Party in the Age of Roosevelt*, 142–8, 156, 172–3; Mason, *The Republican Party and American Politics*, 107–8; "Fashions in Politics," *New York Times*, March 17, 1945, 12.

59   Michael Bowen, *The Roots of Modern Conservatism: Dewey, Taft, and the Battle for the Soul of Republican Party* (Chapel Hill: University of North Carolina Press, 2011), 21–31; Mason, *The Republican Party and American Politics*, 115.

60   Bowen, *The Roots of Modern Conservatism*, 59–68; Mason, *The Republican Party and American Politics*, 120–1.

61   Rosenfeld, *The Polarizers*, 62. Seventy-nine incumbents who supported Taft-Hartley lost in 1948, including nine senators. Schlozman, *When Movements Anchor Parties*, 140.

62   Burch, *Elites in American History, Volume III*, 126–7; Travis Beal Jacobs, "Eisenhower, the American Assembly, and 1952," *Presidential Studies Quarterly* 22:3 (1992), 458; Mason, *The Republican Party and American Politics*, 143. Paul Hoffman, the first head of the CED, had several personal meetings with Eisenhower in 1951 to persuade him to run. Alan R. Raucher, *Paul G. Hoffman: Architect of Foreign Aid* (Lexington: The University Press of Kentucky, 1985), 92.

63   Geoffrey Kabaservice, *Rule and Ruin: The Downfall of Moderation*

and the Destruction of the Republican Party From Eisenhower to the Tea Party (New York: Oxford University Press, 2012), 15; Kevin S. Price, "The Partisan Legacies of Preemptive Leadership: Assessing the Eisenhower Cohorts in the U.S. House," *Political Research Quarterly* 55:3 (2002), 609–31.

64 Kabaservice, 13–14; Bowen, *The Roots of Modern Conservatism*, 85–6.

65 Patrick C. Patton, "Standing at Thermopylae: A History of the American Liberty League" (PhD diss., Temple University, 2015), 168–72. Clarence E. Wunderlin Jr., "'Be Patient and Satisfied with Their Progress Thus Far': Senator Robert A. Taft's Opposition to a Permanent Fair Employment Practices Commission, 1944–1950," *Ohio History* 120 (2013), 92–117. More generally on Liberty League ambitions for the South, see Wolfskill, *The Revolt of the Conservatives*, 189–191.

66 Rosenfeld, *The Polarizers*, 70–1; Scott N. Heidepriem, *A Fair Chance for a Free People: The Biography of Karl E. Mundt, United States Senator* (Madison, SD: Leader Printing, 1988), 158–66.

67 Allan J. Lichteim, *White Protestant Nation: The Rise of the American Conservative Movement* (New York: Atlantic Monthly Press, 2008), chapter 5; Perlstein, *Before the Storm*, chapter 1.

68 For more detailed accounts of the Goldwater campaign, see Perlstein, *Before the Storm*; Mary C. Brennan, *Turning Right in the Sixties: The Conservative Capture of the GOP* (Chapel Hill: University of North Carolina Press, 1995); and Elizabeth Tandy Shermer, ed., *Barry Goldwater and the Remaking of the American Political Landscape* (Tucson: University of Arizona Press, 2013).

69 Klinkner, *The Losing Parties*, 71–7.

70 John H. Fenton, *Midwest Politics* (New York: Holt, Rinehart, and Winston, 1966), 117; Brian M. Conley, *The Rise of the Republican Right: From Goldwater to Reagan* (New York: Routledge, 2019), 41–50.

71 Brian M. Conley, "The Politics of Party Renewal: The 'Service Party' and the Origins of the Post-Goldwater Republican Right," *Studies in American Political Development* 27: 1 (2013), 51–67.

72 Conley, *Rise of the Republican Right*, 99–100, 119–20.

73 Klinkner, *The Losing Parties*, 146–52; Conley, *Rise of the Republican Right*, 116–27. In fact, one of the major initiatives of the RNC under Reagan was to emulate Amway's multilevel marketing structure. Daniel J. Galvin, *Presidential Party Building: Dwight D. Eisenhower to George W. Bush* (Princeton: Princeton University Press, 2010), chapter 6.

74 Klinkner, *The Losing Parties*, 128; David Menefee-Liberty, "Embracing Campaign-Centered Politics at the Democratic Headquarters: Charles Manatt and Paul Kirk in the 1980s," in John C.

Green, ed., *Politics, Professionalism, and Power: Modern Party Organization and the Legacy of Ray C. Bliss* (Lanham: University Press of America, 1994), 167–85.

75 Garvin, *Presidential Party Building*, chapter 9; Sidney Milkis, *The President and the Parties: The Transformation of the American Party System Since the New Deal* (New York: Oxford University Press, 1993), 189; Klinkner, *The Losing Parties*, 93; Zelizer, *On Capitol Hill*, 111.

76 Zelizer, *On Capitol Hill*, chapter 7; Marian Currinder, *Money in the House: Campaign Funds and Congressional Party Politics* (Boulder: Westview Press, 2009), 19–21.

77 Morris Fiorina, "The Decline of Collective Responsibility in American Politics," *Engineering and Science* 44:2 (1980), 14; Paul S. Herrnson, "The Evolution of National Party Organizations," in L. Sandy Maisel and Jeffrey M. Berry, eds., *The Oxford Handbook of American Political Parties and Interest Groups* (Oxford: Oxford University Press, 2010), 234.

78 Gary J. Andres, "Business Involvement in Campaign Finance: Factors Influencing the Decision to Form a Corporate PAC," *PS* 18:2 (1985), 214; Vogel, *Fluctuating Fortunes*, 207; Edwin M. Epstein, "Business and Labor Under the Federal Election Campaign Act of 1971," in Michael J. Malbin, ed., *Parties, Interest Groups, and Campaign Finance Laws* (Washington, DC: American Enterprise Institute, 1980), 110–11, 118.

79 Allan J. Cigler, "Political Parties and Interest Groups: Competitors, Collaborators, and Uneasy Allies," in Eric M. Uslaner, ed., *American Political Parties: A Reader* (Itasca, IL: F. E. Peacock Publishers, 1993), 418–21; Adam Clymer, "New GOP Chairman Criticizes Party's Right Wing," *New York Times*, January 18, 1981, 18; Clymer, "G.O.P Seeking Accord with Conservative Groups," *New York Times*, June 24, 1981, 17; Daniel Schlozman and Sam Rosenfeld, *The Hollow Parties: The Many Pasts and Disordered Present of American Political Parties* (Princeton: Princeton University Press, 2024), chapter 6.

80 Richard S. Katz and Robin Kolodny, "Party Organization as an Empty Vessel: Parties in American Politics," in Richard S. Katz and Peter Mair, eds., *How Parties Organize: Change and Adaptation in Party Organizations in Western Democracies* (London: Sage, 1994), 23–50.

81 Thomas Ferguson, "Legislators Never Bowl Alone: Big Money, Mass Media, and the Polarization of Congress," Institute for New Economic Thinking working paper, 2011, ineteconomics.org.

82 Currinder, *Money in the House*, 24–6, 87–9; Ross K. Baker, *The New Fat Cats: Members of Congress as Political Benefactors* (New York: Priority Press, 1989), 29–40.

83 Currinder, *Money in the House*, 28–31, 124–5.

84 Eric Heberlig, Marc Hetherington, and Bruce Larson, "The Price of Leadership: Campaign Money and the Polarization of Congressional Parties," *The Journal of Politics* 68:4 (2006), 992–1005; Currinder, *Money in the House*; Frances McCall Rosenbluth and Ian Shapiro, *Responsible Parties: Saving Democracy from Itself* (New Haven: Yale University Press, 2018), 114–18.

85 Paul S. Herrnson and David Menefee-Libey, "The Dynamics of Party Organizational Development," *The Midsouth Political Science Journal* 11 (1991), 3–30.

86 Gerald C. Wright, "State Parties Research: The Quest for Strong, Competitive State Parties," in Maisel and Berry, *Oxford Handbook*, 410–13; John J. Coleman, "The Resurgence of Party Organization? A Dissent from the New Orthodoxy," in Daniel M. Shea and John C. Green, eds., *The State of the Parties: The Changing Role of Contemporary American Parties* (Lanham: Rowman and Littlefield, 1994), 318.

87 Daniel Schlozman and Sam Rosenfeld, "The Hollow Parties," in Frances E. Lee and Nolan McCarty, eds., *Can America Govern Itself?* (Cambridge: Cambridge University Press, 2019), 121.

88 Nolan McCarty, Keith T. Poole, and Howard Rosenthal, *Polarized America: The Dance of Ideology and Unequal Riches* (Cambridge, MA: MIT Press, 2006), chapter 2.

3. The Republican Revolution

1 Kabaservice, *Rule and Ruin*, 371–2; Matthew N. Green and Jeffrey Crouch, *Newt Gingrich: The Rise and Fall of a Party Entrepreneur* (Lawrence: University Press of Kansas, 2022), 22, 25.

2 The consultant expanded on his metaphor: "We exist with some support from North Vietnam (the formal Republican Party, the Senate, and the Presidency) on the basis of larger shared goals, but we live under the domination and corruption of the Republic of South Vietnam (the Democrats in the House, and in the majority of the 50 state legislatures, local officials and Governors)." Julian Zelizer, *Burning Down the House: Newt Gingrich, the Fall of a Speaker, and the Rise of the New Republican Party* (New York: Penguin Press, 2020), 54–5, 61; Ferguson and Rogers, *Right Turn*, 155–6; Green and Crouch, *Newt Gingrich*, 34.

3 Zelizer, *Burning Down the House*, 56–7; Green and Crouch, 33–4.

4 Sean M. Theriault, *The Gingrich Senators: The Roots of Partisan Warfare in Congress* (Oxford: Oxford University Press, 2013), 22–3; Green and Crouch, *Newt Gingrich*, 59–74; Randall Strahan, *Leading Representatives: The Agency of Leaders in the*

Politics of the U.S. House (Baltimore: Johns Hopkins University Press, 2007), 139.

5 Nicole Hemmer, *Partisans: The Conservative Revolutionaries Who Remade American Politics in the 1990s* (New York: Basic Books, 2022), 46; Marcus M. Witcher, *Getting Right with Reagan: The Struggle for True Conservatism, 1980–2016* (Lawrence: University Press of Kansas, 2019), 34, 42, 78; Green and Crouch, *Newt Gingrich*, 44.

6 Larry J. Sabato and Glenn R. Simpson, *Dirty Little Secrets: The Persistence of Corruption in American Politics* (New York: Times Books, 1996), 77–8.

7 William Corkery, "Newt Gingrich and GOPAC: Training the Farm Team That Helped Win the Republican Revolution of 1994" (honors thesis, College of William and Mary, 2011), 17–18, 26–7.

8 Corkery, "Newt Gingrich and GOPAC," 27; Green and Crouch, *Newt Gingrich*, 84. On Gingrich's self-image in this regard, see Strahan, *Leading Representatives*, 141–3.

9 Both Julian Zelizer and Randall Strahan, for example, to take two of the most influential recent accounts of Gingrich's career, more or less ignore its role in Republican fundraising to focus on its ideological work. See Zelizer, *Burning Down the House* and Strahan, *Leading Representatives*.

10 Sabato and Simpson, *Dirty Little Secrets*, 78.

11 Sabato and Simpson, 79–81.

12 Sabato and Simpson, 124; Michael Kranish, "The House That Gingrich's PAC Rebuilt," *Seattle Times* November 23, 1994, A3; Green and Crouch, *Newt Gingrich*, 91.

13 Eliza Newlin Carney, "PACMEN" *National Journal*, Oct 1, 1994, 2268; Currinder, *Money in the House*, 123–4. See also Gary Jacobson, "The 1994 House Elections in Perspective," *Political Science Quarterly* 111:2 (1996), 203–23; Thomas Ferguson, "The 1994 Explosion," in Benjamin Ginsberg and Alan Stone, eds., *Do Elections Matter?*, 3rd ed.(New York: Routledge, 1996), 88–9.

14 On Coelho's exploits, see Brooks Jackson, *Honest Graft: Big Money and the American Political Process* (New York: Alfred A. Knopf, 1988).

15 R. H. Melton, "Funds Flock To PAC Controlled by Gingrich," *The Washington Post*, April 10, 1995; Elizabeth Drew, *Showdown: The Struggle Between the Gingrich Congress and the Clinton White House* (New York: Simon and Schuster, 1996), 118; Strahan, *Leading Representatives*, 148–52; Currinder, *Money in the House*, 134–5; Ferguson, "Big Money, Mass Media, and the Polarization of Congress," in William Crotty, ed., *Polarized Politics: The Impact of Divisiveness in the US Political System* (Boulder: Lynne Rienner Publishers, 2015), 99; Jim VandeHei,

"GOP Chairmen Warned About Contributions, Gingrich, Linder Seek More Cash For 'Breakout' Ads" *Roll Call* Oct 1, 1998.

16 Issue One, *The Price Of Power: A Deep-Dive Analysis into How Political Parties Squeeze Influential Lawmakers to Boost Campaign Coffers*, Washington, DC (2017) issueone.org; Eric Heberlig, Marc Hetherington, and Bruce Larson, "The Price of Leadership: Campaign Money and the Polarization of Congressional Parties." *Journal of Politics* 68 (2006), 992–1005; Damon M. Cann, *Sharing the Wealth: Member Contributions and the Exchange Theory of Party Influence in the U.S. House of Representatives* (Albany: SUNY Press, 2008); Eleanor Neff Powell, "Where Money Matters in Congress," unpublished working paper, Yale University, 2010.

17 Lou Dubose and Jan Reid, *The Hammer: Tom DeLay, God, Money, and the Rise of the Republican Congress* (New York: PublicAffairs, 2004), 65, 87; Paul Kane, "Dennis Hastert's Rise Was Based on Being the No 'Skeletons' Guy—Until This Week," *Washington Post*, May 29, 2015; Kabaservice, 375–6; Thomas B. Edsall, *Building Red America: The New Conservative Coalition and the Drive for Permanent Power* (New York: Basic Books, 2006), 135–6.

18 David Maraniss and Michael Weiskopff, "Speaker and His Directors Make the Cash Flow Right," *Washington Post*, November 27, 1995, A1; Linda Killian, *The Freshmen: What Happened to the Republican Revolution* (Boulder: Westview Press, 1998), 118.

19 Killian, *The Freshmen*, 425–6; Green and Crouch, *Newt Gingrich*, 149–56.

20 David Baumann, "Grading the Class of '94," *National Journal*, May 1, 2004, 1323.

21 Katz, *Influence Machine*, 62. For other exponents of this argument, see Hacker and Pierson, *American Amnesia*, 216–7 and Mark S. Mizruchi, "*The Power Elite* in Historical Context: A Reevaluation of Mills' Thesis, Then and Now," *Theory and Society* 42:2 (2017), 95–116.

22 Nelson Lichtenstein and Judith Stein, *A Fabulous Failure: The Clinton Presidency and the Transformation of American Capitalism* (Princeton: Princeton University Press, 2023), 101–7.

23 Katz, *Influence Machine*, 62; John Judis, "Abandoned Surgery: Business and the Failure of Healthcare Reform," *American Prospect*, April 1, 1995; Mizruchi, "*The Power Elite* in Historical Context," 110.

24 Lichtenstein and Stein, *A Fabulous Failure*, 113–117. Even the Democratic Leadership Council, with whose neoliberal politics Clinton has long been identified, began signaling its opposition to the plan. See Jason Stahl, *Right Moves: The Conservative Think*

Tank in American Political Culture Since 1945 (Chapel Hill: University of North Carolina Press, 2016), 158.

25 G. William Domhoff, *The Corporate Rich and the Power Elite in the Twentieth Century: How They Won, Why Liberals and Labor Lost* (New York: Routledge, 2020), 348.

26 Dana Priest and Ann Devroy, "Business Leaders Split with Clinton," *Washington Post*, February 2, 1994. For details on the process that led to the Roundtable's decision, see Judis, "Abandoned Surgery" and Lichtenstein and Stein, *A Fabulous Failure*, 137–43.

27 Dana Priest and Michael Weisskopf, "Healthcare Reform: The Collapse of a Quest," *Washington Post*, October 11, 1994.

28 Priest and Weisskopf, "Healthcare Reform: The Collapse of a Quest."

29 For a discussion of these effects, see Marc Labonte, "The FY2014 Government Shutdown: Economic Effects," *Congressional Research Service*, November 1, 2013.

30 Ferguson and Rogers, *Right Turn*, 185–93; qtd. in John H. Makin, "Perspective on U.S. Fiscal Policy Before and After 1990," *Hearing Before the Subcommittee on Deficits, Debt Management and International Debt of the Committee on Finance United States Senate*, 102nd Congress, 2nd session, June 6, 1992; Mizruchi, *Fracturing of the American Corporate Elite*, 231–2; Seito Hayasaki, "The Unlikely Heroes of Progressive Taxation: CEO Support for Bill Clinton's Tax Increase Package in 1993," *Journal of Policy History* 35:2 (2023), 219–53. The Roundtable had actually begun signaling its concern around 1985, when it argued that cutting the budget deficit was key to addressing the trade deficit. See I. M. Destler and C. Randall Henning, *Dollar Politics: Exchange Rate Policymaking in the United States* (Washington, DC: Institute for International Economics, 1989), 128.

31 Paul Starobin, "Welcome to the Club," *National Journal*, January 28, 1995, 219; Graeme Browning, "Bob Walker's Got an Idea," *National Journal*, August 12, 1995, 2062; Louis Jacobson, "Washington's a Movable Feast for Conservatives," *National Journal*, November 25, 1995, 2928–9.

32 Starobin, "Welcome to the Club"; Drew, *Showdown*, 116.

33 Michael Meeropol, *Surrender: How the Clinton Administration Completed the Republican Revolution* (Ann Arbor: University of Michigan Press, 1998), 242–64; Steven M. Gillon, *The Pact: Bill Clinton, Newt Gingrich, and the Rivalry That Defined a Generation* (Oxford: Oxford University Press, 2008), 148; Bob Woodward, *The Choice: How Bill Clinton Won* (New York: Simon and Schuster, 1996), 410–12. For detailed discussions of how the Clinton administration formulated its balanced budget

policy, see Lichtenstein and Stein, *A Fabulous Failure*, 185–218; and Erik Van Deventer, "The Strong Dollar and the Political Economy of Financialization, from Reagan to Clinton" (PhD diss., New York University, 2020), 365–75.

34 Woodward, *The Choice*, 444; Eric Pianin and John F. Harris, "Clinton Signs Measures to Halt Shutdown," *Washington Post*, January 6, 1996, A1; Ann Devroy, "The End of the Endgame," *Washington Post*, January 7, 1996.

35 "Testimony of Susan Hering, Salomon Brothers Inc Before the Senate Finance Committee," July 28, 1995; Mike McNamee, "Why Everybody Thinks Rubin is Crying Wolf," *Business Week*, November 20, 1995.

36 "An Impressive Beginning for Congress," *Nation's Business*, December 1995, 80; "Our Debt Deepens by $482 Million a Day," *Nation's Business*, January 1996, 64; "Obstructionism is Not Good Policy for 1996," *Nation's Business*, February 1996, 76.

37 Paul Pierson, *Dismantling the Welfare State? Reagan, Thatcher, and the Politics of Retrenchment* (Cambridge: Cambridge University Press, 1994), 126; "Republican Contract with America," house.gov.

38 "Readers' Views on Welfare Reform," *Nation's Business* 80:11 (1992); "Readers' Views on Welfare Bill," *Nation's Business* 83:8 (1995); "Welfare Reform: Undoing the Mistakes," *Nation's Business* 83:6 (1995); Ellen Reese, *Backlash Against Welfare Mothers: Past and Present* (Berkeley: University of California Press, 2005), 168.

39 Ronald Walters, "The Democratic Party and the Politics of Welfare Reform," in Clarence Y. H. Lo and Michael Schwartz, eds., *Social Policy and the Conservative Agenda* (Malden: Blackwell Publishers, 1998), 37–52; Woodward, *The Choice*, 248–50.

40 Peter Baker and Susan Glasser, *The Man Who Ran Washington: The Life and Times of James A. Baker III* (New York: Doubleday, 2020), 485.

41 Thomas Ferguson, "Blowing Smoke: Impeachment, the Clinton Presidency, and the Political Economy," in William J. Crotty, ed., *The State of Democracy in America* (Washington, DC: Georgetown University Press, 2001), 212–21. On industry concern with Gingrich's deregulatory fervor, see Graeme Browning, "Scowls, High-Pitched Whines and Great Grub," *National Journal*, September 2, 1995, 2165. On the impact of the act, see Jay D. Hmielowski, Michael A. Beam, Myiah J. Hutchens, "Structural Changes in Media and Attitude Polarization: Examining the Contributions of TV News Before and After the Telecommunications Act of 1996," *International Journal of Public Opinion Research* 28:2 (2016), 153–72

42 Sara Miles, *How to Hack a Party Line: The Democrats and Silicon Valley* (New York: Macmillan, 2001), 28–30.

43 Miles, *How to Hack a Party Line*, 28–30.

44 Miles, *How to Hack a Party Line*, 35–6; Margaret O'Mara, *The Code: Silicon Valley and the Remaking of America* (New York: Penguin, 2019).

45 James Shoch, *Trading Blows*, chapters 7–9; Lichtenstein and Stein, *A Fabulous Failure*, chapters 8 and 11.

46 Domhoff, *The Corporate Rich and the Power Elite*, 481–2.

47 Shoch, *Trading Blows*, 145–60.

48 Shoch, 179; Domhoff, *The Corporate Rich and the Power Elite*, 484–7.

49 Shoch, *Trading Blows*, 214; Jiwon Choi et al., "Local Economic and Political Effects of Trade Deals: Evidence from NAFTA," *American Economic Review* 114: 6 (2024), 1540–75.

50 Lichtenstein and Stein, *A Fabulous Failure*, chapter 12.

51 Lichtenstein and Stein, *A Fabulous Failure*, chapter 12; Peter H. Stone, "The Bailout Brigade," *National Journal*, January 24, 1998, 174; Peter H. Stone, "A Bailout Agency Bailout," *National Journal*, September 5, 1998, 2032.

52 "Here's One Exec Buchanan Won't Bash," *Chicago Tribune*, March 1, 1996.

53 Ben Wildavsky, "Going Nativist?" *National Journal*, May 27, 1995; Peter Beinart, "The Nationalist Revolt," *The New Republic*, December 1, 1997, 20–6; Robert Weissman, "Rejecting the IMF," *Multinational Monitor*, May 1998, 6–7; Shoch, *Trading Blows*, 222–3.

54 Richard S. Dunham, "Is the GOP the Only Party of Business?" *BusinessWeek*, May 4, 1998, 154; Thomas B. Edsall, "GOP Angers Big Business on Key Issues," *Washington Post*, June 11, 1998; Shoch, *Trading Blows*, 223.

55 Peter H. Stone and Margaret Kriz, "The Bottom-Line Fallout: A GOP Bonanza," *National Journal*, September 9, 1998, 2158–9; Thomas B. Edsall, "Business, GOP Chiefs Reconcile on Agenda," *Washington Post*, July 8, 1998, A4.

56 Lichtenstien and Stein, *A Fabulous Failure*, 317–25; Gillon, *The Pact*, 210–11.

57 Eric Laursen, *The People's Pension: The Struggle to Defend Social Security Since Reagan* (Chico: AK Press, 2012), 246–50, 368.

58 Gillon, *The Pact*, 153.

59 Lee Walczak and Amy Borrus, "Impeachment: Bad for Business?" *BusinessWeek* January 11, 1999, 38–40; David Warner, "Hurdles for Business in the New Congress," *Nation's Business* 87:2 (February 1999), 24.

60 Lichtenstein and Stein, *A Fabulous Failure*, 322–4; Howard

Gleckman and Mike McNamee, "Advantage, Clinton," *Business-Week*, February 1, 1999, p30–1; Gillon, *The Pact*, 224.

61 John Boehner, *On the House: A Washington Memoir* (New York: St. Martin's Press, 2021), 76–7.

62 "Delay, Inc.: A Democracy 21 Report on House Majority Leader Tom DeLay and His Money Machine," Democracy 21, July 22, 2003; Dubose and Reid, *The Hammer*, 126–7; Peter H. Stone, "The Nicotine Network," *Mother Jones*, May/June 1996.

63 Laura E. Tesler and Ruth E. Malone, "'Our Reach Is Wide by Any Corporate Standard': How the Tobacco Industry Helped Defeat the Clinton Health Plan and Why It Matters Now," *American Journal of Public Health* 100:7 (July 2010), 1174–88.

64 David A. Kessler, "Statement on Nicotine-Containing Cigarettes," *Tobacco Control* 3 (1994), 148–58; David A. Kessler, *A Question of Intent: A Great American Battle with a Deadly Industry* (New York: PublicAffairs, 2001), 331–3; Terence Monmaney and John M. Broder, "Clinton Hints at Giving FDA Tobacco-Regulation Power," *Los Angeles Times*, July 14, 1995.

65 Peter H. Stone, "Blowing Smoke at its Critics," *National Journal*, April 20, 1996, 884–8.

66 Ferguson, "Blowing Smoke," 205–9.

67 Bente Tangvik, "President Clinton and the American Tobacco Industry" (master's thesis, University of Oslo, 2007), 82; Jeffrey Klein, "Where There's Smoke," *Mother Jones*, September/October 1998.

4. The Bush II Years

1 William Booth, "How Larry Flynt Changed the Picture," *Washington Post*, January 11, 1999, C1. Livingston wasn't the only GOP official to have his own indiscretions revealed during impeachment. See Margaret Carlson, "The Clinton in Us All," *Time*, December 28–January 4, 1998, 94.

2 Thomas Schaller, *The Stronghold: How Republicans Captured Congress but Surrendered the White House* (New Haven: Yale University Press, 2015), 88; Mark K. Updegrove, *The Last Republicans: Inside the Extraordinary Relationship Between George H. W. Bush and George W. Bush* (New York: HarperCollins, 2017), 239–41.

3 Updegrove, 190–1; Schaller, *The Stronghold*, 88–9; Burt Solomon, "The Other, Softer, GOP," *National Journal*, February 2, 1999, 456–7; Michael Nelson, "George W. Bush's Elections: 2000, 2002, 2004, 2006, and 2008," 43: *Inside the George W. Bush Presidency* (Lawrence: University of Kansas Press, 2022), 37.

4   Jacob Weisberg, *The Bush Tragedy* (New York: Random House, 2008), 92, 96–7. See also Kevin M. Kruse, "Compassionate Conservatism: Religion in the Age of George W. Bush," in Julian Zelizer, ed., *The Presidency of George W. Bush: A First Historical Assessment* (Princeton: Princeton University Press, 2010), 227–51.

5   "George W. Reagan," *New York Post*, November 23, 1999, 38; John Robert Greene, *The Presidency of George W. Bush* (Lawrence: University Press of Kansas, 2021), 59; Robert V. Remini, *The House: The History of the House of Representatives* (New York: HarperCollins, 2006), 463.

6   Nelson Lichtenstein, "Ideology and Interest on the Social Policy Home Front," in Zelizer, ed., *The Presidency of George W. Bush*, 172; Helen Dewar, "GOP Departures Signal Arrival of a New Era For Conservatism," *Washington Post*, September 16, 2002.

7   Lawrence R. Jacobs and Robert Y. Shapiro, "Bush's Democratic Ambivalence: Responsiveness and Policy Promotion in Republican Government," in Colin Campbell, Bert A. Rockman, and Andrew Rudalevige, eds., *The George W. Bush Legacy* (Washington, DC: Congressional Quarterly, 2008), 49; Kruse, "Compassionate Conservatism," 232–3; Edsall, *Building Red America*, chapter 2; Weisberg, *The Bush Tragedy*, 133–6.

8   As his vice president, Dan Quayle, remarked, in Bush's administration "there wasn't any real ideological, conservative, domestic agenda, other than markets and free enterprise and things of that sort." Michael Nelson, "George Bush: Texan, Conservative," in Michael Nelson and Barbara A. Perry, eds., *41: Inside the Presidency of George H. W. Bush* (Ithaca: Cornell University Press, 2014), 28.

9   Paul Burka, "Has Bush Monkeyed Around with Business?" *Texas Monthly*, June 1999; Bob Sechler, "Coming From Texas, Bush Knows New Economy's Clout," *Wall Street Journal*, December 13, 2000.

10 Lee Walczak, "Why Business is Holding its Fire," *BusinessWeek*, May 29, 2000, 82; Bob Dreyfuss, "George W. Bush: Calling for Philip Morris," *The Nation*, October 21, 1999. See also John Mintz, "Big Tobacco Takes Its Chances on Bush," *Washington Post*, February 18, 2000, A6; Laura Cohn "The Bushdaq vs. the Goredex," *BusinessWeek*, November 13, 2000, 84; Edsall, *Building Red America*, 109; Peter H. Stone, "Corporations, K Street Throw a Party," *National Journal*, January 13, 2001, 117.

11 Peter H. Stone, "GOP Jousts with Business Roundtable," *National Journal*, January 11, 1997, 75; Nick Confessore, "Welcome to the Machine," *Washington Monthly*, July 1, 2003; Jeremy Scahill, "Exile on K Street," *The Nation*, February 20, 2006.

12 Sheldon D. Pollack, *Refinancing America: The Republican Antitax Agenda* (Albany: State University of New York Press, 2003), 119–20; "Mr. Bush's Beginning," *New York Times*, April 29, 2001.

13 Jacob M. Schlesinger and John D. McKinnon, "Bush Tax Cuts Send Corporate Lobbyists into a Feeding Frenzy," *Wall Street Journal*, February 2, 2001, A1; Ferguson and Rogers, *Right Turn*, 119–24; Benjamin C. Waterhouse, *Lobbying America: The Politics of Business from Nixon to NAFTA* (Princeton: Princeton University Press, 2014), chapter 7; John Maggs and Peter H. Stone, "Tax Cut Fever," *National Journal*, February 3, 2001, 324–9.

14 Michael J. Graetz and Ian Shapiro, *Death by a Thousand Cuts: The Fight over Taxing Inherited Wealth* (Princeton: Princeton University Press, 2005), chapter 15; Elizabeth Drew, "Bush's Weird Tax Cut," *New York Review of Books*, August 9, 2001.

15 Howard Gleckman and Rich Miller, "Selling the Tax Cut" *BusinessWeek*, February 5, 2001, 34–40; Graetz and Shapiro, *Death by a Thousand Cuts*, chapter 15. On Van Dongen, see Jeffrey Birnbaum, "The Man in the Middle," *Fortune Small Business*, April 1, 2002.

16 Graetz and Shapiro, *Death by a Thousand Cuts*, 165.

17 Corporate Tax Breaks Enacted," in *CQ Almanac 2004*, 60th ed., Washington, DC: Congressional Quarterly, 2005; Jacob S. Hacker and Paul Pierson, "Tax Politics and the Struggle over Activist Government," in Paul Pierson and Theda Skocpol, eds., *The Transformation of American Politics: Activist Government and the Rise of Conservatism* (Princeton: Princeton University Press, 2007), 257. Cheney quoted in James T. Patterson, "Transformative Economic Policies: Tax Cutting, Stimuli, and Bailouts," in Zelizer, ed., *The Presidency of George W. Bush*, 118. On business lobbying in support of the 2003 bill, see Peter H. Stone, "Arm-Twisting on Taxes," *National Journal*, February 1, 2003, 375–6; and Keith Koffler, "Spending Millions on Bush's Tax Plan," *National Journal*, May 3, 2003, 1388–9. For discussions of the new tolerance for deficits among business, see Jonathan Fuerbringer, "Deficits Are Back: But Maybe They Aren't as Dangerous," *New York Times*, August 25, 2002; and David Leonhardt, "That Big Fat Budget Deficit. Yawn," *New York Times*, February 8, 2004; and, suggestively, Martin Vaughn, "K Street Not Wild About Bush Tax Plan," *National Journal*, October 22, 2005, 3283.

18 Steven Greenhouse, "Battle Lines Drawn over Ergonomic Rules: Business Pitted Against Washington" *New York Times*, November 18, 2000; Peter H. Stone, "Block Those Regs!" *National Journal*, February 17, 2001, 484–7; Stephen Labaton, "OSHA Leaves Worker Safety Largely in Hands of Industry," *New York Times* April 25, 2007. See also the interview with the NAM head

Michael E. Baroody: Louis Jacobson, "Baroody's Bottom Line," *National Journal*, March 13, 1999, 700–1.

19   David Marcus, "The History of the Modern Class Action, Part II: Litigation and Legitimacy, 1981–1994" *Fordham Law Review* 86:4 (2018), 1785–845; Terry Carter, "Boosting the Bench," *ABA Journal* 88:10 (2002), 28–30; Myriam E. Gilles, "'A Force Created': The U.S. Chamber of Commerce and the Politics of Corporate Immunity," *DePaul Law Review* 72 (2022), 139–70; David Byrd, "Why Trial Lawyers Have a Beef with Bush" *National Journal*, May 8, 1999, 1256–8; Shawn Zeller, "Tort Reform's Massive War Chest," *National Journal*, March 29, 2003, 1008–9; Edsall, *Building Red America*, 126–7.

20   Jesse Rhodes, *An Education in Politics: The Origin and Evolution of No Child Left Behind* (Ithaca: Cornell University Press, 2012), chapter 6; Susan Crabtree and John Bresnahan, "Boehner Facing Plenty of Heat from Conservatives," *Roll Call*, May 3, 2001, 1; Michael S. Greve, "The End of Education Reform," *Weekly Standard* 6:34 (May 21, 2001), 16–17.

21   Milt Freudenheim, "Employers Seek to Shift Costs of Drugs to U.S." *New York Times*, July 2, 2003; Thomas R. Oliver, Philip R. Lee, and Helene L. Lipton, "A Political History of Medicare and Prescription Drug Coverage," *The Milbank Quarterly* 82:2 (2004), 283–354; Dick Armey, "Say 'No' to the Medicare Bill," *Wall Street Journal*, November 21, 2003; David E. Rosenbaum, "A Final Push in Congress: The Savings Plan" *New York Times*, November 23, 2003; Fred Barnes, "Hey Big Spenders," *Weekly Standard*, December 8, 2003, 9–10.

22   Peter H. Stone, "Power Rangers," *National Journal*, October 30, 2004, 3288–92; Thomas B. Edsall, Sarah Cohen, and James V. Grimaldi, "Pioneers Fill War Chest, Then Capitalize," *Washington Post*, May 16, 2004, A1; Thomas B. Edsall, "In Bush's Policies, Business Wins," *Washington Post*, February 8, 2004.

23   Fred Barnes, "Realignment, Now More Than Ever," *Weekly Standard*, November 22, 2004.

24   Vivek Chibber, "American Militarism and the US Political Establishment," *Socialist Register* 45 (2009), 23–53.

25   Chibber, "American Militarism."

26   Melvyn P. Leffler, *Confronting Saddam Hussein: George W. Bush and the Invasion of Iraq* (Oxford: Oxford University Press, 2023), 46–7.

27   Benjamin W. Cramer, "The Power of Secrecy and the Secrecy of Power: FACA and the National Energy Policy Development Group" *Communication Law and Policy* 13:2 (2008), 183–230; Don van Natta Jr. and Neela Banerjee, "Top G.O.P. Donors in Energy Industry Met Cheney Panel," *New York Times*, March 1, 2002.

28 For more on the CFR, see Lawrence H. Shoup, *Wall Street's Think Tank: The Council on Foreign Relations and the Empire of Neoliberal Geopolitics, 1976–2014* (New York: Monthly Review Press, 2015).

29 *National Energy Policy*, Report of the National Energy Policy Development Group, May 2001; *Strategic Energy Policy Challenges for the 21st Century*, report of an independent task force cosponsored by the James A. Baker III Institute for Public Policy of Rice University and the Council on Foreign Relations, April 2001. By 2004, however, some firms were abandoning the imperial consensus; worried that the anti-Americanism engendered by the war would hurt their brand images, they formed the group Business for Diplomatic Action. Keith Reinhard and Tom Miller, "A Business Problem for U.S. Firms," *International Herald Tribune*, May 27, 2004, 8.

30 Vivek Chibber, "The Iraq Invasion 20 Years Later" *Jacobin* 50 (2023), 11–18; Gary C. Jacobson, *A Divider, Not a Uniter: George W. Bush and the American People* (Boston: Longman, 2011), chapter 8.

31 Mike Davis, "The Democrats After November," *New Left Review* 2:43 (2007), 5–31.

32 Daniel Béland and Alex Waddan, *The Politics of Policy Change: Welfare, Medicare, and Social Security Reform in the United States* (Washington, DC: Georgetown University Press, 2012), 134–5; Ron Suskind, "Without a Doubt," *New York Times Magazine*, October 17, 2004, 102; George C. Edwards, *Governing by Campaigning: The Politics of the Bush Presidency* (New York: Pearson, 2007), 215–6; Mark A. Peterson, "Still a Government of Chums: Bush, Business, and Organized Interests," in Campbell, Rockman, and Rudalevige, eds., *The George W. Bush Legacy*, 302; Peter H. Stone, "The Business Blitz on Social Security," *National Journal*, January 22, 2005, 209–10; Glen Justice, "Social Security Fight Begins, Over a Bill Still Nonexistent," *New York Times*, February 17, 2005; Judy Sarasohn, "Coalition Pushes Social Security Accounts," *Washington Post*, April 6, 2005; Paul Magnusson, "Bush's Reluctant Business Allies" *BusinessWeek*, May 9, 2005, 69–70.

33 For detailed discussions of the evolution of the administration's policy proposals, see Edwards, *Governing by Campaigning*, chapters 6 and 7.

34 Jacob S. Hacker and Paul Pierson, "Abandoning the Middle: The Bush Tax Cuts and the Limits of Democratic Control," *Perspectives on Politics* 3:1 (2005), 33–53; Jacobson, *A Divider*, 160; Mark Preston, "AUPSS Gets Cash Infusion," *Roll Call*, June 27, 2005; John Tierney, "Can Anyone Unseat F. D. R.?" *New York Times*, January 23, 2005.

35 Magnusson, "Bush's Reluctant Business Allies"; "COMPASS Alliance Needs Some Pointers," *National Journal*, May 21, 2005, 1518.

36 Edwards, *Governing by Campaigning*, 274.

37 Andrew Wroe, *The Republican Party and Immigration Politics: From Proposition 187 to George W. Bush* (New York: Palgrave MacMillan, 2008), chapter 8; Daniel J. Tichenor, "The Congressional Dynamics of Immigration Reform," in Tony Payan and Erika de la Garza, eds., *Undecided Nation: Political Gridlock and the Immigration Crisis* (Cham: Springer, 2014), 23–48.

38 Jim Yardley, "Hispanics Give Attentive Bush Mixed Reviews," *New York Times*, August 27, 2000; Tichenor, "Congressional Dynamics," 37–8; Wroe, *Republican Party*, 175.

39 David Bacon, "The Political Economy of Immigration Reform," *Multinational Monitor* 25:11 (2004), 9–13; Judy Holland, "High-Tech Companies Lobbying to Let More Educated Foreigners Stay Here," *Milwaukee Journal Sentinel*, March 21, 2004, 1D; Brian Grow, "Embracing Illegals," *BusinessWeek*, July 18, 2005, 56–64.

40 Wroe, *Republican Party*, 189, 194; Ted Barrett and Steve Turnham, "Moderates Seen As Key To Immigration Reform Passage," *CNN*, January 8, 2004; Tichenor, "Congressional Dynamics," 39.

41 Rachel Morris, "Borderline Catastrophe," *Washington Monthly*, October 1, 2006; Brian Rosenwald, *Talk Radio's America: How an Industry Took Over a Political Party That Took Over the United States* (Cambridge: Harvard University Press, 2019), chapter 16.

42 On the USBIC's history, see Katherine Rye Jewell, *Dollars for Dixie: Business and the Transformation of Conservatism in the Twentieth Century* (Cambridge: Cambridge University Press, 2019).

43 Tyanne Conner, "Nativism or Response to Globalization? Business Reaction to Immigration Reform," *Portland State University McNair Scholars Online Journal* 2 (2006–2008), 18–47; Robert Pear, "Employers Cite Problems with Immigration Bill After Crafting It," *New York Times*, May 20, 2007; Lisa Caruso, "Behind Closed Doors," *National Journal*, June 9, 2007, 60; Wroe, *Republican Party*, 214. While business was dispirited by the course of the bill, they were not entirely without influence on immigration politics. *BusinessWeek* reported that Tom Tancredo dropped a proposal to tax remittances sent home by immigrants when banks in his district supported his opponent in response. Grow, "Embracing Illegals," 64.

44 Wroe, *Republican Party*, 209; Rosenwald, *Talk Radio's America*, 157.

45 Nelson Lichtenstein and Judith Stein, *A Fabulous Failure: The Clinton Presidency and the Transformation of American*

Capitalism (Princeton: Princeton University Press, 2023), chapter 13; Thomas Ferguson and Robert Johnson, "Too Big to Bail: The 'Paulson Put,' Presidential Politics, and the Global Financial Meltdown: Part I: From Shadow Financial System to Shadow Bailout," *International Journal of Political Economy* 38:1 (2009), 3–34.

46 Lichtenstein and Stein, *A Fabulous Failure*, 424; Ferguson and Johnson, "Too Big to Bail, Part I," 11–13; National Commission on the Causes of the Financial and Economic Crisis in the United States, *The Financial Crisis Inquiry Report* (Washington, DC: US Government Printing Office, 2011), *xxii*; Edmund L. Andrews, "Fed Shrugged as Subprime Crisis Spread," *New York Times*, December 18, 2007; Thomas Herndon, "Mortgage Fraud Fueled the Financial Crisis—and Could Again," Institute for New Economic Thinking, September 7, 2018.

47 Manuel Adelino, Antoinette Schoar, and Felipe Severino, "The Role of Housing and Mortgage Markets in the Financial Crisis," *Annual Review of Financial Economics* 10 (2018), 25–41; Thomas Ferguson and Robert Johnson, "Too Big to Bail, Part I"; Ferguson and Johnson, "Too Big to Bail: The 'Paulson Put'; "Presidential Politics, and the Global Financial Meltdown: Part II: Fatal Reversal—Single Payer and Back," *International Journal of Political Economy* 38:2 (2009), 5–45.

48 Ferguson and Johnson, "Too Big to Bail, Part II," 15–16; Henry M. Paulson Jr., *On the Brink: Inside the Race to Stop the Collapse of the Global Financial System* (New York: Business Plus, 2010), chapter 5; Ben S. Bernanke, *The Courage to Act: A Memoir of Crisis and its Aftermath* (New York: W. W. Norton, 2015), chapter 10; Adam Tooze, *Crashed: How a Decade of Financial Crises Changed the World* (New York: Viking, 2018), 171.

49 Steven Lee Myers, "Bush Supports Fed's Intervention," *Pittsburgh Post-Gazette*, March 18, 2008, A4; Maura Reynolds and Janet Hook, "Markets in Turmoil; White House Fallout; Central Bank Action," *Los Angeles Times* March 18, 2008, A1; David M. Herszenhorn, "Homeowners' Pleas Put G.O.P. Lawmakers in Bind on Defaults," *New York Times*, March 30, 2008.

50 Lee Fang, *The Machine: A Field Guide to the Resurgent Right* (New York: The New Press, 2013), 24–5; "FreedomWorks Foundation to Host Policy Luncheon on Subprime Bailout," *Business Wire*, March 21, 2008; Michael M. Phillips, "Mortgage Bailout Infuriates Tenants (And Steve Forbes)," *Wall Street Journal*, May 15, 2008, A1; Patrick O'Connor and Victoria McGrane, "Conservatives Bemoan Mortgage Bailout," *Politico*, December 5, 2007.

51 Edmund L. Andrews, "Democrats Split on Ways to Ease Housing Crisis," *New York Times*, October 4, 2007, C3; *Reuters*, "Mortgage

Bailout Plan Gains Traction in Congress," *Reuters*, March 13, 2008; Tooze, *Crashed*, 172–3; Stephen Labaton and David M. Herszenhorn, "Debating Rebates and Bailouts: A Rescue for Fannie and Freddie Kindles Opposition and Political Duels," *New York Times*, July 15, 2008, C1; Carl Hulse, "Behind a G.O.P. Revolt, Ideology and Politics," *New York Times*, July 26, 2008; "FreedomWorks: No Taxpayer Bailout for Fannie Mae, Freddie Mac," *Business Wire*, July 11, 2008.

52 Ferguson and Johnson, "Too Big to Bail Pt II," 18–23; Tooze, *Crashed*, 176–7; Jon Hilsenrath, Deborah Solomon, and Damian Paletta, "Paulson, Bernanke Strained for Consensus In Bailout," *Wall Street Journal*, November 10, 2008.

53 Steven T. Dennis, "Bailouts Whipsaw House GOP," *Roll Call*, September 22, 2008; John A. Lawrence, *Arc of Power: Inside Nancy Pelosi's Speakership: 2005–2010* (Lawrence: University of Kansas Press, 2023), 112–14; Emily Pierce and Steven T. Dennis, "Wall St. Plan Finds Support: Focus Turns to House GOP," *Roll Call*, September 25, 2008.

54 David M. Herszenhorn, "Politics Take Hold of Bailout Proposal," *New York Times*, September 26, 2008; Tom Petruno and Walter Hamilton, "Financial Crisis; Dissension on Capitol Hill," *Los Angeles Times*, September 27, 2008, A1; Donald Lambro, "Bailout Plan Divides Free-Market Backers," *McClatchy - Tribune Business News*, September 29, 2008; June Kronholz, Sarah Lueck, and Greg Hitt, "'No' Votes Came from All Directions," *Wall Street Journal*, September 30, 2008.

55 Lawrence, *Arc of Power*, 117; Atif Mian, Amir Sufi, and Francesco Trebbi, "The Political Economy of the US Mortgage Default Crisis," *American Economic Review* 100:5 (2010), 1967–98.

56 Sarah Lueck, Damian Paletta, and Greg Hitt, "Bailout Plan Rejected, Markets Plunge, Forcing New Scramble to Solve Crisis," *Wall Street Journal*, September 30, 2008 ; "ELFA Joins 50+ Business/Financial Trade Associations to Urge Congress to Act This Week to Stabilize Credit Markets," *US Fed News Service*, September 30, 2008; Jeanne Cummings, "Chamber Threatens Anti-Bailout Members," *Politico*, September 30, 2008; Jane Mayer, *Dark Money: The Hidden History of the Billionaires Behind the Radical Right* (New York: Doubleday, 2016), 21.

57 Steven T. Dennis and Tory Newmyer, "House Leaders Bullish on Vote: Support Grows on Both Sides," *Roll Call*, October 2, 2008; Lawrence, *Arc of Power*, 117.

5. Politics Outside the Party

1 Cheney's approval rating upon leaving office was 13 percent. Conor Friedersdorf, "Remembering Why Americans Loathe Dick Cheney," *The Atlantic*, August 30, 2011.

2 Cate Doty, "Tancredo Quits Race, Endorses Romney," *New York Times*, December 20, 2007; Richard S. Dunham, "Execs on the Sidelines," *Business Week*, June 4, 2007, 42–3.

3 Matt Grossmann and David A. Hopkins, *Asymmetric Politics: Ideological Republicans and Group Interest Democrats* (Oxford: Oxford University Press, 2016), 215; David Grann, "The Fall," *The New Yorker*, November 8, 2008; Dan Balz and Haynes Johnson, *The Battle for America 2008: The Story of an Extraordinary Election* (New York: Viking, 2009), 227–85.

4 Kenneth P. Vogel, *Big Money: 2.5 Billion Dollars, One Suspicious Vehicle, and a Pimp—On the Trail of the Ultra-Rich Hijacking American Politics* (New York: PublicAffairs, 2014), chapter 6; Tim Alberta, *American Carnage: On the Frontlines of the Republican Civil War and the Rise of President Trump* (Harper: New York, 2020), chapter 1.

5 Balz and Johnson, *The Battle for America*, chapters 19 and 20; Grann, "The Fall."

6 Gary C. Jacobson, "The 2008 Presidential and Congressional Elections: Anti-Bush Referendum and Prospects for the Democratic Majority," *Political Science Quarterly* 124:1 (2009), 13; Michael J. Malbin, "Small Donors, Large Donors and the Internet: The Case for Public Financing after Obama," The Campaign Finance Institute, 2009; Peter H. Stone, "Keeping Those Bundlers Happy," *National Journal*, August 2, 2008; Peter H. Stone, "The McCain Money Chase Matures," *National Journal* April 5, 2008, 64–5.

7 McCain's personal ignorance of economics also didn't help. As John Heileman and Mark Halperin relate, "In one exchange with the Fed chairman, McCain compared the causes of the crisis to some recent management troubles at Home Depot. 'It's kind of like that, isn't it?' he asked Bernanke. 'No, it's not,' a flabbergasted Bernanke replied." John Heileman and Mark Halperin, *Game Change: Obama and the Clintons, McCain and Palin, and the Race of a Lifetime* (New York: Harper Perennial, 2010), 381.

8 Lee Fang, *The Machine: A Field Guide to the Resurgent Right* (New York: The New Press, 2013), 44.

9 Robert Draper, *Do Not Ask What Good We Do: Inside the U.S. House of Representatives* (New York: Free Press, 2012), xv–xxii.

10 Theda Skocpol, "Who Owns the GOP?" *Dissent* (Spring 2016), 142–8; Axel Hertel-Fernandez, Theda Skocpol, and Jason Sclar, "When Political Mega-Donors Join Forces: How the Koch

Network and the Democracy Alliance Influence Organized U.S. Politics on the Right and Left," *Studies in American Political Development* 32:2 (2018), 6–8.

11 Mayer, *Dark Money*, 1–23.

12 Glenn Thrush, "Pete Sessions: House GOP learning from Taliban," *Politico*, On Congress Blog, February 9, 2009.

13 Paul Burka, "Daily 'Bad News for Republicans': The House GOP Memo," *Texas Monthly*, May 18, 2008.

14 Mayer, *Dark Money*, chapter 7.

15 Fang, *The Machine*, chapter 1.

16 Fang, chapter 1; Clarence Lo, "Astroturf Versus Grass Roots: Scenes from Early Tea Party Mobilization," in Lawrence Rosenthal and Christine Trost, eds., *Steep: The Precipitous Rise of the Tea Party* (Berkeley: University of California Press, 2012), 100–101.

17 Lo, "Astroturf Versus Grass Roots"; Patrick Rafail and John D. McCarthy, *The Rise, Fall, and Influence of the Tea Party Insurgency* (Cambridge: Cambridge University Press, 2023), 4; Mayer, *Dark Money*, 183; Theda Skocpol and Vanessa Williamson, *The Tea Party and the Remaking of Republican Conservatism* (Oxford: Oxford University Press, 2012); Rachel Blum, *How the Tea Party Captured the GOP: Insurgent Factions in American Politics* (Chicago: University of Chicago Press, 2020).

18 Rafail and McCarthy, *The Rise, Fall, and Influence of the Tea Party*, 53–6.

19 Tim Dickinson, "The Lie Machine," *Rolling Stone*, October 1, 2009, 45–9.

20 Andy Barr, "'Tea party' Polls Better Than GOP," *Politico*, December 7, 2009; Chris Good, "Tea Party More Popular Than Both Political Parties," *The Atlantic*, May 13, 2010; Skocpol and Williamson, *The Tea Party*, 41; Christopher S. Parker and Matthew Barreto, *Change They Can't Believe In: The Tea Party and Reactionary Politics in America* (Princeton: Princeton University Press, 2013); Blum, *How the Tea Party Captured the GOP*, 27–8.

21 Wendy K. Tam Cho, James G. Gimpel, and Daron R. Shaw, "The Tea Party Movement and the Geography of Collective Action," *Quarterly Journal of Political Science* 7:2 (2012), 105–33.

22 "Tea Party's Image Turns More Negative," Pew Research Center, October 16, 2013; Rafail and McCarthy, *The Rise, Fall, and Influence of the Tea Party*, 102, 111.

23 See, for example, Doug Bandow, "Save Us from Social Security," *Chicago Tribune*, March 22, 1985, 31; Dan Morgan, "Think Tanks: Corporations' Quiet Weapon," *Washington Post*, January 29, 2000. See also Peter H. Stone, "Grass-Roots Group Rakes in the Green," *National Journal*, March 11, 1995, 621.

24 Theda Skocpol and Alexander Hertel-Fernandez, "The Koch

Network and Republican Party Extremism," *Perspectives on Politics* 14:3 (2016), 687; Alexander Hertel-Fernandez and Theda Skocpol, "When Political Mega-Donors Join Forces: How the Koch Network and the Democracy Alliance Influence Organized U.S. Politics on the Right and Left," *Studies in American Political Development* 32:2 (2018), 19; Alexander Hertel-Fernandez and Theda Skocpol, "Billionaires Against Big Business: Growing Tensions in the Republican Party Coalition," paper delivered at the 2016 Midwest Political Science Association Conference, April 8, 2016, 14; Kenneth P. Vogel, "How the Koch Network Rivals the GOP," *Politico*, December 30, 2015.

25 "Group: Bush Allies Illegally Helping Nader in Oregon" CNN. com, July 1, 2004; Jonathan Mummolo, "Nimble Giants: How National Interest Groups Harnessed Tea Party Enthusiasm," in Paul S. Herrnson, Christopher J. Deering, and Clyde Wilcox, eds., *Interest Groups Unleashed* (Los Angeles: Sage, 2013), 193–212; Mike Allen and Jim VandeHei, "The Koch Brothers' Secret Bank," *Politico*, September 11, 2013; Kenneth P. Vogel, "The Koch ATM," *Politico*, November 17, 2015.

26 Julie Bykowicz, "Scott Walker Is King of Kochworld," *Bloomberg*, February 17, 2015; Mayer, *Dark Money*, chapter 10; Tony Carrk, *The Koch Brothers: What You Need to Know About the Financiers of the Radical Right*, Center for American Progress Action Fund, April 2011; Vogel, *Big Money*, chapter 7; Skocpol and Hertel-Fernandez, "The Koch Network and Republican Party Extremism."

27 Charles Post, "Why the Tea Party?" *New Politics* 14:1 (2012); "MEMO: Health Insurance, Banking, Oil Industries Met with Koch, Chamber, Glenn Beck to Plot 2010 Election," *Climate Progress*, October 20, 2010; Mayer, *Dark Money*, 12; Thomas Ferguson, Paul Jorgensen, and Jie Chen, "How Money Drives US Congressional Elections: Linear Models of Money and Outcomes," *Structural Change and Economic Dynamics* 61 (2022), 527–45. For a more detailed breakdown of the sectoral composition of Koch contributors, see Hertel-Fernandez, Skocpol, and Sclar, "When Political Mega-Donors Join Forces," 13.

28 Vogel, *Big Money*, 6; Haley Barbour et al., *Growth and Opportunity Project*, 2013.

29 Vogel, *Big Money*, 37–9.

30 Peter H. Stone, "Conservatives' Johnny Appleseed," *National Journal*, September 8, 2007, 52; Vogel, *Big Money*, chapter 3.

31 Vogel, *Big Money*, chapter 3.

32 Tim Dickinson, "Rove Rides Again," *Rolling Stone*, May 27, 2010, 38–41; Ralph Z. Hallow, "Steele's Side Pursuits Drive Away Big Donors," *Washington Times*, January 7, 2010.

33 Nicholas Confessore, "Ex-Romney Aide Steers Vast Machine of G.O.P. Money," *New York Times*, July 21, 2012; John J. Pitney Jr., "Iron Law of Emulation: American Crossroads and Crossroads GPS," in Herrnson et al., eds., *Interest Groups Unleashed*, 170–92; Alberta, *American Carnage*, 90.

34 Laura Myers, "GOP's Angle Offers Apology to Unemployed," *Las Vegas Review-Journal*, July 23, 2010; Sam Stein, "Sharron Angle's Advice For Rape Victims Considering Abortion: Turn Lemons Into Lemonade," *Huffington Post*, July 8, 2010; Naftali Bendavid, "Insurgents Now Turn to Establishment," *Wall Street Journal*, June 15, 2010, A6.

35 Pitney, "Iron Law of Emulation," 180–5; Gary C. Jacobson, "The Republican Resurgence in 2010," *Political Science Quarterly* 126:1 (2011), 40; "Non-Party Spending Doubled in 2010 but Did Not Dictate the Results," Campaign Finance Institute, November 5, 2010, Table 1, cfinst.org.

36 Nicholas Confessore, "Outside Groups Eclipsing G.O.P. as Hub of Campaigns Next Year," *New York Times*, October 30, 2011, 1; Dave Cook, "Karl Rove 'Super PAC' Won't Favor Any 2012 Candidate During Primaries," *Christian Science Monitor*, June 24, 2011, 16.

37 Eric Rauchway, "Neither a Depression nor a New Deal: Bailout, Stimulus, and the Economy," in Julian Zelizer, ed., *The Presidency of Barack Obama: A First Historical Assessment* (Princeton: Princeton University Press, 2018), 38–9.

38 "Business Roundtable Calls for Immediate Enactment of Economic Stimulus Package," *Tax Notes*, January 18, 2008; Lisa Lerer, "U.S. Chamber Heaps Praise on Dems," *Politico*, March 12, 2009; Greg Hitt, "Businesses Focus on Finding Common Ground," *Wall Street Journal*, January 6, 2009, A6.

39 "Taxpayers Across Country Revolt Against Heralded Stimulus Package," *Courier Post*, February 24, 2009; "AFP Regrets Passage of So-Called Stimulus Bill, Applauds Bipartisan Rejection," *Targeted News Service*, January 29, 2009; Mayer, *Dark Money*, 170; Rauchway, "Neither a Depression nor a New Deal," 39.

40 Domhoff, *The Corporate Rich and the Power Elite*, 353–6.

41 Mayer, *Dark Money*, chapter 7; Dickinson, "The Lie Machine"; Dan Eggen and Philip Rucker, "Loose Network Drives Health Reform Opposition," *NBC News*, April 16, 2009.

42 Michael Beckel, "U.S. Chamber Dominates Third Quarter Lobbying as Large Health, Energy Companies Also Continue to Spend Big," Center for Responsive Politics, October 21, 2009; Peter H. Stone, "Health Insurers Funded Chamber Attack Ads," Under the Influence, *National Journal*, January 12, 2010; Alyssa Katz, *The Influence Machine: The U.S. Chamber of Commerce and*

the Corporate Capture of American Life (New York: Spiegel and Grau, 2015), 24; Domhoff, *The Corporate Rich and the Power Elite*, 362.

43 Rafail and McCarthy, *The Rise, Fall, and Influence of the Tea Party*, 153–6; Christopher F. Karpowitz, J. Quin Monson, Kelly D. Patterson, and Jeremy C. Pope, "Tea Time in America? The Impact of the Tea Party Movement on the 2010 Midterm Elections," *PS: Political Science and Politics* 44:2 (2011), 303–9.

44 Christopher Leonard, *Kochland: The Secret History of Koch Industries and Corporate Power in America* (New York: Simon and Schuster, 2019), chapters 19 and 20; Lee Davidson, "Late Money Pours into U.S. Senate Race in Utah," *Deseret News*, April 30, 2010, B5.

45 Alberta, *American Carnage*, 66, 77; Boatright, "Voice of American Business," 41–2; Josh Kraushaar, "Conservatives Resent NRSC Nods," *Politico*, September 17, 2009; Allison Sherry, "Long-Shot Senate Candidate Buck Hits Bull's-Eye in Colo.," *The Denver Post*, April 14, 2010. On Rubio's centrism, see Michael J. Mishak, "What Kind of Leader Is Marco Rubio? An Investigation," *The Atlantic*, July 10, 2015.

46 Andrea Fuller, "Chamber Starts Ad Campaign Against Obama on Health Care," *New York Times*, July 21, 2009; Michael D. Shear, "Rift between Obama and Chamber of Commerce Widening," *Washington Post*, October 20, 2009, A3; Boatright, "The Voice of American Business," 42; Mayer, *Dark Money*, chapter 10; Vogel, *The Big Money*, 53; "Non-Party Spending Doubled in 2010 but Did not Dictate the Results," Campaign Finance Institute, Table 2.

47 Jacobson, "Republican Resurgence," 27; Skocpol and Williamson, *The Tea Party*, 160–3; Gary C. Jacobson, "The President, the Tea Party, and Voting Behavior in 2010: Insights from the Cooperative Congressional Election Study," paper prepared for delivery at the 2011 Annual Meeting of the American Political Science Association, Seattle, Washington, September 1–4, 2011, 27; Rafail and McCarthy, *The Rise, Fall, and Influence of the Tea Party*, 156–60. The evidence here is not unequivocal when it comes to the 2010 midterms, because, for reasons of statistical research design, most studies have focused on elections to *state*, rather than federal, office. However, these studies have consistently found that the ruling empowered conservatives. See Tilman Klumpp, Hugo M. Mialon, Michael A. Williams, "The Business of American Democracy: Citizens United, Independent Spending, and Elections," *Journal of Law and Economics* 59:1 (2016), 1–43; Anna Harvey and Taylor Mattia, "Does Money Have a Conservative Bias? Estimating the Causal Impact of *Citizens United* on State Legislative Preferences," *Public Choice* 191 (2019), 417–41.

48 Skocpol and Williamson, *The Tea Party*, 169–71; Thomas F. Schaller, *The Stronghold: How Republicans Captured Congress but Surrendered the White House* (New Haven: Yale University Press, 2015), 17; Amy Gardner, "Newcomers Backed by Tea Party Are Urged to Think Small-Government," *Washington Post*, November 12, 2010, A1.

49 Frank Rich, "The Grand Old Plot Against the Tea Party," *New York Times*, October 30, 2010; John McCormick, "Why Business Doesn't Trust the Tea Party" *BusinessWeek*, October 13, 2010.

50 Alberta, *American Carnage*, 84.

51 Joshua Green, "How Dick Gephardt Fixed the Debt-Ceiling Problem," *The Atlantic*, May 9, 2011.

52 Charles G. Koch, "Why Koch Industries Is Speaking Out," *Wall Street Journal*, March 1, 2011, A15; Vogel, *Big Money*, 139; Mayer, *Dark Money*, 298; "Club for Growth Commends Senate GOP for Introducing Balanced Budget Amendment," *Targeted News Service*, April 1, 2011; Jennifer Liberto, "Big Business: Quit Screwing around on Debt Ceiling," CNN Money, May 12, 2011.

53 Kate Ackley, "Business Booming for Finance Lobbyists," *Roll Call*, July 27, 2011. See also Tim Fernholz, "Wall Street: Raising Debt Ceiling Is a Done Deal-Right?" *National Journal*, May 26, 2011; Stan Collender, "Debt Ceiling Questions Remain in the House," *Roll Call*, May 3, 2011; Michael Hirsch, "Where's Wall Street in the Debt Debate?" *National Journal*, July 14, 2011. For more on finance's campaign against Dodd-Frank, see Thomas Ferguson, Paul D. Jorgensen, and Jie Chen, "High Finance, Political Money and the US Congress: A Quantitative Assessment of the Campaign to Roll Back Dodd–Frank," in Louis-Philippe Rochon and Hassan Bougrine, eds., *Credit, Money and Crises in Post-Keynesian Economics* (Cheltenham: Edward Elgar, 2020), 152–205.

54 Alberta, *American Carnage*, 104; Samuel L. Popkin, *Crackup: The Republican Implosion and the Future of Presidential Politics* (Oxford: Oxford University Press, 2023), 50–1.

55 Bryan T. Gervais and Irwin L. Morris, *Reactionary Republicanism: How the Tea Party in the House Paved the Way for Trump's Victory* (Oxford: Oxford University Press, 2018), 57; Emma Dumain, "'Defund Obamacare' Letter to Be Unveiled After Heritage Push," *Roll Call*, August 20, 2013; Sheryl Gay Stolberg, "Republicans Long Planned to Use Budget as a Weapon," *New York Times*, October 7, 2013.

56 Alberta, *American Carnage*, 173; Vogel, *The Big Money*, 23. Even Pete Sessions, the Republican Mullah Omar, was opposed to the strategy.

57 Anna Palmer, "Trade Groups: No Shutdown," *Politico*, September 27, 2013; Neil King Jr., "Poll Finds GOP Blamed More for

Shutdown," *Wall Street Journal*, October 10, 2013; Philip Bump, "Koch Industries Wary of Being Tainted by the Obamacare-Prompted Shutdown," *Atlantic*, October 9, 2013; Eric Lipton and Nicholas Confessore, "Kochs and Other Conservatives Split over Strategy on Health Law," *New York Times*, October 10, 2013; Paige Winfield Cunningham, "Defund Plot Upsets Some on Right," *Politico*, September 11, 2013.

58 Mayer, *Dark Money*, 302–6; Alberta, *American Carnage*, 117–18.

59 Mark Halperin and John Heilemann, *Double Down: Game Change 2012* (New York: Penguin Press, 2013), chapter 11; Alexander Burns, "Crossroads Brass Defend Forti's Role," *Politico*, June 24, 2011; Cook, "Karl Rove 'Super PAC'"; Vogel, *Big Money*, 110–1; Alex Roarty, "Understanding Romney's Base," *National Journal*, March 8, 2012.

60 Santorum technically received the most delegates, but the vagaries of the caucus process led Romney to be declared the winner.

61 Vogel, *Big Money*, 94–5; Connie Bruck, "The Brass Ring," *The New Yorker*, June 23, 2008; James V. Grimaldi, "Sheldon Adelson and Newt Gingrich: One Gained Clout from Friendship, The Other Funding," *Washington Post*, January 19, 2012; Mayer, *Dark Money*, 317–20; "In Iowa, a Plague of Stealth Spending," *Detroit Free Press*, January 4, 2012.

62 Kendra Marr, "Newt's Rough Roll-Out," *Politico*, May 17, 2011; Matt Bai, "Newt Gingrich's Glory Days," *New York Times*, December 28, 2011; Alberta, *American Carnage*, 112; Popkin, *Crackup*, 102–6.

63 Matea Gold, "Koch-Backed Political Network, Built to Shield Donors, Raised $400 Million in 2012 Elections," *Washington Post*, January 5, 2014; Heath Brown, *The Tea Party Divided: The Hidden Diversity of a Maturing Movement* (Santa Barbara: Praeger, 2015), 75–6; Vogel, *Big Money*, chapter 9; Thomas Ferguson, Paul Jorgensen, and Jie Chen, "Party Competition and Industrial Structure in the 2012 Elections: Who's Really Driving the Taxi to the Dark Side?" *International Journal of Political Economy* 42:2 (2013), 3–41.

64 Alberta, *American Carnage*, 135; Ferguson, Jorgensen, and Chen, "Party Competition and Industrial Structure in the 2012 Elections," 25–6; Vogel, *The Big Money*, 176; Dante J. Scala, "Are Super PACs Arms of Political Parties? A Study of Coordination," in R. Ward Holder and Peter B. Josephson, eds., *The American Election 2012: Contexts and Consequences* (London: Palgrave MacMillan, 2014), 69–80; Vogel, *Big Money*, 176, 181.

65 Alberta, *American Carnage*, 135; Karen McVeigh, "Todd Akin and Richard Mourdock Fall to Senate Defeats," *The Guardian*, November 6, 2012.

66 Timothy Noah, "GOPocalypse: A Guide to Republican Purges," *The New Republic*, December 6, 2012; Daniel Newhauser and Alan K. Ota, "Steve Scalise Hopes to Reposition RSC in Next Congress," *Roll Call*, October 25, 2012; Alberta, *American Carnage*,139, 221–2; Gervais and Irwin, *Reactionary Republicanism*, 23; Rafail and McCarthy, *The Rise, Fall, and Influence of the Tea Party*, 160–2.

67 Alberta, *American Carnage*, 137–8; Amy Gardner, "Freedom-Works Tea Party Group Nearly Falls Apart in Fight Between Old and New Guard," *Washington Post*, December 25, 2012; Jeff Zeleny, "Top G.O.P. Donors Seek Greater Say in Senate Races," *New York Times*, February 3, 2013, 1; Eric Lipton, Nicholas Confessore, and Nelson D. Schwartz, "Business Groups See Loss of Sway Over House G.O.P.," *New York Times*, October 9, 2013.

68 Alberta, *American Carnage*, chapter 8.

69 Rhodes Cook, "The Primaries of 2014: More Than Meets the Eye," in Larry J. Sabato, ed., *The Surge: 2014's Big GOP Win and What It Means for the Next Presidential Election* (New York: Rowman and Littlefield, 2015), 37–52; Alberta, *American Carnage*, 194.

70 Karl Rove, "Republicans Won Big, So Now Go Big," *Wall Street Journal*, November 5, 2014.

71 Michael T. Toner and Karen E. Trainer, "The Money Game: Emerging Campaign Finance Trends and Their Impact on 2014 and Beyond," in Sabato, ed., *The Surge*, 111–27.

72 Thomas Ferguson and Walter Dean Burnham, "Americans Are Sick to Death of Both Parties: Why Our Politics Is in Worse Shape Than We Thought," *AlterNet*, December 17, 2014.

6. A Hostile Takeover of the Republican Party

1 See, for example, Dylan Riley, "What Is Trump?" *New Left Review* II/114 (2018), 5–31; Julia R. Azari, "The Scrambled Cycle: Realignment, Political Time, and the Trump Presidency," in Zachary Callen and Philip Rocco, eds., *American Political Development and the Trump Presidency* (Philadelphia: University of Pennsylvania Press, 2020), 13–27.

2 Philip Bump, "It's All but Official: This Will Be the Most Dominant Republican Congress Since 1929," *Washington Post*, November 5, 2014; Aaron Blake, "Nearly Half Of Americans Will Now Live In States Under Total GOP Control," *Washington Post*, November 11, 2014; Alberta, *American Carnage*, 236.

3 Daniel Newhauser, "As Flores Wins RSC Race, Tension Simmers Between Leaders and Conservatives," *National Journal Daily*

A.M., November 19, 2014; Jim Norman, "In U.S., Support for Tea Party Drops to New Low," Gallup, October 26, 2015; Ed O'Keefe and Matea Gold, "Jeb Bush and Allied Super PAC Raise an Unprecedented $114 Million War Chest," *Washington Post*, July 9, 2015; Ben White and Marc Caputo, "Inside Jeb's 'Shock And Awe' Launch," *Politico*, February 18, 2015.

4   Robert Costa, David A. Fahrenthold, and Sean Sullivan, "Boehner Survives Leadership Challenge from Conservative Members," *Washington Post*, January 6, 2015; Alberta, *American Carnage*, 240–3, 250–5.

5   Kenneth P. Vogel, "How the Koch Network Rivals the GOP," *Politico*, December 30, 2015; Nicholas Confessore, "Koch Brothers' Budget of $889 Million for 2016 Is on Par with Both Parties' Spending," *New York Times*, January 26, 2015.

6   Alberta, *American Carnage*, 116, 323; James Oliphant, "CPAC: Donald Trump Says He's Considering 2012 Presidential Run," *Los Angeles Times*, February 10, 2011; Michael Tesler, "Birtherism Was Why So Many Republicans Liked Trump In The First Place," *Washington Post*, September 19, 2016; Popkin, 102–4; John Boehner would later estimate that "there was at least a couple dozen members [of the House] who believed [birtherism was true]." Alberta, *American Carnage*, 94.

7   Maggie Haberman and Alexander Burns, "Donald Trump's Presidential Run Began in an Effort to Gain Stature," *New York Times*, March 12, 2016; Peter Baker and Susan Glasser, *The Divider: Trump in the White House, 2017–2021* (New York: Doubleday, 2022), 16.

8   Popkin, *Crackup*, 72–4; Alberta, *American Carnage*, 226; Mark Halperin, "Exclusive: New Ted Cruz Super-PACs Take in Record Haul," *Bloomberg*, April 8, 2015.

9   Alberta, *American Carnage*, chapter 10.

10   Robert P. Saldin and Steven M. Teles, *Never Trump: The Revolt of the Conservative Elites* (Oxford: Oxford University Press, 2020), 94; Alberta, *American Carnage*, 273.

11   Alberta, *American Carnage*, chapter 12.

12   Jon Herbert, Trevor McCrisken, and Andrew Wroe, *The Ordinary Presidency of Donald J. Trump* (London: Palgrave MacMillan, 2019), 16; Saldin and Teles, *Never Trump*, 97–8; Alberta, *American Carnage*, 288–9; Peter Stone, "Koch Donors Divided over Failure to Stop Donald Trump," *The Guardian*, March 15, 2016.

13   Marty Cohen, David Karol, Hans Noel, and John Zaller, "Party Versus Faction in the Reformed Presidential Nominating System," *PS: Political Science and Politics* 49:4 (2016), 701–8; Popkin, *Crackup*, 113–14. Some have argued that the failure of GOP elites to coordinate is not a compelling explanation of Trump's victory.

They point to polling data that show Trump winning a plurality of voters in every 1-to-1 matchup against his rivals. However, these data themselves, derived from polls in early 2016, reflect the choices GOP elites had already made at that point. If elites had coordinated earlier, it is likely that respondents' answers to these polls would have differed. See Jonathan Woo, Sean Craig, Amanda Leifson, and Matthew Tarpey, "Trump Is Not a (Condorcet) Loser! Primary Voters' Preferences and the 2016 Republican Presidential Nomination," *PS: Political Science and Politics* 53:3 (2020), 407–12.

14 Herbert, McCrisken, and Wroe, *The Ordinary Presidency*, 24; Alberta, *American Carnage*, 310.

15 Theda Skocpol, "The Elite and Popular Roots of Contemporary Republican Extremism," in Theda Skocpol and Caroline Tervo, eds., *Upending American Politics: Polarizing Parties, Ideological Elites, and Citizen Activists from the Tea Party to the Anti-Trump Resistance* (Oxford: Oxford University Press, 2020), 3–27. See also Theda Skocpol, "Who Owns the GOP?" *Dissent* (Spring 2016), 142–8; Thomas Ferguson, Benjamin I. Page, Jacob Rothschild, Arturo Chang, and Jie Chen, "The Roots of Right-Wing Populism: Donald Trump in 2016," *International Journal of Political Economy* 49:2 (2020), 102–23; Patrick Rafail and John D. McCarthy, *The Rise, Fall, and Influence of the Tea Party Insurgency* (Cambridge: Cambridge University Press, 2023), 180–6; Bryan T. Gervais and Irwin L. Morris, *Reactionary Republicanism: How the Tea Party in the House Paved the Way for Trump's Victory* (Oxford: Oxford University Press, 2018), 210–16.

16 There is a very large literature on negative partisanship. For a discussion of the concept in the context of the 2016 election, see Alan Abramowitz and Jennifer McCoy, "United States: Racial Resentment, Negative Partisanship, and Polarization in Trump's America," *Annals of the American Academy of Political and Social Science* 681:1 (2019), 137–56.

17 Gervais and Morris, *Reactionary Republicanism*, chapter 8; Alberta, *American Carnage*, 346.

18 Alberta, *American Carnage*, 392.

19 Herbert, McCrisken, and Wroe, *The Ordinary Presidency*, 55–8; Ross Douthat and Reihan Salam, "The Party of Sam's Club" *Weekly Standard* 11:9 (2005), 21–8.

20 Donald Kinder and Jennifer Chudy, "After Obama" *The Forum* 14:1 (2016), 3–15; John Sides, Michael Tesler, and Lynn Vavreck, *Identity Crisis: The 2016 Presidential Campaign and the Battle for the Meaning of America* (Princeton: Princeton University Press, 2018); Justin Grimmer, William Marble, and Cole Tanigawa-Lau, "Measuring the Contribution of Voting Blocs to Election

Outcomes," SocArXiv, February 28, 2023. There is, however, some evidence that Trump's success in winning endorsements from the police unions, a fact far from unrelated to his racial politics, contributed to his win. See Michael Zoorob and Theda Skocpol, "The Overlooked Organizational Basis of Trump's 2016 Victory," in Skocpol and Tervo, eds., *Upending American Politics*, 79–100.

21 Erika Franklin Fowler, Travis N. Ridout, and Michael M. Franz, "Political Advertising in 2016: The Presidential Election as Outlier?" *The Forum* 14:4 (2017), 445–69.

22 Alberta, *American Carnage*, 322–6, 347; Vogel, *Big Money: 2.5 Billion Dollars*, 53. Trump and Wynn had been rivals in Atlantic City in the 1980s and 1990s, but their similarities led them to leave the acrimony behind them. See Richard D. Bronson, *The War at the Shore: Donald Trump, Steve Wynn, and the Epic Battle to Save Atlantic City* (New York: The Overlook Press, 2010).

23 Alberta, *American Carnage*, 117–18, 332; Jonathan Martin, "Pence Woos Conservatives," *Politico*, October 2, 2009.

24 Alberta, *American Carnage*, 335; Kyle Trygstad, "RNC Looks to Refurbish Ailing State Parties, Build Infrastructure," *Roll Call*, January 24, 2013; Lucia Graves, "Katie Walsh: The RNC's Rainmaker," *National Journal*, March 28, 2015; Shane Goldmacher, "Trump Shatters GOP Records with Small Donors," *Politico*, September 19, 2016; Thomas Ferguson, Paul Jorgensen, and Jie Chen, "Industrial Structure and Political Outcomes: The Case of the 2016 US Presidential Election," in Ivano Cardinale and Roberto Scazzieri, eds., *The Palgrave Handbook of Political Economy* (London: Palgrave MacMillan, 2018), 333–440; Kenneth P. Vogel, "Big-Name Donors Skip Trump Event," *Politico* July 18, 2016; Rich Lord and Paula Reed Ward, "Pence Tries to Unlock GOP Donors," *Pittsburgh Post-Gazette*, July 21, 2016; Peter Stone, "Turned off by Trump: Republican Mega-Donors Focus on Congressional Races," *The Guardian*, August 27, 2016; Josh Rogin, "Inside the Collapse of Trump's D.C. Policy Shop," *Washington Post*, September 8, 2016.

25 Kenneth P. Vogel, "American Crossroads Spends Big," *Politico*, August 20, 2012; Jane Mayer, "The Reclusive Hedge-Fund Tycoon Behind the Trump Presidency," *New Yorker*, March 17, 2017; Terry Gross, "Inside The Wealthy Family That Has Been Funding Steve Bannon's Plan For Years," Fresh Air, National Public Radio, March 22, 2017; Kenneth P. Vogel and Ben Schreckinger, "The Most Powerful Woman in GOP Politics," *Politico*, September 7, 2016.

26 Robert Costa, Jose A. DelReal, and Jenna Johnson, "Trump Shakes Up Campaign, Demotes Top Adviser," *Washington Post*, August 17, 2016.

27 Jonathan Martin, Jim Rutenberg, and Maggie Haberman, "In
    Appointment, Trump Scuttles a Gentler Tone," *New York Times*,
    August 18, 2016; Joshua Green, "Steve Bannon's Plan to Free
    Donald Trump and Save His Campaign," *Bloomberg*, August 18,
    2016; Ferguson, Jorgensen, and Chie, "Industrial Structure and
    Political Outcomes," 422.

28 Matea Gold, "After Opposing Trump in the Primaries, Joe Ricketts
    Will Give at Least $1 Million to Support Him," *Washington Post*,
    September 20, 2016; Theodore Schleifer, "First on CNN: Adelson
    to Spend at Least $45 Million on 2016 Races in Boost for GOP,"
    CNN Wire Service, September 20, 2016.

29 Nicholas Confessore and Maggie Haberman, "Sheldon Adelson
    Focuses on Congressional Races, Despite Donald Trump's Pleas,"
    New York Times, September 20, 2016; Michael C. Bender,
    *"Frankly We Did Win This Election": The Inside Story of How
    Trump Lost* (New York: Grand Central, 2021), 335. Melania
    scoffed at Trump's plan, telling him, "Donald, nobody goes to
    Monte Carlo in November."

30 Sabrina Tavernise, "Many in Milwaukee Neighborhood Didn't
    Vote—and Don't Regret It," *New York Times*, November 20,
    2016; Kevin Robillard, Seung Min Kim, and Alex Isenstadt,
    "Senate GOP Faces Late Cash Crunch," *Politico*, October 15,
    2016; Alex Isenstadt, "Panicking GOP Makes Major Last-Minute
    Senate Investment," *Politico*, October 25, 2016; Ferguson, Jor-
    gensen, and Chie, "Industrial Structure and Political Outcomes,"
    358–61.

31 Mike Davis, "The Great God Trump and the White Working
    Class," *Catalyst*, 1:1 (2017), 151–71; David Autor, David Dorn,
    Gordon Hanson, and Kaveh Majlesi, "Importing Political Polari-
    zation? The Electoral Consequences of Rising Trade Exposure,"
    American Economic Review 110:10 (2020), 3139–83; Leonardo
    Baccini and Stephen Weymouth, "Gone For Good: Deindustri-
    alization, White Voter Backlash, and US Presidential Voting,"
    American Political Science Review, 115:2 (2021), 550–67.

32 My understanding of personalism is indebted to invaluable recent
    work by Erica Frantz, Andrea Kendall-Taylor, and Joseph Wright.
    See *The Origins of Elected Strongmen: How Personalist Parties
    Destroy Democracy from Within* (Oxford: Oxford University
    Press, 2024).

33 Political scientists have recently stressed the contradiction between
    these two roles. See Stephen Skowronek, John A. Dearborn, and
    Desmond King, *Phantoms of a Beleaguered Republic: The Deep
    State and the Unitary Executive* (Oxford: Oxford University
    Press, 2021); and Nicholas F. Jacobs and Sidney Milkis, "Our
    'Undivided Support': Donald Trump, the Republican Party,

and Executive-Centered Partisanship," in Eric M. Patashnik and Wendy J. Schiller, eds., *Dynamics of American Democracy: Partisan Polarization, Political Competition, and Government Performance* (Lawrence: University Press of Kansas, 2021), 291–322.

34 Jonathan Martin and Maggie Haberman, "Fear and Loyalty: How Donald Trump Took Over the Republican Party," *New York Times*, December 21, 2019.

35 John L. Campbell, *American Discontent: The Rise of Donald Trump and the Decline of the Golden Age* (Oxford: Oxford University Press, 2018), 139; "Read Donald Trump's Speech on Trade," *Time*, June 28, 2016; Rick Gates, *Wicked Game: An Insider's Story on How Trump Won, Mueller Failed, and America Lost* (New York: Post Hill Press, 2020), chapter 5. Ironically, Mike Pence ended up being at least as obsequious a vice president as Ivanka probably would have been.

36 Zachary Albert and David J. Barney, "The Party Reacts: The Strategic Nature of Endorsements of Donald Trump," *American Politics Research* 47:6 (2018), 1239–58; Alberta, *American Carnage*, 412; Baker and Glasser, *The Divider*, 34.

37 Alex Isenstadt, Kenneth P. Vogel, and Eliana Johnson, "Trump Likely to Pick McDaniel to Lead RNC," *Politico*, December 9, 2016; Alberta, *American Carnage*, chapter 18; Baker and Glasser, *The Divider*, 53; James Oliphant, "Once on the Outside, Conservative Koch Network Warms to Trump," *Reuters*, June 27, 2017; Jeffrey D. Broxmeyer, "The Patrimonial Turn in the American State," *Clio* 28:2 (2019), 6, 20–4.

38 Alberta, *American Carnage*, 411, 458; Herbert, McCrisken, and Wroe, *The Ordinary Presidency*, 166.

39 Daniel J. Galvin, "Party Domination and Base Mobilization: Donald Trump and Republican Party Building in a Polarized Era," *The Forum* 18:2 (2020), 135–68.

40 Galvin, "Party Domination and Base Mobilization," 154; Nicholas F. Jacobs, Desmond King, and Sidney M. Milkis, "Building a Conservative State: Partisan Polarization and the Redeployment of Administrative Power," *Perspectives on Politics* 17:2 (2019), 453–69; Baker and Glasser, *The Divider*, 503.

41 Baker and Glasser, *The Divider*, 37–8, 234–8.

42 Baker and Glasser, *The Divider*, 187; Bruce Cumings, "Obama, Trump and North Korea," in Oliver Turner and Inderjeet Parmar, eds., *The United States in the Indo-Pacific: Obama's Legacy and the Trump Transition* (Manchester: Manchester University Press, 2020), 7993.

43 Baker and Glasser, *The Divider*, chapters 17 and 19.

44 Michael Deibert, *When the Sky Fell: Hurricane Maria and the United States in Puerto Rico* (New York: Apollo Publishers, 2019);

John Bresnahan, Marianne LeVine, and Andrew Desidario, "How the $2 Trillion Deal Came Together—and Nearly Fell Apart," *Politico*, March 26, 2020.

45 John L. Campbell, *Institutions Under Siege: Donald Trump's Attack on the Deep State* (Cambridge: Cambridge University Press, 2023), 181–22.

46 Amanda Hollis-Brusky and Celia Parry, "'In the Mold of Justice Scalia': The Contours and Consequences of the Trump Judiciary," *The Forum* 19:1 (2021), 117–42; Jonathan M. King, Peter McAndrews, and Ian Ostrander, "President Trump and the Politics of Judicial Nominations," *The Justice System Journal* 43:4 (2022), 524–43.

47 Riley, "What is Trump."

48 Herbert, McCrisken, and Wroe, *The Ordinary Presidency*, 152.

49 Lee Fang, "GOP Lawmakers Now Admit Years of Obamacare Repeal Votes Were a Sham," *The Intercept* March 31, 2017; Daniel Béland, Philip Rocco, and Alex Waddan, "Obamacare in the Trump Era: Where Are We Now, and Where Are We Going?" *The Political Quarterly*, 89:4 (2018), 687–94.

50 Andrew S. Kelly, "Finding Stability and Sustainability in the Trump Era: Medicare and the Affordable Care Act in Historical Perspective," in Callen and Rocco, eds., *American Political Development and the Trump Presidency*, 130–50; "U.S. Chamber Supports American Health Care Act," US Chamber of Commerce, March 21, 2017.

51 Kelly, "Finding Stability and Sustainability," 142–6; Alberta, *American Carnage*, 433; Baker and Glasser, *The Divider*, 130; Sarah Kliff, "Republicans Killed the Obamacare Mandate: New Data Shows It Didn't Really Matter," *New York Times*, September 18, 2020.

52 John W. Schoen, "Trump Touts Sweeping, and Costly, Tax-Cut Plan," *CNBC*, August 8, 2016; Baker and Glasser, *The Divider*, 138–9.

53 Christopher Leonard, *Kochland: The Secret History of Koch Industries and Corporate Power in America* (New York: Simon and Schuster, 2019), 542–3.

54 Leonard, *Kochland*, 543–50; Bernie Becker, "Border Adjustment, Collecting Skeptics," *Politico*, January 5, 2017; Don Lee, "Trump Elevates Border-Tax Idea, but Also the Political and Legal Challenges," *Los Angeles Times*, January 28, 2017; Baker and Glasser, *The Divider*, 141.

55 William Greider, *The Education of David Stockman and Other Americans* (New York: E. P. Dutton, 1981), 58; Monica Prasad, *Starving the Beast: Ronald Reagan and the Tax Cut Revolution* (New York: Russell Sage Foundation, 2018), 124.

56 Jiakun Jack Zhang, "The US Congress and the Business Lobby," in Shiping Hua, ed., *The Political Logic of the US-China Trade War* (Lanham: Lexington Books, 2022), 243, 235–56; James Mann, "Trump's China Policy: The Chaotic End to the Era of Engagement," in Julian Zelizer, ed., *The Presidency of Donald J. Trump: A First Historical Assessment* (Princeton: Princeton University Press, 2022), 259–78; "Schumer, Graham Urge Action Against China's Unfair Currency Manipulation," press release, August 2, 2006; Daniel C. K. Chow, "How the United States Uses the Trans-Pacific Partnership to Contain China in International Trade," *Chicago Journal of International Law*, 17:2 (2016), 370–402.

57 Mann, "Trump's China Policy"; Ana Swanson, "Trump Administration Goes After China over Intellectual Property, Advanced Technology," *Washington Post*, August 14, 2017.

58 Jieun Lee and Iain Osgood, "Firms Fight Back: Production Networks and Corporate Opposition to the China Trade War," in Etel Solingen, ed., *Geopolitics, Supply Chains, and International Relations in East Asia* (Cambridge: Cambridge University Press, 2021), 153–72. Lee and Osgood claim that corporate opposition to Trump's trade war was the "best organized on any trade issue of the past twenty-five years," but their evidence for this claim is extremely thin.

59 Mann, "Trump's China Policy," 262–3; Jiakun Jack Zhang, "American Multinational Corporations and the US-China Trade War," in Ka Zeng and Wei Liang, eds., *Research Handbook on Trade Wars* (Cheltenham: Elgar, 2022), 252–70.

60 Mann, "Trump's China Policy."

61 Mike Davis, "Riot on the Hill," *New Left Review*, Sidecar, January 7, 2021.

62 Amisa Ratliff, "12 Numbers to Know About the Money in the 2020 Presidential Election," *Issue One*, December 14, 2020; Kenneth P. Vogel and Shane Goldmacher, "Democrats Decried Dark Money: Then They Won With It in 2020," *New York Times*, January 29, 2022; Greg Ip and Ken Thomas, "Business on Biden: Not So Bad, Given the Alternatives," *Wall Street Journal*, October 25, 2020; Matt Egan, "America's CEOs Say Trump Failed on Coronavirus – and They're Backing Biden," *CNN Wire Service*, September 29, 2020.

63 Tom Wheeler, "The 2020 Republican Party Platform: 'L'etat, c'est moi,'" *Brookings Institution*, August 25, 2020.

64 Baker and Glasser, *The Divider*, chapters 27 to 29.

65 Baker and Glasser, *The Divider*, chapter 31.

66 Tom Krishner and Paul Wiseman, "Top CEOs Met to Plan Response to Trump's Election Denial," *AP News*, November 13, 2020; "Manufacturers Call on Armed Thugs to Cease Violence at

Capitol," National Association of Manufacturers, press release, January 6, 2021; Zhao Li and Richard DiSalvo, "Can Stakeholders Mobilize Businesses for the Protection of Democracy? Evidence from the U.S. Capitol Insurrection," *American Political Science Review* 117:3 (2023), 1130–6.

67 "MEMO: Political Support for Candidates in Light of Events of January 6th," US Chamber of Commerce, March 5, 2021; Alexander Cohen, "Can Corporations Support Democracy?: The Vanishing Financial Cost of Election Denial Among House Republicans After January 6th," OSF Preprints, April 13; Laura Barrón-López and Shrai Popat, "How 2020 Election Denialism Became a Litmus Test for the GOP," *PBS Newshour*, February 19, 2024.

68 James Oliphant, Jason Lange, Julia Harte, and Tim Reid, "Republican Donations Surge Despite Corporate Boycott After Capitol Riots," *Reuters* March 9, 2021; Jane Mayer, "The Big Money Behind the Big Lie," *The New Yorker*, August 2, 2021; Justin Elliott, Megan O'Matz, and Doris Burke, "Ubiquitous Boxes, Paper Bags from Wisconsin-Based Uline Fueling Election Denial," *Milwaukee Journal-Sentinel*, October 26, 2022; Julia Fishman and Ian Vandewalker, "Big Donors Working to Overturn the 2020 Election Are Backing Election Denial Candidates in 2022," The Brennan Center, November 3, 2022.

69 Adam Bonica, "Mapping the Ideological Marketplace," *American Journal of Political Science* 58:2 (2014), 367–86. That said, it is likely that January 6 played some role in the increasing shift of corporate leaders and the rich more generally towards the Democratic Party. See Sam Zacher, "Polarization of the Rich: The New Democratic Allegiance of Affluent Americans and the Politics of Redistribution," *Perspectives on Politics* 22:2 (2023), 338–56; Eitan Hersh and Sarang Shah, "The Partisan Realignment of American Business: Evidence from a Survey of Corporate Leaders," working paper, August 1, 2023.

70 Josh Dawsey and Michael Scherer, "Trump Asserts His Dominance Inside GOP, Pushing Republicans to Embrace His False Claims of Fraud," *Washington Post*, October 14, 2021; David Siders and Stephanie Murray, "'Get on the Team or Shut Up': How Trump Created an Army of GOP Enforcers," *Politico*, July 13, 2021; Julia Azari, "Trump's Dominance in the GOP Isn't What It Seems," *Politico*, May 18, 2023; Isaac Arnsdorf, Josh Dawsey, Yvonne Wingett Sanchez, Patrick Marley, and Amy Gardner, "MAGA-Dominated State Republican Parties Plagued by Infighting, Money Woes," *Washington Party*, November 13, 2023; Shane Goldmacher and Nick Corasaniti, "Inside the G.O.P.'s State Party Problem," *New York Times*, February 22, 2024; Jon King, "Michigan GOP

Leaders Seek Karamo's Dismissal as Report Alleges the Party Is Facing Bankruptcy," *Michigan Advance*, December 11, 2023.

71 Nicholas Nehamas, "DeSantis Keeps Getting Asked: Why Won't He Directly Criticize Trump?" *New York Times*, January 3, 2024; John McCormick, "Why Business Doesn't Trust the Tea Party," *BusinessWeek,* October 13, 2010; Sara Dorn, "Here Are the Billionaires Backing Nikki Haley as a Trump Alternative: LinkedIn's Reid Hoffman, Charles Koch and More," *Forbes* December 5, 2023; Nidia Cavazos, "Network Founded by Koch Brothers Says It Will Stop Spending on Nikki Haley's Presidential Campaign," *CBS News*, February 26, 2024.

Conclusion

1 Nic Garcia and Jakob Maurer, "Liz Cheney Says Dick Cheney Will Vote for Kamala Harris, and She Will Support Democrat Colin Allred in Texas Senate Race," *Texas Tribune*, September 6, 2024.

2 Jacob S. Hacker and Paul Pierson, "Confronting Asymmetric Polarization," in Nathaniel Persily, ed., *Solutions to Political Polarization in America* (Cambridge: Cambridge University Press, 2015), 59–70.

3 Matt Grossmann and David A. Hopkins, *Asymmetric Politics: Ideological Republicans and Interest Group Democrats* (Oxford: Oxford University Press, 2016), 3.

4 See especially Adam Hilton, *True Blues: The Contentious Transformation of the Democratic Party* (Philadelphia: University of Pennsylvania Press, 2021); Grossmann and Hopkins, *Asymmetric Politics*.

5 For the extent of Democratic dependence on interest group mobilization, see Daniel Schlozman and Sam Rosenfeld, *The Hollow Parties: The Many Pasts and Disordered Present of American Party Politics* (Princeton: Princeton University Press, 2024), chapter 7.

6 On the disorganization of American civic life, see Theda Skocpol, *Diminished Democracy: From Membership to Management in American Civic Life* (Norman: University of Oklahoma Press, 2004).

7 For the most compelling explorations of this process, see Jared Abbott, "Understanding Class Dealignment," *Catalyst* 7:4 (2024), 76–132; Jiwon Choi, Ilyana Kuziemko, Ebonya Washington, and Gavin Wright, "Local Economic and Political Effects of Trade Deals: Evidence from NAFTA," *American Economic Review* 114:6 (2024), 1540–75; and Ilyana Kuziemko, Nicolas Longuet-Marx, and Suresh Naidu, "'Compensate the Losers?' Economic

Policy and Partisan Realignment in the US," National Bureau of Economic Research working paper 31794, October 2023.

8 Matthew Karp, "Power Lines," *Harper's*, October 2024.

9 Alma Cohen, Moshe Hazan, Roberto Tallarita, and David Weiss, "The Politics of CEOs," National Bureau of Economic Research working paper 25815, May 2019; Eitan Hersh and Sarang Shah, "The Partisan Realignment of American Business: Evidence from a Survey of Corporate Leaders," working paper, August 1, 2023; Reilly Steel, "The Political Transformation of Corporate America, 2001–2022" Columbia Law and Economics working paper No. 4974868, October 9, 2024; Sam Zacher, "Polarization of the Rich: The New Democratic Allegiance of Affluent Americans and the Politics of Redistribution," *Perspectives on Politics* 22:2 (2023), 1–19.

10 Some have argued that Joe Manchin, the decisive vote against the legislation, was effectively a scapegoat, taking the blame for killing the bill even though the party leadership secretly agreed with him. The evidence of the political infighting surrounding the bill does not support this account. See John Cassidy, "Joe Manchin Kills the Build Back Better Build," *The New Yorker*, December 19, 2021; Eric Levitz, "Give Manchin What He Wants Already," The Intelligencer, *New York Magazine*, January 20, 2022.

11 Jacob S. Hacker, Amelia Malpas, Paul Pierson, and Sam Zacher, "Bridging the Blue Divide: The Democrats' New Metro Coalition and the Unexpected Prominence of Redistribution," *Perspectives on Politics* 22:3 (2024), 1–21; Amelia Malpas and Adam Hilton, "Retreating from Redistribution? Trends in Democratic Party Fidelity to Economic Equality, 1984–2020," *The Forum: A Journal of Applied Research in Contemporary Politics* 19:2 (2021), 283–316; Michael Auslen and Justin H. Phillips, "Divided by Income? Policy Preferences of the Rich and Poor Within the Democratic and Republican Parties," working paper, February 2024.

12 Ironically, this is the opposite of what is happening on many social issues, where Republican attitudes are liberalizing just as Democratic attitudes did, but at a lag. See Delia Baldassarri and Barum Park, "Was There a Culture War? Partisan Polarization and Secular Trends in US Public Opinion," *The Journal of Politics* 82:3 (2020), 809–27.

13 Doug Henwood, "Soaking the Rich Is a Great Start—but It's Not Enough," *Jacobin*, October 20, 2019.

14 Andrew Prokop, "Why Republicans Didn't Write A Platform for Their Convention This Year," *Vox*, August 24, 2020; Zachary B. Wolf and Curt Merrill, "The GOP's Trump-Centered Platform, Annotated," CNN.com, July 9, 2024; Isaac Maddow-Zimet and Candace Gibson, "Despite Bans, Number of Abortions in

the United States Increased in 2023," The Guttmacher Institute, March 19, 2024; Luke Mullins, "FreedomWorks Is Closing—And Blaming Trump," *Politico*, May 8, 2024.

15 Quinn Slobodian, *Crack-Up Capitalism: Market Radicals and the Dream of a World Without Democracy* (New York: Penguin Books, 2023); Zachary Warmbrodt, "A JD Vance-Aligned Think Tank Is Stirring the Pot with Conservatives," *Politico*, July 25, 2024.

16 Oren Cass, "Trump's Most Misunderstood Policy Proposal," *The Atlantic*, September 26, 2024; Patrick Wyman, "American Gentry," *The Atlantic*, September 23, 2021; Alexander Sammon, "Want to Stare into the Republican Soul in 2023?" *Slate*, May 30, 2023.

17 Meena Venkataramanan, "Trump Is the 'Most Effective Uprooter of Liberalism': Newt Gingrich Talks GOP, Midterms, Space," Good Morning America, June 27, 2018; Alan I. Abramowitz, "Explaining Republican Loyalty to Trump: The Crucial Role of Negative Partisanship," The Center for Politics, August 22, 2023.

18 Tia Mitchell, "Marjorie Taylor Greene Remains a Top House Fundraiser," *The Atlanta Journal-Constitution*, July 14, 2023; David D. Kirkpatrick, "How Marjorie Taylor Greene Raises Money by Attacking Other Republicans," *The New Yorker*, April 27, 2024.

Index

Index